Jacqueline Kennedy Onassis, or Jacqueline
Bouvier Onassis as she prefers to be known,
is a woman who has lived closer to
contemporary history, enjoyed greater
triumphs and greater tragedies than probably
any other woman alive today. She is, and
always has been, rich, beautiful and
controversial. She herself has sought both
privacy and publicity in equal measure, and
Willi Frischauer's remarkable biography
gives us a unique picture of this extraordinary
woman who, now in her late forties, will not
cease to attract world-wide attention,
whatever the future holds for her.

Jackie

WILLI FRISCHAUER

SPHERE BOOKS LIMITED
30/32 Gray's Inn Road, London WC1X 8JL

First published in Great Britain by Michael Joseph Ltd 1976
Copyright © 1976 by Willi Frischauer
Published by Sphere Books 1977

TRADE
MARK

Set in Intertype Lectura

Printed in Great Britain by
Hazell Watson & Viney Ltd
Aylesbury, Bucks

INTRODUCTION

The plan to write the life story of Jackie Kennedy Onassis or Jacqueline Bouvier Onassis, as she prefers to be known until further notice, originated in conversations with the late Aristotle Onassis whose biography I wrote in 1967 before he and Jackie became man and wife, and who wanted to counter the fantastic rumours and reports circulating about their marriage. His contribution was sporadic but significant. He did not live to complete the rounded picture he wanted me to convey of his wife and, relying on other sources, I may not have wholly implemented his intentions.

Instead I have tried to bring together the gist of widely scattered information about Jackie who figures in dozens of books and thousands of magazines and newspaper features, many of them owing more to the imagination of the writers than to the truth. Eliminating untrue stories about her was as arduous a chore as obtaining facts but some of the published fantasies have to be quoted because they have become part of the Jackie myth. The problem was to de-mythologise her without reducing her – and neither friends who see her as a shining heroine nor enemies who regard her as a tedious socialite have been much help in producing a balanced account.

Over the years I have talked to dozens of people who know her well or knew her at some stage in her life. Her real intimates did not want to be quoted even when they were highly complimentary about her, and most of her detractors were not reliable witnesses. My solution was to assimilate all information that came my way whether in personal interviews or previously printed and present the result as one coherent whole. I am still obliged to my numerous informants and can show my gratitude best by preserving their anonymity. I have given credit only where their experiences coincided with material published. Facts and fiction having been handed down for decades and reiterated time and again, it was sometimes impossible to trace statements, true or false, to their origin.

It would be dishonest on my part to pretend that I have zealously striven for total objectivity. Jackie arouses all sorts of emotions, hence the astonishing interest with which her doings have been followed throughout her life. Perhaps, I can best explain my approach by admitting that, in writing about her, I frequently became involved and it is quite possible that some passages reflect my conflicting reactions – respect and admiration, puzzlement and exasperation, doubt and, most of all, pity. My purpose was not to unearth old scandals or recent secrets – there may be secrets, there were no scandals – but to write a popular account of a public figure who has sought privacy and publicity (for various causes) in equal measure, lived closer to contemporary history, enjoyed greater triumphs and suffered greater disasters than any other woman alive. At forty-seven, she has not only a crowded past but a future.

The bibliography lists some of the works, some highly relevant, some marginal to my subject, which I have perused in the course of my research but it is quite impossible to mention all the magazine and newspaper reports which have amused and confused me in the process.

As with my previous work, only more so, I owe a great deal to my wife who has helped tirelessly with research into an inordinate volume of source material. Ted Clark in Washington has been as diligent. My thanks to Gil Pearson who has typed the manuscript.

Willi Frischauer
London, 1976

CHAPTER ONE

Jacqueline Bouvier Kennedy Onassis, for all the accolades life has bestowed on her – beauty, brains, wealth, position – is probably the world's outstanding victim. For no discernible reason, tragedy has buffeted her with disconcerting persistence. She is a classical example of the theory expounded in victimology, a new branch of criminology, which is concerned with the victims rather than the perpetrators of crime, and proceeds from the assumption that there are people who are destined to be victims, most of them more than once in their lives; that there is something in their nature, their character, their behaviour, their attitudes which invites or provokes attack. Extended beyond the frontiers of crime, the theory applies to a great number of people to whom things, similar things, happen again and again – the lucky ones who always draw the winning number in the lottery of life, and again the luckless who suffer misfortune after misfortune. The colloquial 'Why does it always happen to me?' demands an answer which can only be found in themselves though they rarely discover it, and curse fate which seems so unreasonably harsh on them.

Jackie married twice – both times into tragedy. When she met John F. Kennedy, his wealthy and eminent family was already grievously ravaged – his elder brother killed in the war, one sister retarded, another killed in an air accident (and her husband before her). Her first year as the wife of the then Senator from Massachusetts was a desperate struggle to keep him alive as he underwent two major operations and came so near to death that he was given the last sacrament. She lost three babies, one through miscarriage, the second still-born, and baby Patrick within a day of his birth, with all the agonies each loss inflicted on her. Hardly recovered from the death of little Patrick, she rode into Dallas with the President and saw him struck down by an assassin's bullet; five years later she stood at the deathbed of her brother-in-law who was shot while campaigning for high office. The only surviving brother, Senator Edward Kennedy, escaped death in an air crash by a hair's breadth, and was involved in another dramatic incident which cost a life and all but wrecked his political career.

If Jackie thought that marriage to Aristotle Onassis, the immensely wealthy Greek ship-owner, would shield her from further misadventure, she was rudely disappointed. In the course of their brief marriage, her second husband's daughter was caught up in an unhappy marriage tangle and found unconscious, his sister-in-law perished in mysterious circumstances, his son was killed in an air crash, his previous wife (later the Marchioness of Blandford) died in her prime, and Onassis himself was afflicted by a disease which proved fatal leaving her a widow for a second time at the age of forty-six. Such a series of Sophoclean tragedies can destroy or harden the victim. To come through them unmarked requires either total insensitivity or extraordinary strength of character.

The tears Jackie has shed profusely – while desperately trying to follow the precept of her first husband's family, 'Kennedys don't cry' – are evidence that she is not insensitive. Her strength of character has earned her the reputation of a hard woman. Yet her charm has captivated men like de Gaulle and Nehru, and she counts some of the outstanding men of our times among her friends which suggests a certain quality of the heart. She has crammed more experience, some invaluable, some rather spectacular than worthy, into her years than any other woman.

That she has caused a few things to happen while so much has happened to her, only deepens the enigma of her personality which has made her the most fascinating woman in the world.

Jacqueline Lee Bouvier celebrated her second birthday in the manner to which the children of East Hampton's wealthy residents were accustomed. Twenty boys and girls of her age were invited, and a social writer, duly alerted to the event, gushed in her column: 'Little Jackie Bouvier, daughter of Jack Bouvier and the former Janet Lee, was a charming hostess at her second birthday party . . .'

The gossip paragraph was an essential ingredient of the occasion. The Bouviers and the nouveau riche Lees, even more so, would have felt they were slipping if their birthdays, graduations, engagements, marriages – oh yes, and deaths, too – had not been recorded in the public press: 'I'm mentioned, therefore I exist,' was the socialite version then as it is now of the philosopher's self-assertion 'I think, therefore I am.'

Four decades later, Jackie with more column inches to her credit than Greta Garbo, Brigitte Bardot and Elizabeth Taylor between them, is ambivalent about personal publicity. She demands respect for her privacy but will not hide her light under a bushel. She has asked the photographers of a latter-day society magazine into her house in Fifth Avenue but went to law to keep a persistent American paparazzi at arm's length. When she arrived at New York's Colony restaurant which was on the beat of the city's professional Jackie-watchers, the manager, anxious to protect her from the curious, offered her a chair with the back to the door. 'Why do you want to hide me?' she asked a little plaintively. She wanted to sit with her back to the wall facing the door and all who sailed through it. At Claridge's in London, she and Ari lunched at one of the privileged tables near the restaurant entrance where the beautiful and important people can see and be seen. I went over to greet them: 'May I join you?' Usually so gregarious and never other than welcoming to his biographer, Onassis looked positively alarmed. Inviting a writer into his wife's presence was like making common cause with the enemy; allowing a journalist to share her table akin to treason. Most important, he did not want her to suspect that he was in any way aiding and abetting my work in a new edition of his life story in which she would figure prominently, that he was helping, guiding, manoeuvring me to show her in the right light – right being the way he saw her.

Trying to hide his embarrassment, he motioned me feebly to sit down. Jackie nodded gracefully: 'Hello', she whispered with the whimper in her voice which suggests the vulnerable little girl. She, too, looked apprehensive. Two dozen eyes were on us, and an American couple, recognising her as they were leaving the restaurant, stopped in their tracks and stood and stared. It made me feel uncomfortable; it was obviously painful to her.

I recalled an occasion on the Aegean island of Rhodos when Jackie, arriving in one of the *Christina*'s motorboats, joined an English couple at their house for aperitifs. A dozen or so guests, mostly sophisticated cosmopolitans, were in animated conversation. Abruptly, as soon as Jackie entered the room, silence fell. After a few perfunctory exchanges – she needed no introduction, the names of the people meant nothing to her – conversation faltered and ebbed away into another awkward silence. Jackie settled in an easy chair looking bewildered at the expectant faces. Everybody was waiting for her to speak, to say something profound perhaps or, even better, something cute, memorable, well quotable, anyway. A tiny dog nuzzled up to her: 'What a lovely puppy!' she said.

'That's all she had to say,' one of the people muttered when she had gone. He did not explain what exactly he had expected nor why he and the others were too overwhelmed to open their mouths. Since this sort of thing had happened before, it is not surprising that Jackie is not wild about meeting strangers. Conversely, it is not easy for outsiders to relax and be themselves in her company. People not of her own circle are reluctant to approach her lest they be suspected of trying to ingratiate themselves; others keep away because they genuinely do not want to intrude. 'Are they frightened of me?' she asked on one such occasion.

Yet, when you meet her, even among friends, there is the hint of the school mistress about her as if she expected all to be on their best behaviour and as perfectly controlled as she is – or rather appears to be. For it is not unknown for Jackie, having navigated a difficult passage, to burst into tears or explode with pent-up exasperation once she is round the corner and behind closed doors. Her chain-smoking (out of the limelight) is a dead give-away. Nerves.

Calm and controlled? Emotional and explosive? There is not only one Jackie but three or four and, like New York where all four seasons often come together on a single day, she can register within a couple of hours, the gaiety of spring, the warmth of high summer, the mellowness of autumn and the frozen grimace of a hard, hard winter. Puzzling? Not really, when you analyse her – and it does not require the insight of a Freud to trace the key to this enigma. It can be found in her mother's womb and father's personality. No two persons could have been further apart in outlook and temperament. Joined in Jackie's complex emotional and mental make-up they add up to a potent but uneasy mixture.

Though the contradictory strains can no longer be easily separated, once pursued to their origins they soon tell what makes Jackie run. How was she groomed for destiny? How was she able to snap her fingers and lure a future President of the United States? Where did this fragile, delicate society beauty find the resource to mould the White House in her image and usher in the new Camelot? How did she capture the imagination of the people who were prepared to accept her grandfather's claim that the family was of aristocratic, even royal descent, which was, of course, nonsense? How did she cope with the shock and the tragedy of Dallas? How did she become, at her lowest ebb, the most celebrated woman alive? And why, oh why, did she marry again (only the second widow of an American President to do so); and, what's more, 'that Greek', as the American people referred to Aristotle Onassis because they did not like his snatching their dream girl from them, a case of mass libido interrupto.

There is without doubt a strong element of sexuality in Jackie's relationship with the world at large. It is her sexuality which defies bourgeois moral standards when she insists on seeing a blatant sex film like *I'm Curious, Yellow* impervious to the inescapable public *éclat* which followed (she knew there was not a theatre manager she could trust to forego the publicity and not to shout the news of her visit from the rooftops). Yet sexuality was not a likely motive, not a prime motive for marriage to a man twenty-five years older than she, which meant that she must have expected to become a widow for a second time unless the marriage broke up before Onassis' death. These are just a few of the pieces which must be fitted into place to complete the whole mosaic.

In front of me as I write are the notorious colour photographs of Jackie in the nude, a modern version of Goya's *Maja*

11

Desnuda, another high-born lady depicted without her clothes. The pictures were 'snatched' on Skorpios Island and published in the Italian magazine *Playmen.* 'What do you think of these pictures?' a friend asked Onassis at the time when the world was shocked by so much unauthorised disclosure. 'They're rather good,' Ari replied lightly which was a good answer to gloss over the domestic row they caused.

They are indeed pleasant to look at, showing Jackie to be handsomely shaped though her legs could be longer and her torso shorter. Above all they are symbolic in several ways, subjectively and objectively. They reveal a lack of inhibition, an element of exhibitionism, and, at the same time, hint at unsuspected rebellious instincts. How readily she discards the trappings of convention! (Jack Kennedy, incidentally, was known to jump into the White House swimming pool without benefit of bathing trunks and, in Jackie's absence, in the company of similarly uncovered lady friends.)

The interest which these pictures aroused and their reproduction all over the world symbolises the intense curiosity Jackie attracts and the universal desire to strip her, as it were, to the buff and to examine every fibre of her being. Cultivated, or not, the studied reticence of the 'frightened little girl' retreating from the public gaze creates about Jackie a mystery which people of the most heterogeneous interests strive to penetrate. Professor Galbraith's famous quip when meeting Jackie shortly after the publication of the nude photos – 'How nice to see you with your clothes on!' – perfectly expressed the intellectual's knack of reversing the popular trend.

Mystery and tension. In many ways, Jackie is like a nervous, hypersensitive thoroughbred – no accident that her early emotionalism revolved around horses – locked in the starting gate but geared to victory. (Significantly in the oppressive aftermath of Ari's death, she reverted to horses and started a stud farm in New Jersey.) The tension can be almost tangible, compounded of a turbulent childhood beneath a veneer of genteel tranquillity; the tug of war over her and her younger sister between a snobbish father and an ambitious mother who soon went their separate ways; the contrast between outward opulence and hidden but severe financial stresses in a stockbroking family in a period of world-wide economic crisis; life with a wealthy stepfather who handled his money with extreme caution; the sense of competitiveness and high aspiration instilled and carefully nurtured in a shy infant.

Gore Vidal (whose mother having parted from his father married the man who later took Jackie's mother as his next wife) said about Jackie and her sister Caroline Lee, better known as Princess Lee Radziwill: 'They'd been brought up to be adventuresses. Their father had it in mind for them.' But not in his wildest dreams could Jack Bouvier have fathomed what adventures were in store for his little Jackie.

Early 1974. They were talking about publicity, unpleasant, intrusive publicity, Ari, Jackie and a few American friends. A couple of days earlier, a French newspaper had published a picture of Ari leaving a Paris night-club with a very handsome young 'actress'.

'Did it upset you,' one friend asked, 'the picture, I mean?' Eyes were on Jackie who screwed up her pretty face and winced. Ari thought for a moment, and those who knew him well could guess that he was working up one of his folksy epigrams which owed their simplicity to his Anatolian ancestors: 'Look here,' he said at last, 'what does it matter to a man in the pouring rain if someone empties a glass of water over him?'

In spite of being drenched by an incessant flood of publicity, Onassis kept the powder of his humour dry. He often tried to smooth Jackie's ruffled feathers when another absurd rumour about her hit the headlines: 'Jackie pregnant', 'Jackie sterile', 'Jackie jealous of her daughter', 'Jackie's secret visit to specialist' were just a few examples. He went to great lengths not to increase the risk of misrepresentation, misquotation, misunderstanding when talking about Jackie but was quite uninhibited when he told me about their life together, their first meeting and their 'romance' which, by the way, was not a word in his earthy vocabulary although Jackie uses it frequently.

The first time Jackie's name cropped up in our conversation was in the summer of 1967 when we, Ari and I, were sitting on the poop deck of *Christina*, the world's most glamorous private yacht, a 1,600 ton frigate converted into a gleaming white floating palace at the cost of five million dollars. She was anchored at Skorpios, almost dwarfing Ari's treasure island in the Ionian Sea. Maria Callas was stomping around the deck like a tigress waiting for us to finish our session. Dinner was ready and, like a suburban housewife trying to coax her husband from his cronies, she wanted him at the table. Onassis was too engrossed in memories to pay attention to her.

He was talking about his encounters with the Kennedys in the late fifties when Onassis invited John F. Kennedy, the young Senator from Massachusetts in the South of France on a visit to his father Joseph Kennedy, to come and meet Sir Winston. We were sitting in almost the exact spot where the encounter between the ex-Premier of Great Britain and the future President of the United States had taken place: 'So you were already a friend of Jack Kennedy's?' I asked Onassis. 'Never say you are a friend of the King,' Ari retorted. 'The King must say you are his friend!'

After dinner we returned to the subject but this time Onassis talked of Jackie Kennedy and their cruise together in his yacht in 1963 after she had lost her baby boy. I did not attach any significance to the lyrical faraway look in Ari's eye when he mentioned her name; had I been more alert, it should have given me an early warning. It was on this cruise that Ari fell in love with Jackie though he did not, at this stage, admit it to himself. And not even a man as undaunted as Onassis could have perceived the glimmer of a hope that his affection could ever be reciprocated.

Back to Skorpios. In the sixth year of her second marriage, Jackie is the perfect hostess for Ari Onassis. Flying in from the military airfield on the west coast of Greece (which is as far as four-engined aircraft can go), a helicopter brings a party of guests to the island: an English industrialist, an American banker, a Canadian politician. Jackie is on the landing stage to welcome them and ride with them up the steep road to show them to their chalets.

The second helicopter approaches carrying luggage and Ari's London man, Nigel Neilson, his wife, son and daughter. Familiar as he is with the Skorpios routine, Nigel prepares to make his own way to the top of the island but no, Jackie is back on the landing stage to greet the new arrival; her husband's employee or not, he is a guest and she insists on doing the honours: 'Impeccable!' an appreciative Nigel Neilson commented.

A good time is had by all culminating in dinner, wine and talk flowing as freely as always when Onassis presides. The cigars are emitting their bluish smoke, the brandy glasses tinkle gently, the dinner is coming to an end when Jackie speaks up briskly, confidently: 'I have arranged for you to see a film . . . I am sure you will like it.'

Post-prandial private cinema, ugh! An American upper-class social stereotype, the more recent the film, the more prestigious for the hosts. As far as Jackie is concerned, it also discourages too much liquor. Nor, unlike Onassis's first wife of yore, daughter of a shipowner, or, for that matter Callas, Jackie's predecessor in Ari's affections, who revels in men's business chat, is Jackie over-eager to participate much longer in the decidedly non-intellectual conversation.

Murmurs, their meaning difficult to determine, acknowledge her announcement. For an instant, the talk flags. The men wait for Ari who speaks in a low key as always until he erupts in a noisy crescendo, though not this time: 'I don't think so, darling,' he says very quietly.

Jackie looks perplexed. She does not like being turned down, not in front of the guests. Ari rises, Jackie rises and everybody with them. They follow him as he makes his way to one of the boathouses: 'Anybody got a guitar?' he asks. Servants with their ears cocked to his every request quickly produce a guitar, and Nigel Neilson, a lapsed showman of great talent, strums it with gusto.

Ari's full-throated baritone leads the singing, the others sitting crosslegged on the floor join in, only Jackie is silent and takes umbrage. Greek tunes pierce the air, a chorus more enthusiastic than melodious. Much laughter all around. Not Jackie's. Twenty minutes later the theme switches from Greek to American and the strains of popular, rhythmic hillbilly airs replace the soulful twangs. And, lo and behold, Jackie, shedding her bad temper like a snake sheds its skin, joins in with a voice much stronger and better modulated than anyone would have expected.

Wine, fruit, nuts, olives from the groves of Skorpios 'The best in Greece,' Onassis boasts. Evening turns into night and the early hours and, across the water on neighbouring Lefkas Island, they can still hear Jackie, Ari and their guests whooping it up. No question, Jackie has had a most enjoyable evening.

'Jackie tried to get her own way and do the things she wanted,' a friend says. 'But she gave in when she came up against Ari. She seemed surprised every time it happened, put up a short fight but accepted defeat when it could not be avoided.'

This became the pattern of their lives. Ari and Jackie were apart for long periods, going their own way, few questions asked, few complaints voiced. When they were together and their inclinations clashed, it was not Ari's lifestyle that changed. While remaining himself and refusing – being unwilling or unable – to adapt, there was nothing he would deny his wife. He thought that fate owed her a great deal.

In the autumn of 1970, Jackie and Ari flew into London, were quickly whisked through airport formalities and, via the VIP route, reached their waiting limousine unobserved. They made for Claridge's Hotel where they settled into a spacious five-room apartment, two bedrooms, two sitting rooms, one conference room.

Fate – and ominous memories – are present wherever Jackie goes, whatever she does. It raised a warning finger on this occasion, the first time she publicly involved herself in her husband's business. I say publicly because, while it did not greatly amuse her, she frequently entertained his business associates from all over the world.

The purpose of their London visit was to advance Ari's plan to acquire a majority stake in the Belfast shipyard of Harland and Wolff in which he already had a twenty-five percent interest. It was a tricky transaction because the British government was not keen on a foreigner obtaining control. The shipyard workers would have to be won over for without their co-operation the Onassis bid had little chance of succeeding.

16

How to woo the workers? There was no easy answer. Or perhaps there was. Jackie! Of course, Jackie!

While high-level negotiations were conducted by Ari's top aides, a neat little public relations exercise was mounted by another Onassis platoon. In its concept and execution it was not difficult to detect the touch of Nigel Neilson. The idea was for Jackie to fly to Belfast with Ari and mingle with the workers and their wives. Conveniently, a new social club for workers was about to be opened and, even more conveniently, Bill Currie, the club's secretary, telephoned to ask whether Mr and Mrs Onassis would care to inaugurate the new premises and stay for lunch. The answer was a prompt and eager 'Yes.'

It was only on second thoughts that the political, religious and very personal implications of the enterprise dawned on Onassis. What was he letting Jackie in for? She had, of course, visited Ireland, Catholic Ireland, the cradle of the Kennedys, and, three years earlier, spent a holiday in Wexford with Caroline and John-John. A Catholic Kennedy in Catholic Ireland – no problem. But Northern Ireland, strife-torn Belfast, Harland and Wolff, a Protestant stronghold, where the few remaining Catholics walked in fear, Northern Ireland, prone to exploding bombs, snipers' rifles, fanatical gatherings and violent riots, was a different proposition.

For the former Mrs John F. Kennedy to be thrust into this cauldron of political and religious emotion presented an obvious hazard. English friends hearing of the project, strongly advised that it should be called off. The danger was very real, they said. A prominent Catholic woman in the den of the Protestant lions! Anything could happen. It only needed one crackpot, one Protestant extremist, and what about the odd Catholic objecting to her fraternising with the Protestants? Shades of Dallas inescapably loomed.

Ari who had greeted the idea with enthusiasm, drew back: 'Let's skip it,' he said without going into details. But Jackie would not hear of it: 'I'd rather like to go,' she declared. 'In fact, I insist on going. I will not allow my life to be governed by fear.'

She spent the afternoon before her trip to Belfast with sister Lee touring antique shops in Knightsbridge. That evening, wearing a stunning outfit, a fringed poncho with gaucho pants and boots, she went to the theatre, minus Ari, to see *The Philanthropist*. In the meantime, Onassis aides were busily conferring with the police about security arrangements for the trip.

Discarding plans for a massive police guard, they opted for low-profile protection, a couple of plainclothes men to cover Jackie at all times, other policemen to be judiciously and unobtrusively placed along the route Jackie, Ari and their party would be taking.

After an uneventful flight to Belfast during which Jackie boned up on a few topical aspects of the Ulster situation, she carried out the social parts of the programme with great aplomb. She took lunch with the workers and their wives and got on famously with them, talked freely and easily with neither affectation nor condescension about the kind of clothes she liked, the kind of food that kept her figure trim, about the children . . . Not in a long time had she been so relaxed in public: 'Such pleasant people,' she whispered into Ari's ear. While police guarded the club and watched from the rooftops and other strategic positions, Jackie seemed impervious to any danger. If others nursed memories of Dallas, they did not seem to burden her mind. As a parting gift, she was handed a golden key to the club; Ari was presented with a shillelagh.

It was nearly all over when a detective approached Nigel Neilson: 'Finish your coffee quickly!' he said. Neilson thought he could detect a hint of underlying panic.

'What's up?' he asked.

'We've had a warning – at the moment six of our boys are looking for the bomb.'

Jackie was warned but did not flinch. She showed no reaction, moved easily towards the door shaking hands all round while detectives and aides steered her towards the car. Only when they were on their way, did she become emotional. The strain must have been severe: 'She went through a great ordeal,' Neilson said. The way she had acted, nobody would have guessed. No bomb was found.

The next day, Jackie had fully recovered her composure and was in high spirits as if close contact with ordinary people had stimulated her. Crowds lined the pavement opposite Claridge's to catch a glimpse of her. A phalanx of photographers, cameras at the ready, waited to snap her in yet another startling outfit. Police kept the street clear and the onlookers in order. There was a cheer when Jackie emerged in trousers and raincoat, smiling and waving.

Recognising a familiar face among the photographers, she turned and – unheard of, unbelievably – crossed the street to shake hands with him: 'Didn't we meet in Ireland two or three years ago?' she asked him. 'Quite right,' he replied. It was as if Jackie Bouvier, the enquiring photographer of the *Washington Herald-Times* of twenty years earlier was meeting up with a colleague. Never before had she been so matey with a member of the press. It was the release from the tension of Belfast.

A personal triumph for Jackie, the excursion to Northern Ireland yielded no result for her husband. The Onassis bid for Harland and Wolff was turned down. But years later the ship-yard workers and their wives were still swopping stories about the time they had lunch with the fabulous Jackie.

Ships are like women, women are like ships. How often Onassis has talked about 'courting a ship' or inquiring whether the 'lady' (a certain ship) 'was free and available'. Did this apply to Jackie, too? Well, actually, yes!

When contemplating a big deal such as commissioning half a dozen supertankers costing more than a hundred million dollars, Onassis always studied an analysis prepared by his staff covering every aspect of the transaction. The essentials of the project reduced to a few sentences were put before him on a single sheet of paper.

Among close associates it was no secret that Onassis ap-proached his second marriage in a similar manner which was not surprising since it would be no less costly than a tanker fleet. He did, in fact, carefully study the implications of his personal project which was more complex than any enterprise he had ever considered. In the first instance, he wanted Jackie to see his history as he saw it himself. He persuaded her to disregard the mass of conflicting and biased reports of his acti-vities which appeared in newspapers and magazines all over the world, and instead to read the story of his life which I had written, on which he had co-operated so assiduously with just this prospect in mind and which – by his design, not mine – was published a few weeks before they finally decided to marry.

For him it was a matter of learning about Jackie's past without reading the millions of words that had been produced about her – he had never acquired the habit of sustained reading and it was not possible to encapsulate the life of Jacqueline Lee Bouvier Kennedy in a few sentences on a single sheet of paper. He concentrated on some of the rather superficial accounts which she had inspired, but was already thinking of a comprehensive biography of Jackie to take its place by the side of his: 'I'll help you as much as I can,' he said, 'but Jackie must not know until the job is done.' Alas, he did not live to see the result.

CHAPTER TWO

The friendship between Jackie Kennedy and Aristotle Onassis was still young when she first drew his attention to a slim volume which had pride of place on her shelf almost next to the Bible – and Jackie swore by it. On second glance, Ari noticed that there were several editions of the same book in her library. Though not a bookish man, he insisted on borrowing and reading it. She would not have parted with the little book except to a close friend and for a definite purpose.

Jackie had treasured it since childhood. She was only six when it was presented to her, as to every Bouvier sprite, by her much-loved, (then) seventy-year-old Grampy, the late John Vernou Bouvier Jr (JVB Jr). Privately produced in 1925 and re-issued several times, *The Forebears* traced the history of the Bouviers to their origin. JVB Jr attached tremendous importance to the family tree nursed by decades of research.

The significance of the account was that it showed the Bouvier family to be of French aristocratic descent which was a matter of pride to all Bouviers including Jackie. Whether Onassis was similarly impressed is open to doubt. At the time, Jackie did not know Ari well enough to appreciate how much more he valued the aura of the American presidency than the dubious prestige attaching to some obscure French aristocratic ancestry. French aristocrats? To a shipping tycoon of his calibre, the current crop of comtes, vicomtes, barons was ten a penny (not to speak of the female of the species), at best mildly amusing hangers-on for a night out in the *boîtes* of Paris.

Still, he listened loyally to Jackie's running commentary explaining that Grampy, leaning heavily on the official record of French noble families, settled for one Francois Bouvier (*c.* 1553) of the 'ancient house of Fontaine' as a suitable forebear. He had a coat of arms, was a councillor in parliament, a most worthy minor nobleman. The Bouviers revelled in the reflected glory of their aristocratic descent and their claim achieved popular currency when John F. Kennedy was elected President and Jackie moved into the White House as First Lady. Nothing could have flattered the American psyche more than the combination of a Democratic President and an aristocratic wife.

As it happened, it was the indiscriminate publicity about Jackie's background which led a distinguished historian to look more closely into the family history. In the event, he suggested in an oblique context that the account of the Bouvier history was so full of errors that it ought to be checked against other sources.

It soon turned out that the noble sixteenth-century Francois Bouvier had nothing, nothing at all, to do with Jackie's forebear, a gentleman of the same name but much lowlier station who lived two hundred years later and kept an ironmonger's shop in Grenoble. His wife came from a family of charcoal burners and woodcutters, and the couple worshipped in the Parish of Saint Laurent but there is no connection either with the contemporary Monsieur Yves Saint Laurent at whose altar in Paris Jackie has worshipped in her time.

As there were twenty-four families bearing the name of Bouvier, it is by no means certain, as another version of the family history suggests, that a descendant of Francois Bouvier, the ironmonger, came to America with General Lafayette to fight against the British. Another blank in Jackie's family history? Like the link between the aristocratic and the American Bouviers, the name of this soldierly Bouvier is missing. It does not appear on the roll of honour of Frenchmen who fought for American independence because the records of his regiment were lost. Whatever his pedigree, he was believed to have been there when the British surrendered at Yorktown.

It has been suggested that Jackie's thinking has been affected by the inconsistency in her family history. Nonsense! By the time the aristocratic myth was exploded, it was so deeply ingrained in the consciousness of the clan that they brushed the facts aside and continued to regard themselves as aristocrats. Kennedy acolytes blithely reproduced the fragile evidence as if it were the gospel truth. Yet, *The Forebears*, whether or not deliberately misleading, instilled pride in a noble line and, in perverse fashion, achieved its objective: 'The book,' a new-comer to the Bouvier clan said, 'had some beneficial effect.' The confidence it built up greatly helped the Bouviers to realise their social ambitions. Believing themselves to be aristocrats, they felt and behaved like aristocrats. Jackie adopted the loftiest of aristocratic principles, *Noblesse oblige*, and tried to live up to it.

Ancestry, tradition, looking back with pride were guidelines which Grampy JVB Jr set for the family but it was a trend he had inherited. The name Vernou, for instance, which Jackie's ancestors linked with that of Bouvier, went back to Louise Vernou, second wife of Michel Bouvier, 1792–1874. The French Michel (rather than Michael) was also handed down to future generations. The seventh of the couple's ten children (to add to Michel's two from his first marriage) was John Vernou Bouvier, 1843–1926 – note the longevity of most of the Bouviers.

He, in turn, married Caroline Maslin Ewing, so called after Caroline County, Maryland, where she was born, another name that turns up again and again. It is the first name of the lady known as Princess Lee Radziwill, though she has dropped it, and of Jackie's daughter who carries on the tradition. The early John and Caroline Vernou Bouvier were the parents of Jackie's grandfather, JVB Jr who played such a dominant part in her life.

When Jackie and Ari first exchanged confidences and memories which always marks the early stage of a developing relationship, Jackie often talked about her grandfather, finding it, for a very real reason, easier than to talk about her father. Well-off, eminently respectable and respected, albeit not aristocratic, JVB Jr was a passionate American patriot, a chauvinist, to use the word derived from the French, an enthusiastic 'joiner'; to emphasise his love of America, he joined every conceivable patriotic group, society, association which marched under the Stars and Stripes. To Jackie, too, as her second husband found out, America means as much as the few droplets of European blood, blue or otherwise, which run in her veins.

Conventional, very erudite, grandfather was, perhaps, a bit pompous in the eyes of the younger generation. A *belles lettres* dilettante, he adopted and invented slogans to express his philosophy: 'He that dies, pays all debts' was one he appropriated from Shakespeare, 'An idler is a human clotheshorse' was one of his own. His jottings indicate a preoccupation with the sex lives of great men, Napoleon's mistresses, Byron's incestuous relationships, Goethe's promiscuity . . . but, then, aging men are often preoccupied with sex.

JVB Jr also dabbled in poetry, hammering out verses for every occasion, most of them going with books or presents to his grandchildren. Jackie was at the receiving end of many, and was inspired, or rather expected, to reply in poetic kind. A child's versifying always delights the family but tends to sound fatuous to outsiders as does the little poem which Jackie and several of her cousins put together and which starts:

> Here's to Grampy, they call him Jack,
> He's the best of all the pack!

It was grandfather's rock-like solidity which spelt security for his grandchildren, particularly Jackie, a little bundle of emotionalism kept in check by the iron grip of good manners and, from childhood, an unshakeable resolve not to lose face. How much does a child sense of the instability in a family which keeps its strains and stresses under wraps (*Pas devant les enfants! Pas devant les domestiques!*)?

Jackie herself is not clear when she first noticed the cracks, the pressures and tensions at home. It was years before she admitted even to herself that something could possibly have been wrong with the best of all worlds and with parents who did their conventional best to hide their problems. Little Jackie never betrayed her feelings, not even when her parents parted and she and her younger sister became pawns in a running fight between mother and father.

It was some years before she became aware that father was losing the battle and that she had not done much to help him. The complex father-daughter relationship which developed left a mark and is probably responsible for her preference for older men — for father-figures like Onassis. From the beginning Jackie was struck by certain similarities between Ari and her late father. Her father was a tall fine figure of a man and

24

though short Onassis's manner enabled him to look down on men two foot taller than he. The overall impression of Onassis, a Levantine from Smyrna, inescapably recalled her father whose levantine looks were part of his glamour. The swarthy skin, her father's darkened by daily sunray treatment, Ari's by the Mediterranean and Caribbean sun, strengthened the remarkable resemblance of the two men from such disparate backgrounds. The soulful eyes, the expressive features, the innate gaiety, father more polished, Ari much wittier, the ability to captivate men and women, the gambler's instincts which paid off for Ari but not for father . . . Jackie only knew her father as a mature man, he was thirty-eight when she was born, and a granite maturity was one of Ari's outstanding characteristics. It is no coincidence that Lee Radziwill when she first met Onassis, and she did meet him first, responded much like her elder sister.

Jackie's father, born in 1891, was the eldest of Grampy's five children – John Vernou Bouvier Jr was married to the former Maude Frances Sergeant – and they called him Jack, too. His younger brother, William Sergeant (Bud) was born in 1893, then came Edith (1895) and twin girls, Maude and Michelle, ten years later. As befitted their social station, the family spent the summer months and most weekends in East Hampton at their house, Lasata (Place of Peace) which was too lively to deserve the name. Lasata witnessed most of the Bouviers' romances and, incidentally, was only a stone's throw from where, in the passage of time, Onassis bid for the affection of his first wife, Athina (Tina) Livanos.

In the tightly-knit East Hampton community of the rich and privileged, Jack III and Bud grew into handsome and privileged youths without any particular talents except the most important, a talent for making friends and influencing people. They went to all the right schools but were not very scholarly. Jack played a fair game of cards, the only trouble being that he played too much. He changed colleges several times, struggled on and just made it to Yale.

There his progress was erratic and Bud's was not impressive either, a disappointment to a father who looked back proudly on his own outstanding academic career. Still, Jack managed to graduate from Yale in 1914 (Bud made the grade two years later) by which time sister Edith was married to a stockbroker who found him a job with a reputable banking firm – several of the older Bouviers were bankers. With his charm, his easy manner, his way with people and his family connections, Jack was eminently suited to the profession. Quick-thinking, interested in figures and more interested still in money, he made an ideal dealer.

The only cloud in the sky, a big cloud, was the war in Europe in which the United States became increasingly involved. Infected with the older Bouvier's inveterate patriotism, Bud joined up but, much to his father's distress, Jack held back until the draft threatened and only beat it by a short head. In August 1917 within days of America entering the war he was commissioned a second lieutenant in the Army Aviation Corps. While Bud was posted overseas and fought in France, Lieutenant John V. Bouvier III served in the United States until peace rescued him from a most uncongenial activity.

He resumed his career, acquired a seat on the Stock Exchange with some financial help from the family, specialising in certain stocks which he bought and sold for broking firms. He was doing very well. With an apartment in Park Avenue, the personable bachelor was a typical figure of the 'roaring twenties', convivial, generous, hospitable to a fault, an enormously successful young tycoon, one of those Hollywood screen stereotypes come to life – except for an uncharacteristic penchant for the company of less socially eminent, less pecunious, less inhibited and more amusing friends (an inclination which Jackie inherited though she does not often give in to it).

Such social deviation was the only black mark against Jack. No, not the only one. Some of the older brokers thought John V. Bouvier III was too good-looking, too italianate, too levantine (or *Provençal* which was more to the point), too well dressed and stylish in a continental fashion. They called their deep-tanned colleague Black Jack or, more sarcastically, Black Prince or, with his active love life in mind, the Sheikh.

Girls fluttered around him like pretty and love-hungry moths; most of them belonged to élite families with prestige, money, or both. There were hints of forthcoming engagements almost every other week but, as far as surviving friends remember, only one or two went as far as to be announced in the newspapers before being called off. The family looked on apprehensively as Jack went around creating emotional havoc.

His style did not fit in with the conventional East Hampton code by which most of the Bouviers lived. For the twins, Maude and Michelle, strawberry redheads with all the social graces, life was one long round of parties, dances, functions, horses, dogs but their older sister Edith indulged in a few mild eccentricities, opening her house to Bohemian writers and artists and dressing in what can be best described as premature hippie fashion.

Below the surface there were symptoms of deep-seated troubles; not long ago, they were revealed by John H. Davis, a fifth-generation scion of the Bouviers, who drew the veil from some family secrets which has not endeared him to his cousin Jackie. Son of one of the twins (Maude), John H. Davis frankly discussed the strained relations which existed between Jackie's father and his brother Bud. They were constantly bickering, Jack being the more forceful and aggressive and Bud the more vulnerable. Both brothers drank heavily, Bud certainly to excess – the root of Jackie's understandably violent reaction, decades later, to excessive drinking at White House parties.

Bud had cause to seek oblivion in drink. His marriage broke up while his only son was still a little boy, and his finances were so shaky that he was being sued for back alimony. When his difficulties were duly reported in the press, the Bouviers were incensed about the stain on their honour and their public image. Treating Bud's alcoholism as a social disgrace rather than a serious illness, the two Jacks, father and son, pondered whether to throw him out and at one point decided never to speak to him again. JVB Jr described his unfortunate younger son as 'a contemptible parasite and a dirty nuisance'.

Jack III, in the meantime, was riding high, making a lot of money and enjoying life which meant largely – girls. That one of them would net him sooner or later was a foregone conclusion. The first evidence that his resistance was breaking down came in the summer of 1927 when he suddenly discovered the attractions of a younger generation, the age-group of his twin

27

sisters. Among the twins' friends were the three daughters of James T. Lee, property and finance multi-millionaire of Irish descent (as was his wife) and something of a phenomenon in East Hampton society because he had made his money the hard way by his own efforts.

If the Lee family was made to appear in some way inferior, the aristocratic (or slightly decadent) Bouviers could only profit from a touch of Irish grit. If there was a gap, the Bouvier twins helped the three charming Lee girls to bridge it. Janet, the one in the middle, was just twenty when Black Jack's eye fell upon her. In New York and East Hampton, they were soon inseparable. No longer would the swarthy Sheikh cultivate the harem. Jack was in love.

In the spring of 1928, Jack and Janet became officially engaged. They made a fine couple. At thirty-seven, Jack, to quote a contemporary pen-picture, 'had a smouldering Levantine handsomeness, the wild rakish look of a Barbary pirate . . .' Janet, a tiny girl, was described as 'a vivacious beauty with a slightly one-sided smile' (a hint of which she bequeathed to Jackie). Her strong face betrayed a lot of determination; she was a first-class horsewoman, an excellent dancer, a lively companion.

With his record of broken engagements, Jack's friends would not trust such uncharacteristic attachment. Engagement, perhaps. Marriage, never! Before the summer was out, they were proved wrong, yet even when James T. Lee announced the impending marriage of his daughter they still had their doubts. Might not Jack wriggle out of it at the last moment? Janet guessed what was being whispered behind her back but never faltered. She was confidently looking forward to the day she would land the finest catch in East Hampton.

When the Bouviers, the Lees and their friends assembled at St Philomena Church, East Hampton, on 7 July 1928, for the wedding of the season, it was a formidable assembly of wealth and influence, bankers, financiers, property owners and their families, bevies of nubile girls and eligible young men. The green straw hats of half a dozen bridesmaids (in contrasting yellow dresses) bobbed up and down excitedly until they formed up behind the bride who was attended by her two

28

sisters, and the groom with his best man – yes, to everybody's immense relief, Bud had made it. He performed his duties well, did not lose the ring or put a foot wrong.

Five hundred guests attended the reception on the spacious lawns of the Lee's family residence. The fashionable Meyer Davis Orchestra played; in years to come when Jackie was First Lady there would be few public functions for which she would not call on the same orchestra to entertain her guests. The couple slipped away early to spend the night in a New York hotel, next morning boarded the *Aquitania* for a European honeymoon. They returned to New York to an apartment Jack had rented, an elegant place in keeping with his income, an impressive 75,000 dollars a year. The only shadow was news of Bud whose condition was rapidly deteriorating. Within a month, he was dead. Among the Bouviers, alcohol became a dirty word but Bud's death meant that, with luck, there would be no more scandals. Jack and Janet, anyway, had other, more pleasant thoughts to occupy their mind for Janet was expecting a baby. Her father was jubilant. To assure the child a suitable reception in this world, he installed his daughter and her husband in a sumptuous duplex in one of his Park Avenue properties.

For the Bouviers whose family tree was constantly shedding autumnal leaves and sprouting new blossoms, this was a period of change. Grandmother Caroline Bouvier did not live to see 1929 but both Bouvier twins were expecting as well as Janet. As her husband was the eldest of the fourth-generation Bouviers, JVB Jr awaited Jack III's first offspring with proprietorial interest. Surely, there would soon be another Jack – Jack IV!

Arrangements were made for Janet to have her baby in a New York clinic but the child was a long time coming. One week after the estimated time of arrival, when nothing had happened, Jack took Janet to East Hampton for the weekend; they spent the next weekend again in the Bouviers' summer house – and the next. The baby kept everybody waiting, altogether five weeks passed and Janet, though big and a bit cumbersome, was so reconciled to the delay that she accompanied her husband on yet another East Hampton weekend.

She felt fine on Saturday, 27 July, but when she woke up on

Sunday she was in pain. Since her doctor was also spending the weekend in Oyster Bay and there was no time to get her to New York, Janet was rushed to a hospital in Southampton. There, six weeks behind the right time and not in the right place, the new Bouvier baby, big but well formed, with tiny, finely-chiselled features and dark hair, greeted the world with the traditional lusty cry.

Wrong time, wrong place! Yes, but also wrong sex! Grampy may have been looking forward to another grandson but Janet's baby was no boy. There was only one answer. The girl would be called Jacqueline.

CHAPTER THREE

Jacqueline Lee Bouvier was not really a pretty baby . . . She possessed four teeth when she had aged as many months. She could talk, and really talk, before she was a year old.

Mary van Rensselaer Thayer

On one of her regular morning walks in Central park, three-year-old Jackie was separated from her nurse, Bertha Newey. It was shortly after the kidnapping of the Lindberg baby and nurse was frantically searching for her little charge. Unruffled and perfectly composed, the child went up to a policeman and announced: 'My nurse is lost.'

Even at this tender age, it was inconceivable to Jackie that *she* might be lost; like many accounts of her childhood, the story reflects the mental attitude of the fully grown former First Lady. Not only did she reveal some significant characteristics unusually early but she has also retained many childlike qualities in adult life.

Indeed, had the little girl not survived so obtrusively in the glamorous *dame du monde*, there would be little point to the tales from the family circle, the early impressions, accounts – and myths – so assiduously cultivated by the Jackie clan even though, far from enhancing her stature, most of them tend to diminish her.

Because her childhood has survived into middle age, she looks back on her past with almost total recall, buttressed, if at all necessary, by a jackdaw treasure (drawer upon drawer, shelf upon shelf, packing case upon packing case) of mementoes, photographs, jottings, letters, press cuttings, assembled – one cannot escape the impression – with an instinctive confidence that an admiring posterity would wish to know every detail.

The family albums bristle with pictures depicting every phase of her young life long before marriage to a rising politician qualified her for special attention. Her first formal photograph taken before she was five months old already shows the languid eyes, pursed lips and superior mien of the most publicised woman of our times.

She has meticulously annotated and supplemented most pictures with witty remarks and facetious little poems. It was not the poor child's fault – it was Grampy who encouraged introspection, self-observation and projection among his grandchildren as a kind of educational aid. From John Vernou Bouvier Jr Jackie inherited the Bouvier's compulsive preoccupation with themselves.

Fascination with clothes is one of the traits Jackie seems to have acquired with her mother's milk. Thanks to publicity-hungry stores which feed on her custom, it is common knowledge that Mrs Jacqueline Onassis rarely shops for just one of a kind – sweater, blouse, scarf – but, with the colour of several outfits in mind, buys a dozen at a time in every shade of the rainbow to make sure of perfect ensembles.

Her first garment to attract public attention was her christening robe. It was described as 'long-skirted with puffed sleeves gathered at the wrists, fashioned in gossamer lawn, frilled with fine lace and strewn with miniature bouquets hand-embroidered in microscopic stitches'. Made in Paris, it was worn by her grandfather and her mother and, after Jackie, by her daughter. Thus draped, Jackie was christened at the Church of St Ignatius Loyola in New York. Godfather was ten-year-old cousin Michel who took the place of his recently departed father Bud Bouvier.

Jackie was only one year old when her mother, an accomplished horsewoman, first planted her on the back of a pony. From this time on Jackie and horses became inseparable. Having made her début as a hostess at her second birthday party, she was promptly initiated into one of the seasonal upper-class rites of East Hampton. Gritting her teeth and tightening the muscles of her jaws – which she still does when tense although it distorts her handsome features – she paraded her pet puppy Hootchie before benevolent judges at a local show and won her first prize. ('Little two-year-old Jackie Bouvier', wrote an observer, 'toddled to the show platform and exhibited with a great pride a wee Scotch terrier of about her own size.') There were other dogs and more prizes before horses became her abiding passion; the family owned seven ponies and hunters.

Jackie competed at horse shows and was encouraged to strive for victory. A regular at events in Long Island before she was six, she could reel off the names of every thoroughbred and every rider in the neighbourhood. (Curiously, as a girl, the first Mrs Onassis was equally dedicated to horses; when Ari first set eyes on Tina Livanos she was hobbling on crutches after a nasty riding accident at Oyster Bay, not far from where Jackie was exercising her horse.) So long and so obstinately did Jackie's reputation as a horsey girl persist that she encouraged magazine stories about her other youthful activities to prove that horses were not her sole interest in life.

Jack Bouvier was proud of his daughter's equestrian progress. In his eyes Jackie could do no wrong. It was as if her achievements compensated for his difficulties and the tensions in the life of a glorified gambler. Even when he joined the assembled Bouviers at Lasata at weekends or in the summer holidays, his thoughts were in Wall Street. He was gambling for high stakes.

Confident that he could multiply any amount available to him, he borrowed $25,000 from his wealthy great-uncle Michel Charles Bouvier to increase his basic investment. He did very well. In the first two years of Jackie's life, her father continued to earn $75,000 per annum. He spent as freely as he earned. The duplex in Park Avenue, East Hampton, servants, cars, horses, Janet, with the extravagant tastes of an heiress, a daughter for whom the best was only just good enough added up to a formidable personal expenditure. Depression was already round the corner but it did not seem as if it could ever engulf Long Island and sweep away the good life.

With the gambler's outlook and the stockbroker's inveterate optimism, Jack Bouvier looked upon the sharp drop in share prices simply as a good opportunity to buy. He was unprepared for the catastrophe of 27 November 1931 (Black Friday) when the bottom dropped out of the stock market. In the wake of the crash, the country was plunged into economic chaos, unemployment and political uncertainty.

Attempts to conceal the extent of his personal losses put a

strain on Jack and affected his married life. He did not find it easy to share his burden with an ambitious and demanding wife. There was a rift – no more than a rift – but Jack would not give up his marriage nor the hope of battling back and securing his future. He was determined to make his pile come what may, and fear of becoming dependent on a hard-faced father-in-law acted as a spur and made him run ever faster after success.

He invested heavily in liquor shares and cashed in when prohibition ended and legal liquor became big business. His gamble paid off to the tune of two million dollars which he deposited in the bank avowing not to touch it. The windfall would help to put him on a more equal footing with the wealthier Bouviers, one of them related to J. Pierpont Morgan's partner.

Jackie's most treasured possessions were her stuffed animals. Her collection grew as father showered presents on her but her favourite was a cheap rag doll she called Sammy. Presently another 'doll' – a live doll – arrived and demanded her attention. On 3 March 1933, the day before the inauguration of President Roosevelt, Janet Bouvier gave birth to a second daughter who was named (Caroline) Lee. Though not yet four, Jackie looked poised and self-assured as she posed by the side of Lee's crib and contemplated the newcomer with quizzical eyes. She clearly did not begrudge the baby a share of mother's studied, clinical but still generous affection.

Jack and Janet Bouvier with their delightful children made a most pleasing group on which society photographers never tired of focusing their lenses. Black Jack was as handsome as ever, no wonder so many wild stories about his extra-marital amours were in circulation, and motherhood had not added an inch to the slim waistline of his delicately-built petite wife.

The year 1933 was not much older before the ephemeral bubble of Jack's financial security and domestic bliss burst. One of his nephews has given a depressing account of the decline. Unable to resist the lure of those two million dollars in the bank, he used them to gamble – invest was the word – with disastrous results. By the end of the year, a volatile, unpredictable market had swallowed up nine-tenths of his assets.

Like many a stockbroker, Jack Bouvier blamed his misfortune on the Security Exchange Commission created by Roosevelt to reduce gambling and speculation and headed by Joseph P. Kennedy, father of the future President of the United States, a poacher turned gamekeeper who had amassed millions by the kind of speculation he was now charged with preventing. That John Kennedy's father should contribute to the misfortune of Jackie's father was an extraordinary twist in her twisted family history. As John H. Davis remarked wryly: 'In 1934, Jack's tan would momentarily fade at the mention of Kennedy's name.'

It was not easy to disguise the financial troubles from such a sensitive and perceptive child as Jackie. Jack and Janet tried to pretend that all was well but any moment the bad-tempered silences between them were liable to erupt in a row. Whenever a storm threatened, Jackie received her marching orders. 'Why don't you go and exercise your pony?' was an unfailing device to get her out of the firing line.

She did not mind at all. She was currently infatuated with a sterling piebald pony named Dance Step, on which she lavished much care. Her sister did not share her high opinion of the horse: 'This is the dreadful Dance Step,' was how Lee later captioned a picture of the horse. Jackie was disgusted with Lee who would obviously not be a success in the horse world.

It was a serious handicap in a family whose life revolved around horse shows. Jackie was expected to emulate her mother who even competed at Madison Square Gardens, drawing as much praise from sportswriters as from fashion experts. Her daughter's plucky performances were applauded even when her horse unseated her: 'Why', she asked with perfect logic, 'did they clap me when I fell off?' Public responses to her would puzzle her many more times.

Even at such an early age, she seemed to glow when Jack was around. She was much more in tune with her warm-hearted, extrovert father than with her coolly methodical, less emotional mother. If, outwardly, she did not react to the situation between her parents whose marriage was heading for the rocks, the explanation can be found in a comment she made about her teachers' reprimands: 'I don't listen,' she said blandly. As in later life, little Jackie would not allow unpleasantnesses to get at her.

It has been suggested that Janet drifted away from Jack because she feared that he might not be able to keep her in the style to which she was accustomed, because she had not been brought up to accept failure and because she did not want her children to be contaminated with the hazards of a gambler's existence. But it so happened that at the very moment when Jack was at his lowest ebb and parted from Janet for a trial separation, the gambler's wheel turned up a lucky number for him. Not another stock exchange coup, though, but the death of wealthy Michel C. Bouvier who left a million and a quarter dollars to Grampy and his flourishing brokerage business to Black Jack.

This second windfall swept Jack and Janet briefly back into each other's arms but Jackie was spared the unsettling experience of this on-and-off marriage because she attended Miss Yates' School, a kindergarten which opened up a new busy world for her. Her schoolmates and the new generation of the proliferating Bouviers enveloped her in a social whirl which absorbed her totally. When the brief six-months' reunion of her parents failed to end the deep-rooted conflicts, divorce became inevitable.

Although prayers and church were part of the children's upbringing there was greater emphasis on the trappings than on the substance of the Roman church. Disregard for the most sacred tenets of the faith did not encourage respect. Janet Bouvier travelled to Reno and that was the end of Jack's marriage. As the Catholic establishment is inclined to be indulgent towards its prominent members, he did not fear divine retribution for defaulting on the holy sacrament. In the large Bouvier family, marital break-ups were not infrequent; around the same time, aunts Edith Beale and Michelle Scott also parted from their husbands.

Under the divorce settlement Jackie and Lee remained with their mother in the Park Avenue duplex while father went to live in a single room in an hotel. Harassed by tax demands and debts, among them the 25,000 dollar loan from the late Michel Bouvier whose executors pressed for repayment, he undertook to pay his wife a thousand dollars a month alimony and was given 'reasonable access' to his daughters at weekends and during the school holidays. It would be a poor substitute for the intimate contact they had enjoyed with their father and the warmth and excitement he generated.

For Jack, separation from the children was even more painful. He loved them with a ferocity that owed more to his Mediterranean origin than to his stockbroking background. Though he devoted much time to his numerous woman friends, the girls were the most important thing in his life. Black Jack and his darling Jackie would exchange affectionate glances, and cling to each other, suggesting a passionate love affair containing the obvious, if suppressed, sexual overtones so frequent in father-daughter relationships. Because Jackie was older and more mature, Jack was drawn closer to her than to Lee who was condemned to play forever second fiddle to her sister. Jackie was supposed to be the romantic, poetic child while Lee was described – with a touch of condescending euphemism – as the practical, down-to-earth one. When asked what she wanted to be, Jackie replied: 'A circus queen on a flying trapeze.'

For the benefit of the world at large, Jackie always talks of her 'dear, sweet mother' but life with mother in those days was uninspiring. Presiding over a well organised but dull household, mother never tired of impressing the value of money and the virtue of economy on Jackie: 'Money does not grow on trees,' was her recurring theme. Father by contrast, however hard-pressed for funds, was uninhibitedly extravagant and outrageously generous.

In her conventional mould, Janet dressed conservatively and favoured a similar style for Jackie. Father encouraged the growing girl's more flamboyant tastes. Mother continued to treat Jackie as a child long after father began to see her as a young woman. Janet was anxious for the girls to fit into her own social environment and conform while father wanted them to stand out and be noticed.

Determined to impose their own ideas on the children, the parents competed with each other and only succeeded in confusing the girls who were mother's darlings one day and father's favourites the next. Superimposed on the conflicting influences was the philosophy of Grampy whose faith in Jackie's creative ability was rewarded with her output of little fables such as *The Adventures of George Woofty, Esquire*, the story of a romance between a terrier and her own schnauzer Caprice. Each tale, like her poems, was embroidered with drawings, mostly decorative but sometimes illustrating her theme.

When Jackie transferred from the Yates kindergarten to Miss Chaplin's Classes, her mother moved from the feudal Park Avenue duplex to an apartment in Gracie Street which was not only closer to the school (the reason she gave for the move) but also cheaper. Yates, Chaplin – there would be five more schools in the next fifteen years before Jackie's education was complete. She was a bright child, not beyond indulging in some educational private enterprise and read Chekov – well, a short story by Chekov – before she was six. Her intellectual ambition continued to race ahead of her age and ability but determined efforts to catch up raised her standards well above the average.

She was not easy to handle, could be obstreperous, obstinately doing her own thing, and impervious to admonition but nobody at the time associated her rebellious attitude with the domestic situation. One way to deal with her was to relate her problems to those of a horse – like any good horse, the headmistress told her, she, too, would have to be broken in. It was a curious approach to education but the kind of language Jackie understood.

For the first time, death rudely intruded. Grandmother died and Jackie with the other grandchildren was taken to see her lying in state in Grampy's apartment. Her loss was a blow to Jackie's father who had basked in his mother's adoration all his life. Grampy was taken over by the Bouvier twins, Maude and Michelle who ran his town house and Lasata, the family watering place.

Having forged the marriage of Jack and Janet, the twins were not too pleased to see their handiwork undone and naturally blamed Janet for the breakup. She was expelled from the fold, no longer belonged and was cut dead by the Bouviers and their friends. With affection to spare, they lavished it on Jackie, the most appealing of the younger generation. Constantly in each other's pockets (in every sense of the word since Grampy

38

provided financial help all round), the Bouviers added another dimension to Jackie's ambivalent feelings, endemic divided loyalties. Before long, the family tangle would become even more intractable. No wonder that when eventually another ultra-clannish family, the Kennedys, claimed Jackie and tried to mould her in their image, she resisted all attempts to swamp her individuality.

According to the Bouviers, Janet and the children could hardly make ends meet on their small allowance from Jack but Janet's wealthy, if not too open-handed, father could provide her with all she needed. In her isolation from the Bouviers she clung more tightly to Jackie and Lee while Jack on his part, as his fortunes improved once more, tried to strengthen his hold on the children. They were bound to be spoilt. Jackie, in particular, quickly sensed that if mother did not give her what she wanted father was sure to step into the breach and vice versa.

The book which made the strongest impact on Jackie's young mind was *Gone with the Wind*, although she was not aware that, when the film of the book was shown, Jack Bouvier was instantly identified with Rhett Butler and Clark Gable who portrayed the character. Her admiration for her father needed no such comparisons, and admiration, anyway, was common currency in inter-Bouvier relations. Still, Jackie's cousins, even her bosom pal Scotty, Auntie Michelle's son, poked fun at what they called her regular injection of vitamin P – P for Praise. Not only father, Grampy too, showered praise on her, only occasionally spiced with mild admonition and gentle advice. When Jackie asked him to pronounce on one of her poems, his reply, stripped of the fulsome verbiage, was that the perfect could not be perfected.

Ballet lessons were added to Jackie's crowded curriculum; horses, friends and family kept her fully occupied. She would not gladly miss a party, yet often appeared reticent and aloof even in a crowd and certainly less convivial than her younger sister. She was well behaved, easy on the eye and, perhaps because she seemed, or played, hard to get, was much sought after – and knew she was.

In the summer East Hampton was swarming with Bouviers;

sometimes there were as many as eighteen of them gathered at Lasata and at a second family property, spreading out over the beaches, the golf course, the tennis courts. Jackie, mostly in jodhpurs, led a cavalcade of youngsters on cross-country rides. Her elder cousins introduced their first girl and boy friends into the family circle which also embraced neighbours and acquaintances from New York. Leisure was pursued with unflagging energy.

Sex was not yet a factor in Jackie's life except for her father's philandering, a subject which began to interest her soon and provoked some amusing comments. But she will not dwell on the critical period when her mother became involved with another man, which threatened her established order. Tactfully and certainly more discreetly than Jack with his ladies, Janet Bouvier was going out with Hugh Dudley Auchincloss, a genial, big cheerful man with smiling eyes.

After the ruin of her marriage and the strain of internecine warfare with the Bouviers, Janet found the company of this strong, informal man relaxing. With his casual clothes, Hughdie, as everybody called him, looked and behaved more like a farmer than the tycoon he was – Hammersmith Farm was the name of his big house in Newport, Rhode Island, set in seventy-five rolling acres with a magnificent view of Narragansett Bay. Though younger than Jack Bouvier, Hughdie was forty-three at the time, he was infinitely more mature and stable emanating solidity and security which Janet had not found with her erstwhile husband.

He told her that his family hailed from Scotland where his ancestors had produced yarn in their native city of Paisley. The first Auchincloss to settle in America had quickly established a flourishing business importing and distributing yarn. Grandfather Auchincloss, one of thirteen children, had married into a great New England family and had nine children, the youngest of them shrewdly invested in nitrate and railroads, went into banking and married even better – his bride Emma Brewster Jennings was the daughter of the man who had founded Standard Oil with Rockefeller. Through marriage, he, Hughdie, was related to some of America's outstanding families: du Pont, Rockefeller, Vanderbilt, Tiffany among them. Janet was well aware that the name of Auchincloss was dotted all over the social register.

Hughdie presided over his vast inheritance with traditional Scottish thrift. Like Janet, he had been married before and divorced not once but twice. Janet met Yusha, Hugh Dudley Jr, Hughdie's son from his first marriage to Maria Chrapovitsky, a Russian naval officer's daughter. They had parted amicably. Another member of the family she came to know – it was getting a bit complicated – was Eugene, a son of Hughdie's second wife, Nina Gore (daughter of T. B. Gore, the blind Senator from Oklahoma) by her own previous marriage.

Eugene soon changed his name to Gore, Gore Vidal, the talented, bitchy writer whose acid comments about the new members of the family burned away some of the fine enamel on the Bouvier escutcheon. By Gore Vidal's mother, Hughdie had two more children, Nina Gore and Thomas Gore, who stayed with him after this second marriage was also dissolved.

Undaunted by this ready-made, two-tier family, Janet Bouvier accepted Hughdie's proposal of marriage. He was confident that his three children would welcome her two little girls as sisters and that, Janet willing, there might even be additions to the family before long.

Jackie and Lee were less enthusiastic about the changes which their mother's marriage would bring about. Jackie would have to leave Chaplin's School, New York and the Bouviers. Worst of all, as she learned to think of her mother as Mrs Hugh D. Auchincloss and to follow her into a new life, an ominous gap opened up between her and her father whose place was being taken by a stranger with a vastly different outlook.

Janet, who had not only found a man after her own heart but had made it to the highest echelons of American society, was euphoric; Jackie and Lee, their routine interrupted, were bewildered and despondent. For Jackie the change came at a most inopportune and awkward moment. Already beset by the psychological and physiological disturbance of incipient womanhood, she became difficult and withdrawn like any youngster with a problem of adjustment.

However amiable and welcoming, the stepfather never

really won her affection; deep down in her young and vulnerable heart, she could not reconcile herself to the man who put her father in the shade and claimed such a large share of her mother's attention. That mother might have married this enormously wealthy man not only because she loved him dearly but also because he could provide for her girls dawned on Jackie only later when her father began to harp on the importance of status and wealth and encouraged his daughters to use their talents and attractions to make their way in the world. Gore Vidal put a harsh construction on Jack Bouvier's influence: 'They were pubescent when they moved in,' Vidal remarked referring to the arrival of Jackie and Lee in Washington, and went on to describe them as adventuresses in the making.

Gore Vidal later wrote *Two Sisters*, which would have been recognised as an autobiographical *roman à clef* even if he had not described it as 'A memoir in the form of a novel'. A classical drama with contemporary passages, it tells the story of two sisters of newly-acquired royal (read: presidential) status, narrated by their half-brother, Herostratus, who makes love to one of the sisters. To some people this episode suggested that Gore Vidal had had an affair with Jackie, one of the more insidious rumours which tormented her.

Such harassment was as yet in the distant future when Jackie was busy acquainting herself with her new environment. Emotions and impressions crowded in on her as she explored Hammersmith Farm, one of her new homes. She said that she fell in love with it as soon as she moved in for the summer after her mother's wedding in June 1942. Uncle Hughdie, as she called her stepfather, explained that his father had built the house not in the fashionable Bellevue Avenue with its imposing mansions but on the wrong side of Newport starting a trend from the flashy to the discreet which others soon followed.

The Victorian-type building at the end of a long drive was crowned with gables and cupolas and looked out on a perfectly manicured lawn and deep green pastures with the owner's herd of black Angus cattle grazing in the sun, soon to be joined by the new mistress's hunters and her daughter's ponies. Stepping through the big french windows on to the terrace, Jackie took in the view of the Atlantic – 'The prettiest place on the whole seaboard,' Jack Kennedy said when he, too, came to love the place which held some melancholy memories for Jackie and became an unofficial shrine to the late President.

At the end of the summer, as after every summer, Hughdie sold his herd (only to replace it the following year) and took his new wife, her daughters and his own three children to Merrywood, the other even more impressive Auchincloss estate, forty-six acres high in the woods and facing Washington across the Potomac. There were stables and a big swimming pool. When Jackie moved in, Merrywood was on war footing and only one of the dozen servants who used to look after it had survived the economy drive.

Like all the family, Jackie was allocated certain domestic duties which included operating the telephone switchboard. It was part of a new life-style which bore the strong Auchincloss stamp. Soft living and extravagance were frowned upon. A gust of Scottish Presbyterian puritanism blew cold on the Bouviers' self-indulgence. The newcomers were soon introduced to some of the family peculiarities. Jackie was expected to stand to attention before each meal and recite, prayer-like, the Auchincloss motto 'Obedience to the Unenforceable'. She responded with an almost inaudible mumble.

Many of her early days at Merrywood were spent alone in her room expressing her thoughts and feelings in poems and drawings which she committed to her sketchbook: 'We were seven people with separate lives thrown together,' she noted, a thought she recalled when the slow process of integration had been all but accomplished. Among her new relatives, the one she found most congenial was Yusha whose Russian soulfulness appealed to her romantic imagination. He became her confidant and separation in later years did not detract from their friendship. They exchanged hundreds of letters over the years.

Jackie was enrolled at Holton Arms, a day school not too far from Merrywood. Miss Shearman, the headmistress, was strict but fair and taught Latin with such panache that it became Jackie's favourite subject. Teacher and pupil had an instinctive liking for each other which led to a closer association later on. In the meantime, Jackie learned French and Spanish as well.

At her mother's subtle prompting she opted to spend Christmas with the Auchincloss family in Washington, the first time ever she had not joined her father and the Bouviers at East Hampton for the traditional celebrations. For Black Jack it was a terrible blow. Throughout the holiday he was uncharacteristically despondent and even Grampy, though there were plenty of grandchildren about, sorely missed Jackie. Jack Bouvier made up his mind to stake his claim to his daughters more energetically in future. Christmas 1942 was hardly over when he arranged for them to spend several weeks with him in the summer of 1943.

Before she was fifteen, Jackie moved up to Miss Porter's School in Farmington, Connecticut, where daughters of wealthy families were moulded into little society ladies. Jack Bouvier was responsible for the school fees and, however short of funds, insisted on paying for as much as possible of his daughter's needs – allowances, clothes, medical expenses – if only to cement his paternal rights.

Miss Porter's School provided facilities for pupils to keep their own horses – naturally Jackie wanted her horse in Farmington. She pleaded with her mother to send 'Donny' – Danseuse, her favourite mare. From Merrywood there was no response. When Jackie persisted, mother echoed Hughdie's view that twenty-five dollars a month was too much to spend for the horse's upkeep at Miss Porter's. Father, Jack Bouvier, could not be expected to fork out more than he already did. That left only Grampy. Surely, Grampy would foot the bill?

Jackie knew how to get round the old gentleman. She composed a letter explaining that mother and Uncle Hughdie had refused her request as too extravagant and enclosed her latest poem which could not fail to please Grampy. His reply came by return of post: 'What in one aspect might be viewed as a singular extravagance', he wrote in his peculiar prose, 'may on the other hand from the mental and physical standpoint be regarded as a justifiable necessity.' Danseuse would aid her psychologically and release her spiritually from sordid worldly cares: 'Therefore will I engage to meet her keep of $25 a month until April next.'

Donny was welcomed at Farmington with great joy. Jackie

groomed her loyally and fussed over her whenever she had a free moment. What grieved her was that Donny had no blanket but this was not the time to ask for another costly favour. How she solved the problem, she told her mother in a letter: 'Donny is very happy', she wrote, 'and is wearing a stolen blanket which I snitched from another horse'.

CHAPTER FOUR

As a schoolgirl . . . she was, rather cruelly, dubbed 'Jacqueline Borgia'.

Deane and David Heller

With Jackie at school in Farmington, so much closer to New York than to Washington, Jack Bouvier put up a valiant fight to prevent her slipping away from him. His visits to Miss Porter's school were events in his life. He mingled with other parents, partnered Jackie at tennis tournaments, took her to lunch at a nearby inn with several school friends who envied her such a presentable father: 'He was a very handsome man,' one of them said years later. Jackie basked in his reflected glory. But much as she enjoyed his visits, whenever he asked her to come and see him in New York, she often pleaded a previous engagement in Washington. Jack was convinced that Janet was keeping her away from him.

Competition between Jack and his former wife for the girls' mind and company escalated and their petty warfare created absurd, unedifying situations which embittered Jackie. Whoever was to blame, father or mother, it was equally painful. When she developed toothache, mother arranged for her to see a dentist in Washington. Jack did not like it at all. Since he was the one who would foot the bill, he demanded that Jackie be treated in New York which was nearer and would give him an opportunity of seeing her. There was a row. Jackie had her teeth stopped in Washington but Jack refused to pay for another session unless she transferred to a New York dentist. As with teeth, so with clothes and other items; if things were not done his way, Jack threatened to tighten the purse-strings.

In a happier vein, the Auchincloss family provided Jackie with new human interest. Mother was expecting Uncle Hughdie's child, and, in 1945, gave birth to a baby girl who was christened Janet Jennings after her paternal grandmother. In the best Bouvier tradition, Jackie celebrated the happy event with a rather extravagant poem. The emphasis, as in most of her poems, was on rhyme with a stanza which began: 'Listen my children and you shall hear, a thing that delighted the hemisphere.' Within a year she could record another addition to the family, the birth of her half-brother James Lee. For Hugh and Janet Auchincloss it was now the classical comic-cuts case of 'my children, your children and our children', making seven (not counting Hughdie's stepson Gora Vidal and his sister Nina).

With so much going on at home, Jackie tried – but did not quite succeed – to close her mind to the news of rifts and quarrels among the Bouviers, the worst of which was between her father and her grandfather who viewed Jack's erratic professional and private life, gambling and women, with growing disapproval. (That Jack cajoled his father into lending him $50,000 did not improve tempers.) They fell out, made it up and quarrelled again with Bouvier senior changing his will half a dozen times to exclude Jack and reinstate him after reconciliation. It was impossible to gauge the state of play at any given moment.

Turning away from trouble, not acknowledging that anything was amiss were among Jackie's outstanding characteristics. Among themselves – 'Please do not quote us!' – her contemporaries recall her distant, reserved manner: 'She was aloof but she was not arrogant!' as one of them put it. The girls at Miss Porter's remarked that she was ill at ease and restrained in private conversations, yet, perversely, outgoing and radiant at large gatherings as if determined to shine. She was an excellent swimmer, played tennis well and was the belle of every dance she attended.

Her family were as puzzled as the girls at school by her double-headed personality. The contradiction has survived to this day. Jackie demands privacy as much as she needs public acclaim: 'She wants it both ways,' one life-long friend insisted. Some of her schoolmates saw something sinister in Jackie's lone-wolf style, hence the bitchy references to her as 'Jacqueline Borgia'.

Others more charitable, and with hindsight, assumed that she carried a heavy psychological burden of many conflicting pressures and bottled up her feelings of shame, embarrassment, perhaps also guilt, about her parents' conflicts, about the Bouvier-Auchincloss rivalries and the problem of a family with three sets of children with little in common except the bewildering permutation of short-lived marriages.

But there is evidence that memories are not always impeccable. Otherwise Jackie would not have formed friendships at Miss Porter's which survived the school years. One of her roommates, Nancy Tuckerman, became her secretary and 'spokeswoman' and still helps to manage her affairs. Others she still sees regularly thirty years later. Neither is her reputation for aloofness easily reconciled with her enthusiastic participation in school activities. She wrote poems and drew sketches for the school magazine, joined in dramatics and was a stalwart of the annual Christmas pantomimes. (Camouflaged as party games, pantomimes organised by Jackie became a feature of White House post-prandial entertainment.)

In her second year she was permitted to receive 'callers' and several undergraduates, mostly Yale, who beat a track to Miss Porter's open afternoons, sought her out and were not discouraged, headmaster Ward L. Johnson keeping a wary eye on the proceedings until the decorous get-togethers ended after high tea. 'An original girl,' was the verdict; 'different' would be a more accurate assessment, a girl not in the mould of the majority, with an invisible barrier between herself and a world that could be hard and demanding but also challenging and beautiful. Jackie herself was all of these things.

After three years at Farmington, she graduated from Miss Porter's School. In the class Yearbook she figured with the following entry:

Jacqueline Lee Bouvier
Merrywood
McLean, Virginia
'Jackie'

Favourite song: Lime House Blues
Always saying: 'Play a Rumba next'
Most known for: Wit

Aversion: People who ask her if her horse is still alive.
Where found: Laughing with Tucky
Ambition: Not to be a housewife

At Hammersmith Farm her graduation was celebrated with a *thé dansant* for three hundred, first of several débutante parties to introduce her into society. It was, a little incongruously, combined with a family gathering for the christening of her baby brother, Jamie. A gossip paragraph in the local rag reported that 'Miss Bouvier was deluged with floral gifts'. After the party, Jackie with most of the younger guests repaired to a nearby social club.

At a second débutante party, Jackie who, according to her knowledgeable friend, Mary Thayer, was 'never a spender', appeared in a simple dress she had bought for $59. It was not as glamorous as her mother would have wished. By contrast, Lee, only just fourteen, wore a glittering strapless satin gown which caught all eyes. Jackie borrowed it for yet another party from which she emerged as Queen Deb of 1947, a title apparently in the giving of King Gossip, the columnist Cholly Knickerbocker. As a result, another scribe taking up the theme, noted: 'Jacqueline Bouvier, Queen Deb of the Year, is being besieged with offers of all sorts and demands for interviews and pictures . . .' The family put a stop to it all before Jackie was swamped by publicity.

Still, young beaux queued up to take her out to dances at the Plaza and St Regis – a contemporary described them as 'a beardless stag line who were known as the Grottlesex set'. Jackie saw no future in them: 'I didn't want to marry any of the young men I grew up with,' she said later. She did not know what she wanted. 'I was still floundering,' she recalled. Jonathan Ishan who escorted her frequently summed up his own impression when he said: 'She had the reputation of being very frigid. She was aloof and reserved and seemed to talk an awful lot about animals.'

She was ready to move on to higher things. The school suggested Vassar for her, a prestige college for 'the right people' or, as has been said, for 'brainy socialites', a category into which Jackie fitted well. Jack Bouvier took up the suggestion eagerly –

he was still paying for her education – because Vassar was at Poughkeepsie and so conveniently close to New York, much closer at any rate than to the Auchincloss home in Washington. He was looking forward to Jackie spending weekends with him at his spacious new apartment at 125 East Seventy-Fourth Street rather than with her mother and step-father.

Jackie threw herself into the busy college life with great gusto. Much to her regret she joined too late to hear Simone de Beauvoir lecturing at Vassar on 'The Literary Life in France – The Writer's Place in Society' but she could look forward to a programme which promised a great deal of intellectual stimulation. One of the items she noticed in the Alumnae Magazine was a comment on post-war fashions, Dior's New Look: 'Most Vassar girls don't like it,' it said. 'Long skirts win more approval than sloping shoulders and padded hips but, like it or not, Vassar intends to be *à la mode!*' Not Jackie. She was no fashion plate. Too time-wasting, too expensive: 'She never wore anything of special distinction,' one of her contemporaries recalls.

Whether it was a reaction to her father's notorious extravagance and the problems it caused or the Auchincloss example of extreme thrift (not to say stinginess), she was very careful with her money and would not gladly waste her allowance on frivolities. Jack Bouvier was often critical of his daughter's appearance, told her bluntly how to improve it and, when there was no change, took her out to buy more glamorous outfits. In later life Jackie became ambivalent about spending – economy drives alternated with bursts of outrageous extravagance when she would buy, buy, buy, like no other woman.

The first time she announced that she was coming to New York and asked her father to put her up for the weekend, he was jubilant – just what he had hoped for. They spent a day together, went out to lunch, saw a show. Jackie teased him about his lady friends and asked a lot of questions which betrayed concern. He, in turn, wanted to know all about her boyfriends. There was precious little to tell but he offered some fatherly advice: 'Let *them* go after you!' he insisted, 'Never take the initiative and make yourself scarce!' It added up to a seminar on how to attract men, the right kind of men.

Jack looked forward to many more such weekends but, instead, the next time she came to New York, she blew into his apartment with only just enough time to change for a day out with her own friends. Jack was in bed long before she returned home and not up the next morning when she took off for the day. In the evening she arrived, said goodbye and was off again to Poughkeepsie. That was the pattern for most of her visits in the months to come.

Even such fleeting encounters were better than the weekends when she could not or would not make it to New York and cancelled her visit at the last moment. Jackie was following the Vassar trail to football weekends at Yale, Harvard, Princeton or attending Vassar functions with the young bloods from the universities who came to Poughkeepsie. Jack was seeing less and less of his daughter.

The Vassar curriculum kept her busy. One of the first lectures she attended was on the subject of 'The Creative Arts in Contemporary Society' with Irwin Shaw among the speakers. There were regular political debates in which she took part. Though her voice was soft, if sometimes inaudible, she spoke with confidence on her pet subjects, art and literature – Shakespeare and *Antony and Cleopatra* in particular she found inspiring – and was listened to with respect. She was an impressive young lady, more attractive every day but with just a hint of masculinity and, curiously, not really sexy, although she enjoyed the company of boys. They tried to get close but she kept them at arm's length.

Jack worried about the attention men paid to his daughter: 'I suppose it won't be long before I lose you to some funny-looking gunk,' he wrote in one letter which she later surprisingly released for publication. Surely she would wait until she was at least twenty-one before marrying? To draw her to New York or East Hampton became an obsession. Now that Hammersmith Farm had so much more to offer than his own establishment, he dreamed up ever new devices to attract her, occasionally stooping to some gentle blackmail. His trump card was that ancient family favourite, Danseuse. Although Jackie seemed to be growing out of her craze for horses, she never did really, and she was strongly attached to her old pet which had partnered her in so many equestrian exploits. Jack was keeping Danseuse at East Hampton – if Jackie was not too eager to visit him, she was certain to come and see the horse! In another ploy, Jack even withheld her allowance and, instead of sending her a cheque, insisted on her coming in person to collect it. He was getting pretty desperate.

His schemes did not work out well. While he laid elaborate plans to give Jackie a good time in the summer vacation of 1948, she informed him that she was off to Europe with three school friends for at least six weeks to do the grand tour in traditional *fin de siècle* style. Suspecting another wicked manoeuvre by Janet to keep his daughter from him he protested but it was of no avail. By the time she received a rather lachrymonious letter from him advising against the trip, Jackie was already busy preparing for her new adventure, reading up on Europe and getting together outfits for all the spectacular events in store for her. The head-on clash between Jackie's enthusiasm and her father's jaundiced view only widened the gulf between them and clouded their last brief encounter before she and her friends went off in the *Queen Mary*.

Her companions were Helen and Judy Bowdoin, Julia Bissel and Jackie's Holton Arms teacher, the redoubtable Miss Shearman, whom Janet Auchincloss persuaded to go along as chaperon. The Bowdoin girls' stepfather, Treasury Under-Secretary Edward F. Foley, alerted American embassies all along the route to smooth their progress across Europe.

First stop London. Jackie and her friends dined at the American Embassy but the thrill of the visit was a royal garden party at Buckingham Palace to which the American ambassador's protégées were invited. The pouring rain did not dampen Jackie's enjoyment and she gawped with the best at the King and Queen who gracefully smiled in their direction. There was no formal introduction which was disappointing but by way of compensation Jackie saw Winston Churchill at close quarters. He made a deep impression on her.

From London, the five American travellers went on to Paris, then toured the valley of the Loire with its magnificent castles before moving on to the South of France, Switzerland and Italy, the canals of Venice, the gardens of Rome, art galleries, churches, restaurants. Jackie was enchanted and anxious to retain every impression. Perhaps it was the call of the Bouvier blood or the family mythology but the impact of France was strongest. All she wanted was to come back again and again.

By the time she returned home, Grampy was in a bad way. In the last years of his life, the old man, so proud of his family, had seen it changing and disintegrating with divorces all round, family quarrels and financial difficulties. What had not changed was his love and admiration for his favourite granddaughter who basked in his flattery and returned his deep affection. When he died at the end of 1948, the last pillar holding up the Bouvier tradition collapsed. For once Jackie allowed her sorrow to show and the tears to flow. Unlike the older Bouviers she was not interested in his estate which, according to family records, was much smaller than expected, a mere $824,000 to be divided among four children and ten grandchildren. Jack received $100,000, and the $50,000 he owed his father were wiped off the slate. Jackie's share, just under $40,000, was invested in her name.

As sad as Grampy's death was the loss of Lasata which was sold. For Jackie, even at nineteen, it was as if part of her youth had gone up in smoke. The much more modest cottage which her father rented at East Hampton was further from the sea and could not compare as a base for the summer vacation. It was rather depressing and Jackie, already shaken by her grandfather's death, seemed to retreat into herself behaving with a new solemnity, dignity and self-sufficiency as if she had lost her mainstay and was all on her own.

Happily, an opportunity to visit France again came earlier than she had dared to hope. Returning to Vassar, she discovered that the so-called Smith College Group's Junior Year programme offered students a year's tuition at foreign universities, among them Grenoble and the Sorbonne in Paris. She was determined to go and joined a special course to qualify for the requisite examination. The Vassar authorities supported her. She passed the exams easily.

For his own perverse reasons, Jack this time fully approved his daughter's plan to spend a year in Europe. It would take her away from him but, he reasoned, the rival Auchincloss clan would not have her either. He turned to his younger daughter who spent a few weeks with him at East Hampton. More outgoing, less independent and self-willed but also generating less emotion than Jackie, Lee made a good companion, consulted her father and listened to his advice. Then it was Jackie's turn for a farewell visit. Her mind racing ahead to France, she talked of nothing but her forthcoming trip. Jack told her that she was following in the footsteps of a great-grandaunt, Louise Bouvier, who had been a student at the Sorbonne some fifty years earlier.

Travelling cabin class, Jackie and her colleagues of the Smith Group spent nine days at sea which were, if anything, more stimulating than her previous stylish voyage in the *Queen Mary*. At Le Havre they took the boat train to Paris where a brief interlude admirably set the mood of Jackie's *année Française*. The first Frenchman she encountered was a porter at the Gare St Lazare who studied her luggage label with intense interest: 'Ah – Jacqueline!' he exclaimed. 'That's my daughter's name!' Was it his delight at serving his daughter's namesake or was it Jackie's opulent appearance which promised a generous tip? He fussed over her and showed her his badge, Numero 27, insisting that she ask for him whenever she returned to his station.

She continued the trip to Grenoble where she and her fellow students were billeted on a French family ('They get nicer every day,' she reported) who had seen better days but made their American lodgers very welcome. It was a happy home, comfortable and secure, to return to after the day at the university. Jackie's French improved rapidly but examination papers still posed problems for – to quote her – 'some dumb foreigner who could not do her homework'. The family helped where they could.

With their hosts to guide them, the American girls explored the countryside, discovered exquisite little restaurants and talked to people whose *accent du Midi* appealed to Jackie's ear. She never tired of listening to tales about local customs and history. With insatiable curiosity she found out more about this part of France in a few months than others learn in a lifetime.

In the relaxed atmosphere, her companions came to know

her better than her Vassar contemporaries ever did. They could feel the warmth of her personality breaking through her ice-cool exterior as she responded to the Gallic ambience: 'I want to come back and soak it all up,' she said when her course at the University came to an end, and it was time to move on to Paris.

Family life in Grenoble had been so satisfying that Jackie, turning her back on the dormitory which most of the Sorbonne's American students favoured, went in search of an equally congenial home in Paris. She found exactly what she was looking for in the household of the elderly Comtesse de Renty, a cultured impoverished lady who, with her husband, had been imprisoned by the Germans in a concentration camp from which the Comte did not come out alive. Her two daughters, Claude, the younger, of Jackie's age, and two other American girls shared the apartment at 78 Avenue Mozart. Conversation was in French only which suited Jackie: 'I have a mania to speak French perfectly,' she wrote home.

Sharing an ordinary home, and there was nothing extra-ordinary about the widow of a minor French aristocrat, broadened Jackie's horizon. Nothing that had happened to her before she came to France, nothing she experienced afterwards, opened her mind so profitably to the interests and concerns of average people, the price of bread, overcrowding in the Metro, mending and making do, small cabarets, the local cinema, the non-esoteric things that make up the lives of millions. Jackie reacted as she had at Grenoble: 'They are the most wonderful family,' she told her mother in one of her regular reports.

Poverty was easier to bear when borne by choice and Jackie did not mind living as the other half lived. The apartment was often so cold that she had to wear gloves and ear-muffs while doing her homework, and the hot water system was truly explosive. But the de Rentys goodwill made up for such minor drawbacks. Jackie and Claude became close friends. Though at the Sorbonne Jackie mixed freely with her fellow students she was not so much at ease with them as with the de Rentys and saw little of them outside classes.

In spite of all this austerity and the hard work she put into her studies, Jackie did not lose touch with her own background. Family friends from New York and Washington looked her up — Janet Auchincloss seems to have given her daughter's name and address to every acquaintance bound for Paris. Many of them asked her out and Jackie, exchanging her every-day tweed jacket for an expensive fur coat, made for the Ritz, home from home of rich Americans, to lunch or dine in the style to which she had been accustomed and reward her hosts with a most knowledgeable discourse on *la vie Parisienne*. Pleasurable as these excursions were, Jackie was never sorry to return to the humdrum routine in the Avenue Mozart and her studies in the Boulevard St Michel.

Among messages signalling arrivals from the States was one from her father who wrote that he was planning to visit her in Paris. During their separation, relations between them had greatly improved, fond letters passing back and forth between Paris and New York. She looked forward to seeing him after such a long time, but he never made it. Was he afraid that a personal encounter might break the spell of their harmony?

Instead, Janet, Hugh and Yusha came for a joyful family reunion. They went to the Opera, took in several shows and the obligatory Montparnasse night-clubs. Jackie overwhelmed them with her perceptive commentaries. The family was no sooner on their way back to the States than Jackie was off on a trip of her own. An element of restlessness, a quest for change and a craving for new impressions began to foreshadow her future honorary membership of the jet-set. She was not strictly on her own because she teamed up with Claude de Renty for a tour of Austria and Germany. Travelling second class without sleeper, Jackie once more, and very consciously, rubbed shoulders with ordinary people among whom, she remarked with inverted snobbery, she felt more comfortable than with the more elevated friends of her family. It was an affectation to which she clung tenaciously until quite some time after her return to the United States.

In Vienna which was still under four-power control, the girls made forays into the Soviet sector where Jackie saw her first Russians, sentries of the Soviet Army of occupation in their shoddy uniforms, crumpled boots and menacing tommy-guns which sent a shiver down her spine. Promenading in the inner city with its Gothic churches and baroque palaces, they encountered the *Four Men in a Jeep* patrols of the victorious allies (American, English, French, Russian). This was something to write home about to her half-Russian half-brother!

From Vienna to the glorious festival city of Salzburg and, just across the German border, Berchtesgaden and the ruins of Hitler's house, and Munich with nearby Dachau concentration camp where tens of thousands of Nazi victims had been exterminated in the gas chambers. In the stereotype phraseology of the American tourist she described her excursions to these sombre memorials of recent history as 'great fun'.

Another letter from her father awaiting her on her return to Paris announced that he would have to undergo an eye operation which would keep him away from work for at least two months. It suggested subtly that she might perhaps wish to come back and, if not nurse him, stay with him while he recuperated at East Hampton. Lee, he added, a little petulantly, was off on a vacation in Wyoming . . . Jackie's conscience stirred. Should she break off her studies and go home to father? As so often before when it was a question of joining him, she decided against it. His condition was not all that serious, she told herself. She wrote back explaining coolly and rationally that leaving Paris at this stage would irretrievably damage her academic progress.

Her mother wrote to draw her attention to the celebrated annual *Prix de Paris* contest for American students, sponsored by *Vogue*, the world's leading fashion magazine, offering the winner a six months' job at their Paris H.Q. followed by a spell on the American sister publication. Now that her year in France was coming to an end it seemed to offer an ideal opportunity of another spell in Paris, provided she won. The prospect made the farewell from the de Rentys easier and gave her something to look forward to at a time when she was uncertain what to do next.

It did not take her long to re-integrate herself into the family set-up in Washington and resume her old life. The prodigal daughter went to see her father and some of the other Bouviers, and contacted a few Vassar friends but, no, she would not be returning to Poughkeepsie although this had been the idea.

After a year of independence and freedom in Paris, she did not want to become a schoolgirl among schoolgirls again.

Happily there was the *Vogue* contest to occupy her mind. Conditions were clear-cut and demanding. Contestants were required to produce four essays on fashions, a personality piece and a lay-out for a complete *Vogue* issue. In later years *Vogue* developed the idea by handing over editorial control of special issues to prominent outsiders (Marlene Dietrich among them). Another task was to write an essay on 'People I wish I had known', an excursion into history.

While working on the set themes, Jackie explored the American academic landscape to find a university to complete her studies. She surprised her family and friends, by enrolling at George Washington, not the kind of campus for sons and daughters of the well-born they had expected her to choose. An urban university much like the Sorbonne, the explanation for her choice, with a good and growing academic reputation, George Washington required students to work and work hard. Janet and Hugh Auchincloss were puzzled but did not object. Father, as might be expected, protested. It was not the university which he disliked but the advantage George Washington, or rather Washington D.C., would give the Auchinclosses over the Bouviers. Living and studying in Washington, would Jackie ever come to see him?

She found work on the *Vogue* project congenial. Using a commonsense approach, she dealt competently with each subject in turn and produced eminently reasonable essays. Her predilections showed up most clearly in her choice of people she wished she had known: the great Serge Diaghilev, immortal producer of Russian ballet; a French poet, Charles Pierre Baudelaire and an English poet, Oscar Wilde. She was remarkably confident of victory.

When the *Vogue* editors handed down their verdict on the contributions of 1,280 contestants, the winner was Miss Jacqueline Lee Bouvier. It was a great triumph. The prospect of six months in Paris and working on *Vogue* with the assurance of at least another six months on the American edition, what more could Jackie wish for herself?

Her mother was proud but Uncle Hughdie was not so sure.

He felt that another long stay in Paris would alienate Jackie from the American way of life. It would be better for her if she did not go! He converted Janet to his view and they joined forces to persuade Jackie to decline the prize. It almost broke her heart but she did not want to go against the family's wishes and later conceded that Uncle Hughdie had had a point: had she accepted she would have wanted to settle in Paris for good.

By way of consolation, Uncle Hughdie suggested a short holiday in Scotland in search of the Auchincloss heritage, and a brief look at Ireland. While her thoughts were in Paris, Jackie, accompanied by Yusha, made for Paisley ending up where Scotland ends at John O'Groats before crossing to Ireland where she kissed the Blarney Stone.

Sister Lee having been left behind not once but twice, decided it was her turn to venture out into the big world beyond. As the new season approached she had Jackie's enthusiastic support. Lee recalls how she and Jackie pleaded, pestered and plagued for months before Janet gave in and allowed the girls to travel to Europe on their own.

Relying on her previous experiences, Jackie mapped out the trip, first stage London and Paris for a nostalgic view of landmarks of her earlier visits. She took her responsibility very seriously, acting the big sister, not to say governess, and preparing the ground with a terrifying thoroughness. When the two girls finally went off, they carried shoulder bags stuffed with documents, twenty-six of them, including passports, letters to American Express branches in half a dozen countries and membership cards of various motoring organisations for the plan was to hire a self-drive car in Paris and go on to Italy for sun and culture.

They recorded their progress in a spirited, light-hearted diary which was amusing if a bit little-girlish for two young ladies aged twenty-two and eighteen respectively, and, among equally noteworthy incidents, described their exploration of such mysteries as *oeufs en cocotte* (soft-boiled eggs in little cups). They asked mother not to worry that they might come back with liver trouble ('We eat and drink terribly sensibly, plenty of water and fresh vegetables') and assured her that, being good girls, 'we never talk to strangers.' They did, however, meet some nice English boys, snapped them with their box camera and sent the photographs home to mother.

The trip rekindled Jackie's infatuation with France but Lee was much more attracted by Italy which they toured in their hired car. What Paris was for Jackie, Florence became for Lee. She could hardly tear herself away from the city of the Medici. She wanted to return as soon as possible, and did eventually spend a year in Florence studying art. Jackie was a little bossy at times but Lee was too easy-going to mind and the sisters were genuinely fond of each other. The tour was a huge success.

Jack Bouvier was pleasantly surprised when Jackie, on her return, although resuming at George Washington, was much more freqently in evidence in New York than ever before. The magnet attracting her was young John G. W. Husted Jr, son of a banker and, like Jack himself, a Yaleman, New Yorker and stockbroker. Jackie and her new beau spent every weekend together. If she did not come to New York, he went to Washington where he was put up at Merrywood. It was not long before it was official.

The press announcement of the engagement said that Jackie's fiancé had attended Summerfield School, England, and graduated from St Paul's School, Concord, New Hampshire, and Yale University, had served in the war with the American Field Service attached to the British Forces in Italy, France, Germany and India: 'The wedding will take place in June.' According to Mimi Rhea, the prospective bride ordered a whole wardrobe of new outfits and sported a glittering engagement ring. Jack Bouvier was jubilant. Once married, Jackie would obviously come to live in New York.

Alas, it was not to be. Compared with the passionate affairs of some of their friends and fellow students, Jackie's emotional entanglement was on a decidedly low key. Unlike most other girls of her age, she was certainly not prepared to consummate the relationship without the benefit of marriage. Nor, unlike her ardent suitor, was she in a hurry to set the date. For her fiancé it was a frustrating experience, for Jackie too much of an effort to defend 'her honour'. Her visits to New York grew rarer and John Husted did not travel to Washington as often as before. The engagement was petering out long before it was called off. As an incident in Jackie's love-life, it was first pooh-poohed, then hushed up so as not to discourage other suitors.

Janet Auchincloss was not sorry; the young man was not really good enough for her Jackie. There were surely bigger fish in the Washington pond. While she kept her eyes open and bided her time, Jack was dreaming up another trick to tempt the elusive young lady to New York. As her term at university was ending, he came up with the suggestion that she should move to New York and work in his office in Wall Street. Jackie was impatient to start a career and become independent of her small allowance but the world of stockbroking, investing, gambling, and losing, was not for her.

Even before she formally declined her father's invitation, the Auchincloss brigade went into action. New York was out of the question! Jack fought but they won. Their victory assured Jackie a place in the history books.

CHAPTER FIVE

Over lunch I asked Jackie if there was anything to the rumours
I had heard that she was going to become engaged to Kennedy
and was surprised to hear her dismiss him as quixotic because he
had confided to her that he 'intended to become President'.

John H. Davis

Washington was the seat of power. Washington was where it
was all happening. Washington was the city for Jackie! Hugh
D. Auchincloss was so committed to Washington that his arguments carried conviction. Politics, public service, the fifth
estate; writing was Jackie's thing. Poems, essays, letters, her
Vogue triumph. Journalism, of course! Perhaps he could make
it up to Jackie for having stopped her taking the job with
Vogue.

Uncle Hughdie knew everybody who was anybody in Washington. He asked one of his friends, the great Arthur Krock,
Washington correspondent of the *New York Times*, whether he
could find Jackie a job. Was he thinking of the *New York
Times'* Washington Bureaux? What happened next has become
one of the Kennedy lores which have developed in the telling,
one of the pleasant little Jackie anecdotes which *si non e vero,
e ben trovato*. Krock is said to have telephoned Frank Waldrop,
Editor of the Washington *Times-Herald* (now defunct) who
had once employed ex-Ambassador Joseph P. Kennedy's daughter Kathleen as a secretary.

'Are you still hiring little girls?' Krock asked Waldrop and
added without waiting for an answer: 'I have a wonder for you.
She's round-eyed, clever and wants to go into journalism.'

He also mentioned casually that 'the little girl' he had in
mind was the step-daughter of a man of some consequence.
Waldrop promptly asked Jackie to come and see him. Krock
had not exaggerated. She was a beauty but looked suspiciously
like the kind of girl who just wanted to hang around editorial
offices until she got married. How about that, he asked her.

'No Sir,' Jackie replied. 'I want to take up journalism as a career.'

Although it was difficult to see why a young socialite who lived in a million-dollar luxury home should want to enter the rough and tumble of low-level journalism, Waldrop was prepared to give her a try: 'O.K.,' he said, 'but don't come back to me in six months and tell me that you're engaged!'

The rate for the job was only forty-two dollars a week but Jackie would not have exchanged her modest salary for three times the amount of pocket-money: 'I never imagined the daughter of a millionaire could be so cock-a-hoop getting a lowly paid job like this,' one of her new colleagues remarked. He did not know that her millionaire stepfather was rather tight with his cash, and that she was desperately anxious to free herself from the emotional strings attached to the fifty dollars a week allowance from her father.

Reporting for duty at the *Times-Herald* offices, the first snag she encountered was that there seemed to be no suitable work for her. The city editor scratched his greying head when a thought struck him: 'Do you know how to take pictures?' he asked.

'Yes, I do,' she answered blithely.

The only position vacant, he explained, was that of an 'Inquiring Photographer'.

'Inquiring photographer?' 'She knew which end of the camera to point at a subject,' a *Times-Herald* reporter remarked. He still remembered her puzzled, worried expression when she was handed her first Speed Graphic. But there was no shortage of experts eager to teach the attractive brunette who brightened up the male-dominated city room. Ace photographer Joe Heilberger appointed himself chief instructor and showed her how to adjust the camera: 'Take all your pictures at six feet – that way you won't have to change the aperture,' he advised.

'We welcomed her with open arms,' another photographer recalled. 'It wasn't so much that she was young and good-looking. It was just because we had all been afraid we would get stuck with the job!' The job was to set questions and put them to people in the street, their answers to be published alongside their pictures.

Jackie would not allow her lack of technical knowledge and experience to stand in her way. What the chaps in the city room did not know was that, without breathing a word to anyone, she joined a class for a crash course in photography, and went out exploring public places to which she had never before paid much attention: police stations, court rooms, hospitals, and the like where she expected to find the raw material for her column. She spent hours every day pondering suitable questions: 'You could make a column about anything,' she said later. To establish her position, she asked for the name of the column to be changed to 'Inquiring Camera Girl'.

Relations with her colleagues on the *Times-Herald* were cordial – up to a point. Her good looks were a natural asset and for a reporter, for one of them, she dressed very well although her sensible, inexpensive plaids and checks, the turtle-neck sweaters and low-heeled black shoes did not suggest a fashion plate. Nor did the outsize shoulder bag in which she carried the tools of her trade, flash-bulbs, pads and pencils. Most of her clothes came off the peg though some were made by Mimi Rhea, her friend and dressmaker.

However pleasing the total effect on the eye of her colleagues, her manner made it abundantly clear that she did not regard herself as 'one of the boys'. One after another, the younger men asked her out for a drink or a snack, one after another was told politely but firmly that there was nothing doing. A disappointed escort described the even-tempered finality of her refusal: 'She told me quite clearly, if not in so many words, that I was wasting my time.'

He was not alone wondering how she spent her evenings and was intrigued by her private telephone conversations, obviously with boy-friends, no doubt some weeds of the social élite. There were boy-friends, of course, but also the family, former school friends and their husbands, who would come up with young men to make a foursome. With Lee away, studying art in Florence, Janet was watching Jackie's extramural activities as intently as the *Times-Herald* staff. Behind the scenes and one hoped beyond Jackie's ken, a lot of matchmaking went on. Janet and her circle were forever scanning the horizon for suitable young males; prominent family, wealth and good looks being the essential qualifications they sought in likely candidates.

When they discovered someone who satisfied their high standards, there was much scheming and organising of dinner parties, weekend outings, visits to restaurants, theatres, cinemas with the hosts trying to push Jackie into a prospective husband's arms. She needed all her charms and social graces to keep the wolves at bay without causing offence. Among the most active marriage brokers were Charles Bartlett, the Pulitzer prize-winning newspaperman, and his wife Martha. Dinners at their small house in Georgetown were amusing, pleasant gatherings of people who were well-suited to each other. Jackie was delighted whenever she was asked.

At a dinner party for eight, one of the guests, not by accident, of that Jackie was quite certain, was Charles Bartlett's friend, John F. Kennedy, baby-faced son of Joseph P. Kennedy, Catholic Irish-American, pre-war ambassador in London. The date of the dinner, firmly inscribed in Jackie's diary and mind, was 8 May 1952. Jackie liked Jack's open features and eager eyes but could not easily reconcile his looks with a man of thirty-five and a Congressman of five years' standing.

Jack Kennedy had seen Jackie before across the proverbial crowded rooms but had never been introduced. Now he could not take his eyes off the sparkling girl; the Bartletts were jubilant to see them hitting it off so well. Jack and Jackie talked about their travels, about their schools (Jack had been to Canterbury, a Catholic College, and to Harvard), about London where he had stayed with his father, about his war service with the U.S. Navy but he did not enlarge on his exploits as commander of PT 109 in the Pacific nor on the injury to his spine which was damaged when his boat was rammed in a naval skirmish. It was only much later that he mentioned the metal disc which held his vertebrae together and often caused him a great deal of pain.

The young Representative (11th Congressional District of Massachusetts) who had recently announced his candidature for the Senate shared a house in Georgetown, not far from the Bartletts, with his sister Eunice and their housekeeper, Margaret Ambrose, an old Kennedy retainer. When Jackie mentioned that she had seen him several times in the company of good-looking girls, he confessed that most of them complained that he was too preoccupied with politics to be an ideal companion. Jackie laughed, he did remind her of an absent-minded professor. He was not a natty dresser by any means, and certainly not the run-of-the-mill millionaire's son. His ambition, he said, was to be President of the United States – well, that's why one went into politics.

Shielded by their hosts against intrusion from the other guests, Jackie and Jack spent most of the evening talking to each other. Such was the empathy between them, Jack later admitted, that had he had any intention of marrying, which he did not at the time, Jackie would have been the girl for him. At the end of the evening, he asked her to go on with him to have a nightcap, and their host escorted them to the forecourt of the house where Jackie's car was parked. She was still considering Jack's invitation when the Bartlett's dog pounced on a dark figure lurking in the back seat of her old Mercury. Jack Kennedy was startled, the dog was barking, Jackie looked embarrassed. Before she could collect herself and explain that the interloper was an old boy-friend who, seeing her car, had decided, without invitation or encouragement, to wait for her, her companion of the evening had disappeared into the night. She did not see Jack Kennedy again for over half a year.

Her work took up most of her time. If her technical skill still left something to be desired, she quickly developed a useful knack of contrast and a tongue-in-cheek approach which testified to her sense of humour and produced amusing copy. One of her earlier efforts was to ask five truck drivers their opinions on Paris fashions; no wonder she received some salty replies. On another occasion she walked boldly into the locker-room of Griffiths Stadium to point her camera, from the standard six-foot distance, at the star of the Washington Senators baseball team. She sought out children whose answers were original and unexpected: 'She was a businesslike girl,' her boss testified, 'nice, quiet, very earnest, anxious to be professional, a good listener, very efficient.' He soon raised her salary to 56.75 dollars a week.

Inevitably, in Washington's incestuously self-contained social circles, Jackie ran into Jack Kennedy again, and this time there was no old boy-friend to come between them. They went for a drink, followed up with a dinner-dance a few days later, then met again and again. Sometimes the Bartletts joined them, or Jack brought his younger brother Robert (Bobby) and Bobby's wife Ethel along. More often than Jackie liked, Jack was accompanied by one of his political associates.

When Jack went to spend a weekend with his family at their Palm Beach house he asked Jackie to join him. Rose Kennedy was away and Jackie did not meet the grand old lady but wrote her a thank-you letter anyhow, signed Jackie: 'I thought it was from a boy,' Rose Kennedy wrote in her memoirs. It was the first time she had heard of Jackie.

While Jack Kennedy was in Massachusetts campaigning for the Senate on the Democratic ticket against Henry Cabot Lodge, the incumbent Republican, he telephoned Jackie most days at her office; whenever his schedule permitted, he came to Washington to take her out. Some weekends they went sailing in Jack's boat *Victura*. Jackie, who had hitherto shown little interest in politics and, like her family, was Republican by tradition and inclination, followed the Democratic candidate's progress with growing personal involvement. He told her that his sisters were giving tea parties to rally the women voters to his cause. Jackie wished there was something she could do to help.

Preoccupied as he was with politics, Jack was amused by her vivid accounts of life as an inquiring camera girl. She was shrewd enough to realise, and he agreed, that one way of advancing her career was to spice her column with celebrities; and so prominent personalities began to figure more frequently in her column. It was in keeping with the Bouviers' regard for excellence which, save for her brief flirtation with the ordinary people of France, guided her. It happened to coincide with the philosophy of the Kennedys.

With a foot in each camp, Jackie was happy with the outcome of the presidental election. Although the Republicans won and General Dwight (Ike) Eisenhower moved into the White House as President, John F. Kennedy was returned to Capitol Hill as Democratic Senator from Massachusetts. He and Jackie celebrated his victory with Bobby, Ethel and the Bartletts.

A new era began for the *Times-Herald* girl reporter.

Aiming at the top, Jackie chose Mamie Eisenhower as her next target but the First Lady would not play. Instead Jackie approached Pat Nixon, the new Vice President's wife, who was willing to be interviewed and photographed. The questions Jackie put to her were not exactly searching: 'Now that the Republicans are back in power,' she asked, 'who will be Washington's number one hostess?'

The answer was fairly predictable: 'Why, Mrs Eisenhower, of course!' Jackie carefully noted Pat Nixon's eulogy of the First Lady: 'Friendly manner . . . sparkling personality . . . equally gracious in small groups or long receiving lines . . .'

Telephone conversations between Jack and Jackie had not remained unobserved at the *Times-Herald* where Jackie's colleagues pricked up their ears whenever she spoke to him. Irreverently, they referred to the freshman senator as Baby-Face and, when a correspondent reported from Capitol Hill that visitors frequently mistook Kennedy for one of the young Senate pages, the city editor mischievously devised a new assignment for Jackie. Why not seek out Vice-President Nixon whose wife she had already interviewed, and Senator John F. Kennedy whom she knew quite well, didn't she? and ask them what it was like observing the Senate pages at close range; and, conversely, ask some of the pages what it was like observing senators at close range.

Disregarding the personal implication with the straightest of straight faces, Jackie made her appointments. The Vice-President was pleased to receive her, the Senator delighted to give her an interview. The result was a column which has become a piquant historic document. Opposite is the full text:

INQUIRING CAMERA GIRL

by Jacqueline Bouvier

THE QUESTION
What's it like observing the pages at close range? Asked of senators and the Vice-President.

THE QUESTION
What's it like observing senators at close range? Asked of Senate pages.

THE ANSWERS

Vice-President Richard M. Nixon: I would predict that some future statesman will come from the ranks of the page corps. During my time as a senator, I noticed that they are very quick boys, most of whom have a definite interest in politics. I feel they could not get a better political grounding than by witnessing the Senate in session day after day as they do.

Senator John F. Kennedy (D) of Massachusetts: I've often thought that the country might be better off if we Senators and the pages traded jobs. If such legislation is ever enacted I'll be glad to hand over the reins to Jerry Hoobler. In the meantime, I think he might be just the fellow to help me straighten out my relationships with the cops. I've often mistaken Jerry for a senator because he looks so old.

THE ANSWERS

Gary Hegelson, Wisconsin: We've got this book with pictures of senators in it and I'm trying to get their autographs. I didn't know when I could get Nixon, he's so busy. One day when he was presiding over the Senate and I was sitting on the rostrum I decided that was my chance. He signed it right away.

Jerry Hoobler, of Ohio: Senator Kennedy always brings his lunch in a brown paper bag. I guess he eats it in his office. I see him with it every morning when I'm on the elevator. He's always being mistaken for a tourist by the cops because he looks so young. The other day he wanted to use the special phones and they told him, 'Sorry, mister, but these are reserved for senators.'

The column has since been reproduced a hundred times. Jack and Jackie talked about it – he thought it was very funny. He carried the clipping in his wallet for years, and Jackie still keeps several copies of the original *Times-Herald* issue.

On other occasions Jackie's approaches met with less favour. Having been snubbed by Mamie, she conceived a ploy to extract information about the Eisenhower family from Mamie's little nieces (daughters of Mamie's sister, Mrs George G. Moore) whom she cornered on their way home from school: 'And how have your lives been affected by your uncle's election to the Presidency?' she asked eleven-year-old Ellen Moore. With a child's lack of inhibition, Ellen told her: 'I've been charging fifty cents an hour as baby-sitter. Now that my uncle is President of the United States, don't you think I should get seventy-five?' She confided to Jackie that a girl in her class had advised her to demand good marks from teacher, or else Uncle Ike would throw her off the school board.

Ten-year-old Mamie Moore told Jackie that only three people in school realised that the President was her uncle, the others wouldn't believe it: 'But I've got brown hair,' she added, 'and bangs and now everybody says I look like Aunty Mamie . . .' The First Lady was not pleased when this tittle-tattle appeared in Jackie's column. The inquiring camera girl shrugged off the incident but if a reporter, a dozen years later, had approached her children and published this sort of thing about them she would have hit the roof.

Gradually her job was beginning to take second place to her understanding with Jack Kennedy. Yet, though the subject of marriage did occasionally crop up, no proposal was forthcoming. Jack was clearly in love with her but there were still other girls in his life, and Jackie, too, retained her independence and was seen in the company of all manner of eligible young men. Was it a scheme to put the snooping gossip columnists off the scent? Friends thought that while Jackie was only waiting to be asked Jack was still wrestling with doubts. But it was difficult to tell because he was as discreet and uncommunicative as Jackie.

They saw a great deal of each other. Jackie visited him at his Boston apartment-cum-office in Bowdoin Street, brushing past his two secretaries, Evelyn Lincoln and Mary Barelli Gallagher both of whom eventually capitalised on the Kennedy connection with revelations which were a poor reward for the kindness and generosity Jackie had shown, particularly to Mary. Soon the tardy suitor invited Jackie to join him for a long weekend at Hyannis Port, Cape Cod, in the Kennedy compound where the family foregathered much as the Bouviers had done at Lasata. Jackie confessed that she was nervous. Though she knew Bobby and Ethel (who was expecting her first baby) and had met Jack's sisters, there was the formidable Rose Kennedy and her husband whom her own father regarded as something of an ogre. She thought she started off badly because her evening gown was a shade too grand for a country weekend. Jack poked gentle fun at her: 'Where do you think you are going?' he asked. Rose Kennedy came to her rescue. 'Don't be mean to her,' she warned her son and added: 'She looks lovely.'

Though they went out of their way to put her at ease and she warmed to them instinctively, the whole family together, energetic, self-confident, secure in all-for-one one-for-all spirit, could not fail to overwhelm a newcomer to their closely-knit ranks. Jack's sister Eunice was there with her new husband, Sargent Shriver, Jean and Pat were not as yet married. Jackie knew that one sister, Kathleen (Marchioness of Hartington) had perished in an aircrash four years earlier and that another, Rosemary, was a chronic invalid. Jack's older brother, Joseph Junior, had lost his life in action in the war but there was Bobby and the youngest, Ted, as handsome as Jack and with a similar intensity. By now, Jackie adored the head of the clan, never mind what her own father thought of him. They were all vital, stimulating, wonderful. When Jackie was caught up in one of her enthusiasms, no words were adequate to describe her feelings.

She was swept along in the energetic activities; the Kennedys never did nothing. When they did not play, they discussed politics, picked up the telephone and talked to friends and associates in the four corners of the country. They thought nothing of calling Europe which baffled Jackie who had been brought up to assume that transatlantic calls were made only in an emergency. She tried hard to keep up with the exhilarating Kennedy pace until there came a time when she decided to revert to her old style and her more tranquil and reflective manner.

At the same time she suspected and noticed, without admitting it even to herself until much later, that there was an element of reserve in the Kennedy attitude towards her which kept her apart and which, in spite of all the wonderful welcoming noises, made her feel as if she was on probation. She need not have worried. As Jack explained later, there was not the slightest hint of antagonism, only concern for her and doubt whether this fey, delicate creature could measure up to the stern standards of the Kennedys and keep up with a family in perpetual motion.

After this private gathering, Jack Kennedy almost gave the game away and came near to a public commitment when, in January 1953, he escorted Jackie to the President's Inaugural Ball. If he had not made up his mind, a lot of other people made up theirs that Jacqueline Bouvier would be Mrs John F. Kennedy before long. Jackie often turned up at the Senate Chambers with hot box lunches, enough for two, to share with the Senator from Massachusetts.

As he was still not biting, she used her column cunningly to nudge him in the right direction. 'Can you give any reasons why a contented bachelor should marry?' was one of the questions she put to passers-by outside the Senate. Surely, Jack would take a hint! On another occasion she took her cue from Sean O'Faolin and asked what people thought of his view that 'the Irish are deficient in the art of love.'

The Senator's associates were watching developments. Dave Powers was the first to suspect that Jack was seriously considering marriage when the Senator asked him in the spring of 1953: 'Do you think there is really much of a problem in getting married to a girl twelve years younger than you are?' Powers replied that he was himself married to a woman twelve years younger than he.

Jack Bouvier, when he became aware of his daughter's problem, was in two minds. Should not Jackie, instead of prodding him, let Jack Kennedy run after her; or was he a prize worth fighting for? Before he could decide in his own mind, Jackie took her tardy suitor to meet him. She was greatly relieved when the two Jacks got on well with each other. Jack Bouvier, man of the world, good talker and well informed about economic affairs, quickly broke down Jack Kennedy's reserve. Confronting yet another rival for his daughter's affections, he was anxious to show himself at his very best. He was in a dilemma, wanting Jackie to marry well but at the same time afraid of losing her.

At this precise moment, it was not Jackie but Lee who was getting away from him. Since her return from Italy, she had been leading an active social life and, like Jackie, dabbling in journalism. While working for *Harper's Bazaar*, she met the owner's son, Michael Canfield, who became her constant companion. They soon announced their engagement and set an early date for the wedding. Rose Kennedy was a little confused about her son's girl-friends and, reading about Lee's engagement, thought that Jack had lost the Bouvier girl he had brought home. Lee's wedding took place in Washington and Jack Bouvier, however great the ordeal, was obliged to venture into Auchincloss territory and visit Merrywood which was so much more grandiose than Lasata had been.

In the meantime, Jack Kennedy was still dithering until Jackie almost slipped through his fingers. Out of the blue she announced that she was going off to London which was running a high Coronation fever and spreading the infection far and wide. Americans who could afford to travel would not gladly miss the historic spectacle and the romantic ceremony, starring handsome young Queen Elizabeth II and her consort, or fail to enjoy the panoply of a British royal occasion, the horse guards with their glittering breastplates and plumed helmets, the state coaches, the gathering of princes, princesses and statesmen from all over the world, or the round of parties in the finest London season in a lifetime.

When one of the Bowdoin girls, companion of her earlier overseas trip, asked Jackie to join her on a jaunt to London, she agreed on the spot. It was a matter of leaving the day after tomorrow, just enough time to make her farewells and to persuade the *Times-Herald* to give her a formal editorial assign-

73

ment to cover the Coronation. They readily agreed to hold the front page for their inquiring camera girl's reports from London, England.

A brisk wave to Jack, and Jackie was off, once more in the *Queen Mary*. No more enthusiastic society reporter had ever set out on a greater mission. Jackie would not wait with her inquiries until she set foot on English soil. So as not to waste a day, she inspected the dog kennels in the ocean liner and caught some engaging canines in the crossfire of her question and her lens, including the Duke and Duchess of Windsor's pooches en route for Paris.

Jackie and her friend were given the use of an apartment in London and, with the help of the embassy, obtained the most desirable social invitations as well as the necessary reporting facilities. She was as partial to the social whirl as to the official functions. Pearl Mesta's Ball (Mesta Fiesta, she dubbed it) at Londonderry House was a goldmine of good copy. An avid celebrity watcher, she observed Lauren Bacall waltzing with General Omar Bradley, was introduced to the young Marquess of Milford Haven who gave her a useful bit of secret information, that a special mark had to be made on the crown of St Edward the Confessor so that it would not be placed the wrong way round on the Queen's head. Ladies-in-waiting, Jackie discovered, were arranging for their hair to be done at three a.m. on Coronation Day because they were due at Westminster Abbey at six-thirty a.m.

One reader of the *Times-Herald* in Washington, rather more than others, awaited Jackie's despatches impatiently but perused the accounts of her visits to theatres, dances and night-clubs with growing irritation. Who were her escorts, Senator Kennedy wondered? What if she, like his late sister, fell for one of those smooth English aristocrats? He sensed danger. With some thought, he composed a short cable to Jackie: 'Articles excellent but you are missed.' As one of his friends remarked: 'From Jack Kennedy, this was more than a declaration of love. It was a proposal!'

Actually, Jack was much in Jackie's mind. What time she could spare from her engrossing duties were spent scouring bookshops for political tomes that might interest him. In the event she gathered up so many that on her return flight her luggage was overweight to the tune of one hundred dollars. Jack was at the airport to welcome her. Absence had made his heart grow so fond that he could no longer hold back. There and then he asked her to marry him.

Though she would have liked to shout the happy news from the rooftops, the only person to whom she confided it was Aunt Maudie whom she swore to secrecy. The reason was a fellow feeling for the Editor of the *Saturday Evening Post* which had already gone to press with a major article entitled: 'Jack Kennedy – The Senate's Gay Young Bachelor'. Had the news of the engagement leaked out, the *Saturday Evening Post* would have appeared with egg on its type-face. Jack and Jackie waited until the issue was on the news stands. Then the Inquiring Camera Girl went to see her boss, Frank Waldrop, and with mock contrition handed in her resignation. He had been right in the first place, she admitted and told him that she would be getting married soon. On 25 June 1953, the engagement of Senator John F. Kennedy and Miss Jacqueline Lee Bouvier was officially announced.

Jackie proudly showed the emerald and diamond engagement ring to all who wanted to see it. Jack also gave her a diamond bracelet, the first major piece of jewellery she had ever owned. She gave him a gold Saint Christopher medal which he wore until he parted with it on one of the saddest days of his life. They fixed the place and date of the wedding – Newport, September 12. The first thing was for the couple's mothers to get together to discuss details. A meeting was duly arranged and greatly amused Jackie who recorded it with wit and good humour describing the two ladies decked out in their fineries meeting for lunch at a posh Newport beach club where they were joined by Jack in a T-shirt and carpet slippers, and Jackie wearing what she described as 'a knockabout dress'. Later in the car, the mothers sat together in front and Jack and Jackie in the back seats – 'sort of like two bad children'.

Friends and relatives threw several engagement parties, the one at Hyannis Port enlivened by party games (no Kennedy party was ever without games) during which, according to Rose Kennedy, a bus was abducted and a policeman's hat captured;

like Jackie, the Kennedys were truly young at heart. At a bachelor party in Boston, attended by secretaries of Massachusetts cities who had organised the Kennedy committees in the previous year's campaign, Jack was ribbed over Jackie's French antecedents. Had his choice of a bride been motivated by political considerations? Jack's friends presented him with a reproduction in oils of a *Life* magazine cover picture of him and Jackie in his sailing boat.

As arrangements for the wedding were in the hands of the bride's 'parents', Janet and Hugh D. Auchincloss, Jack Bouvier was effectively excluded from active participation. He felt terrible about it. Smarting under the memory of Lee's wedding at which he had only played a minor role, he was determined to make an impression on Jackie's wedding day, make her proud of him as he was of her, show the Bouvier flag in the heart of the Auchincloss stronghold.

He spent weeks selecting a suitable wardrobe, a perfect cutaway specially tailored for the day, his father's pearl tiepin, shoes and gloves of the finest quality and, to complete the ensemble, acquired a deep tan at long sessions on the beach. He booked an apartment at the Viking Hotel while his twin sisters and their families chose another inn. On the eve of the wedding, he travelled to Newport accompanied by a stockbroker friend for support. Like an actor preparing for his grand entry, he concentrated his thoughts on the moment he would lead his daughter down the aisle and give her away. Let Hugh Auchincloss preen himself as much as he liked, Jack Bouvier would not leave anyone in doubt as to who was the father of the bride.

At Hammersmith Farm, on the dawn of the wedding day, Jackie was as serene and organised as ever. With Janet and Lee to assist her she put on her wedding dress of cream taffeta faille which decorously showed off her figure and the creamy lace veil decorated with orange blossom which framed her face. Not a flicker of her eyes betrayed her tension as she waited to be driven to the church.

At the Viking Hotel, the situation was far from serene. With growing agitation Jack Bouvier looked out of the window on a beautiful summer's day, warm and dry with a slight breeze. He left his breakfast untouched but, contemplating the scene in church with Janet and Hugh in the front pew and all eyes watching how he acquitted himself, he needed reassurance. To steady himself, he ordered a drink, took another and another but, far from working up courage, lost his nerve completely. It was shortly before ten a.m. that word went out from the Viking to his sisters and to Hammersmith Farm that Jack was incapable, well, that he would be unable to make it to the wedding. Someone else would have to give Jackie away.

When the news was conveyed to her she was distressed. That father had flunked it on her wedding day, that he was disgracing himself, for no other interpretation could be put on his indisposition, was a blow which, for all her surface composure, hurt her deeply. Only the steely nerve under the gentle exterior enabled her to hide her agony.

It was an impressive ceremony Jack Bouvier was missing. Facing the assembled Lees, Auchinclosses, Bouviers and Kennedys, the ornate figure of Archbishop (later Cardinal) Cushing was waiting to officiate and, special honour for an eminent Catholic family, bestow the Apostolic Blessing of Pope Pius XII on the couple. With brother Bobby as his best man, the bridegroom looked handsome and happy, Lee Bouvier Canfield led the gaggle of pretty bridesmaids in pink taffeta dresses with claret sashes, and then, gorgeous to look at, Jackie on the arm of Hugh D. Auchincloss, earnest, her eyes downcast but with the ghost of a smile on her full lips . . .

Traffic in Newport almost came to a standstill as the small army of guests in an unending line of limousines made their way to the wedding reception at Hammersmith Farm. It was a gargantuan affair. Having signed the wedding register, the couple took their place in the receiving line while twelve hundred guests queued to shake their hands, senators, congressmen, socialites, bankers, political aides, a cross section of the vast and variegated association of the four families involved. It took them over two hours to file by.

Radiant, the undisputed star of the show, Jackie stood close to Jack who looked tanned and fit, perhaps deceptively so. Although she suspected that some of those offering their congratulations were wondering what had become of her father, she appeared perfectly at ease accepting their good wishes and smiling obligingly for the photographers. She danced with her groom, then with her stepfather unaware that, at this moment, Jack Bouvier was packing his bags and decamping though not (according to John Davis) before telling one of his brothers-in-law that, much as he liked and admired Jack Kennedy, he loved Jackie too much to see her 'commandeered' by another man.

When Jackie went to change, her reserves of self-control threatened to run out. If only to make up for past omissions, she had dearly wanted her father to be part of her joy and to re-assure him that he had not lost out to his rivals, be their name Auchincloss or Kennedy. As tears came to her eyes she remembered the Kennedys' watchword 'Kennedys don't cry'. She was one of them now. By the time she returned to her guests in her going-away outfit, she seemed perfectly at ease. She took a fond farewell from her mother, her sister and as many of her assembled relatives as could reach her, threw her bouquet into the crowd and joined Jack in the car.

But the pain in her heart lingered on. When they arrived at their honeymoon villa in Acapulco, Jackie sat down to write to her father. He did not show her note to anyone but told a friend that it was magnificent, a noble letter, understanding and forgiving.

CHAPTER SIX

'O Johnny, We hardly Knew Ye . . .'
Irish Folk Song

Jackie's courtship had been active and satisfying but both she and her bridegroom were intensely private and reticent persons, and the laborious process of getting to know each other was only at an early stage. There was still much that she wanted to find out about Jack, much that only became apparent once they started to live together. Their honeymoon in an attractive villa in Acapulco was not quite the auspicious beginning to their marriage that Jackie had hoped for. Although she had been aware of the handicap resulting from his severe spinal injury, like any young man in love he did not dwell on his infirmity during their courtship. Only now did she begin to understand how it all started and how serious it was. Jack had first damaged his spine playing football at the age of eleven which had probably made him more vulnerable when it came under severe strain in the wartime incident in the Pacific. The metal disc, the clip, which had been inserted in an intricate operation, kept him in one piece but he was often plagued by pain and, besides, suffered from an adrenalin insufficiency which was soon to produce a desperate crisis.

It so happened that there was a deterioration just when a young husband would most wish to be fit and strong and would be reluctant to let his wife know that exertion aggravated his agony. Jackie was most considerate and helped him to make the most of his trouble-free spells. They swam, sailed, made excursions, read and talked and painted; Jackie had brought her brushes and sketchbooks and soon had Jack trying his hand. She read political books he gave her so she could share his thoughts. But it was not a honeymoon without obstacles.

What struck Jackie most forcibly was Jack's strong sense of family which was in marked contrast with the bickering Bouviers and the complicated, heterogeneous Auchincloss set-up. Desperately anxious to work her passage into Jack's world – she called him Jack though he was Johnny to many of his friends – and demonstrate her total loyalty to her new clan in true Bouvier fashion she composed a poem in praise of her husband, a long, deeply-felt well-constructed panegyric extolling his virtues and his purpose in life: 'Part he must serve, a part he must lead.' When the family read it, the poem rather than her marriage lines became her passport to the self-contained realm of the Kennedys.

The honeymoon over, Jack and Jackie went to live with Hugh and Janet Auchincloss at Merrywood: 'No point having a home of your own until you have children,' Jackie was reported as saying. Since they wanted a child and hoped to have one before long, they were looking for a house and eventually bought one in Hickory Hill, McLean, Virginia. When it came to furnishing and decorating it, money was no object. After living so long on strictly limited funds, the Kennedys' financial resources seemed inexhaustible. For the first time in her life, Jackie was able to spend and spend.

Spending became a way of life with her because she knew how rich Jack's family was although she never bothered to analyse the Kennedy fortune. The Ambassador (as everybody had called Kennedy senior since his term at the Court of St James) was probably worth more than a hundred million dollars, accumulated from a succession of deals which would be frowned upon nowadays but were commonplace, if not always as successful, among brokers and wheeler-dealers in his day: from huge imports of 'medicinal whisky' from Scotland during the prohibition, from ingenious stock transactions and shrewd investments. The elder Kennedy had settled a million dollars on Jack, as on each of his children, at birth, and, when the presidency beckoned, funded him with ten million dollars, much of which was spent on the campaign. Though well off, Jack was not enormously wealthy in his own right and was soon forced to check Jackie's expenditure, not always to great effect.

Money was of little concern to Jack in the first year of his marriage. He was preoccupied with his health and inhibited by the weakness of his spine. It was no laughing matter but Jackie could not help smiling on one of the occasions when her father came to stay with them and the very first words he uttered were to complain about his aching back. Jackie had not been aware that he had a slipped disc but soon found her two Jacks engrossed in conversation about their ailments which, at least in their symptoms, seemed very similar.

Politics presently intruded on Jackie's young married life. Jack had a difficult passage in the Senate. One problem was the administration's plan for a seaway to bring ocean shipping to Chicago by-passing Boston. After much heart searching, he supported the measure although it went against the grain of his Massachusetts constituents. Jackie, who frequently listened to Senate debates, was in the gallery to hear him make a brilliant speech 'One of the most thrilling moments of my life,' she said. Much more critical for Jack Kennedy was the matter of the motion to censure Joe McCarthy, the 'Reds-under-the-bed' Senator from Wisconsin whose Committee of Un-American Activities poisoned the political atmosphere. Jack Kennedy disapproved of McCarthy and his vicious campaign but, since Bobby Kennedy had been the Committee's counsel, could not very well stand up in public and condemn his own brother. With her limited experience of politics, Jackie could not be of much help however hard she racked her brain for a way out of Jack's dilemma – principle versus family. In the event, Jack wrote a speech supporting the censure while evading the critical issue.

The subject was the main topic of conversation at Hyannis Port when Jack and Jackie came for a visit. It did not put the Kennedys off their games. Touch football was not in Jackie's line but she joined in eagerly and cut a dashing figure. Perhaps she was a little too ambitious when she took the field another day because, after a short run, she fell over and clutched her leg. A broken bone? It turned out to be only a sprained ankle but it cut short her career as a footballer. She was still hobbling when the doctor diagnosed that she was pregnant. The prospect of motherhood delighted her and, with her features more rounded and her figure filling out, she looked lovelier than ever.

At the same time she was deeply worried about Jack's condition which grew worse and worse. He suffered constant pain and, unable to support himself on his legs, had to use crutches – and hated them. His frustration was almost worse. The glow of the young marriage turned into a nightmare when one team of doctors advised that Jack's only hope of recovery, the only way to relieve him of the agony, was an operation to remove the metal clip from his spine and fuse the damaged vertebrae together.

The family physician, Dr Sara Jordan, of the Leahy Clinic, and some of her colleagues were against the operation. They thought that Jack's adrenal insufficiency was liable to produce shock, infection and other serious complications. The operation would put his life at risk; he would at best have only a fifty-fifty chance of survival. Jack and Jackie spent hours weighing the cruel alternatives. She feared for his life but could not bear to see him suffering. In the end she said she would accept whatever he decided. 'I'd rather be dead than spend the rest of my life on crutches!' Jack exclaimed. In the face of all the grim forebodings, he opted for surgical remedy.

Once the issue was settled, Jackie thought only of keeping up Jack's morale. For a young woman who was often regarded as no more than a social butterfly, her strength of character was astonishing. When Jack entered the Hospital for Special Surgery in New York, she travelled with him and moved in with his sister Jean (Mrs Stephen Smith) at her New York home.

The delicate operation was performed on October 21 and Jackie was thankful that it went off without the dreaded shock effect which could have been fatal. She was told that the spinal fusion had been successfully accomplished but this, alas, was not the end of it. Within days infection set in and Jack's condition worsened dramatically. By the middle of November hope of recovery faded. Jack was so close to death that the family gathered around his bedside and Jackie called in a priest to give him the last rites. The Kennedys did not cry but even their strong nerves were sorely tested.

Coping as well as her in-laws, Jackie's energy never flagged. She sat with her husband for hours on end, held his hand and willed him to live. Later she said she had not given up hope for one moment. Her confidence was rewarded when Jack turned the corner and improved steadily. To help him while away the time, she encouraged friends to visit him as much as possible. Incredibly enough, she carried on a full social life, so to speak, on the side, met people and went out to dinner, very much as she was to do twenty years later when she was criticised for socialising in Paris while her second husband lay gravely ill.

Jack was never far from her mind and, one evening, meeting Grace Kelly at a dinner party, she persuaded her to come with her to see Jack in hospital ('I'm the new night nurse,' Grace announced herself). Jackie made friends with Grace which had an echo in the early seventies, when she was instrumental in making up the old quarrel between Onassis and Rainier of Monaco.

Visits like Grace's helped to speed Jack's recovery. By the end of November, his doctors suggested that he would be better off in the familiar surroundings of one of the family's homes. He was carried to the airport on a stretcher and flown to the Kennedy summer residence in Palm Beach. Still, it was a dismal Christmas. The decorations were hardly down when the infection flared up again and Jack had to return to the New York hospital for another operation. He came out of it in much better shape, was discharged once more and again went to Palm Beach with Jackie, brother Ted and a political associate in attendance. For the first couple of weeks a nurse looked after him and, before leaving, taught Jackie how to dress his wound, a hole in the back big enough for her fist to disappear in it. She was with him for twenty hours a day: 'It seemed she hardly slept at all,' a friend said.

As Jack regained his strength, Jackie encouraged him to read and work. He started writing a book on the subject of political courage about which he had previously published a magazine article. Jackie helped with research, scanning historical volumes from the Library of Congress, taking notes and writing out long passages. Jack concentrated on eight notable figures and their achievements in the face of daunting obstacles. He called it *Profiles in Courage* and in the preface paid a glowing tribute to Jackie: 'This book,' he wrote, 'would not have been possible without the encouragement, assistance and criticisms offered from the very beginning by my wife, Jacqueline, whose help during all the days of my convalescence, I cannot ever adequately acknowledge.' *Profiles in Courage* was a testimonial to his own courage in adversity. It became a bestseller and won him the Pulitzer Prize.

While he was at his lowest ebb, the Senate discussed the censure motion on McCarthy but Jack was, of course, unable to deliver the speech he had prepared. Several senators were disappointed and reproached him for not recording his vote in favour of the motion after the event: 'There was no point,' he argued. 'It would have looked as if I were kicking a man while he was down.'

As Jack emerged from the crisis, Jackie suffered a sad setback. After a troublesome pregnancy she had a miscarriage and doctors hinted that it might not be easy for her to have children. She was dismayed but would not accept that a Bouvier girl could not give birth and that she could not produce an heir. She was certainly not giving up.

There was no time for self-pity. After seven months' absence, Jack returned to Washington. He would not use his crutches, refused a wheelchair and walked to his car unaided. But he was far from well. His spine still hurt, the pain never subsided completely, he was forced to wear a corset and slept with a board under the mattress. It was at this time that he acquired a rocking-chair which, when he was photographed in it, was regarded as an amusing quirk. He had to wear corrective shoes, one a quarter of an inch higher than the other.

This was not the end of his handicaps. His eyesight left something to be desired but he took care not to be photographed wearing his reading glasses. His hearing was not good either and, much worse, his stomach was hyper-sensitive and allergic to certain foods (he was also allergic to dogs) but Jackie never found out exactly to which. Though she took a course in French cooking, she could not practise it on her husband who mainly ate steak, baked potatoes, ice-cream, and drank hot chocolate and milk, lots of milk. When he returned to the Senate, to a warm welcome from his colleagues, Jackie sent prepared lunches to his office to make sure he did not eat anything untoward.

Fully occupied with her husband and reluctant to leave him for any length of time, she saw little, virtually nothing, of her father who, having sold his stock exchange seat, led a quiet, lonely life, attended by Esther, an old retainer, most of the time waiting for a visit or at least a telephone call from his daughter. It rarely came. But, if Jackie neglected her father, she readily attended other Bouvier occasions and acted as godmother to another John Vernou Bouvier (Jack IV), baby son of Michel Bouvier, her own godfather. A less happy family event was Lee's divorce from Michael Canfield but a new husband was already standing in the wings, Polish Prince Stanislas Radziwill, a businessman living in England. They were married and set up house in London in the shadow of Buckingham Palace.

Once Senator Kennedy resumed full-time politics, Jackie's life was even more caught up in his multifarious activities. In the media-conscious atmosphere of Washington, a beautiful wife was an inestimable asset for a politician. Photographs of the handsome couple decorated newspapers and magazines and, without actively intervening, Jackie helped to advance her husband's popularity and standing in Massachusetts and beyond. To fill some of the gaps in her knowledge of subjects with which Jack was intimately concerned, she took a course in American history without neglecting her study of languages, a lifelong passion.

When Jack travelled to Europe she often went with him, acting as secretary and interpreter, and was handsomely complimented for her labour. 'Never,' wrote French Premier Georges Bidault, 'have I encountered so much wisdom invested with so much charm.' In Rome, they were entertained by the ambassador, Claire Booth Luce, but there was little love lost between the Republican Luce family and the Democratic Kennedys. Jackie's abiding interests on all her trips were antique shops. 'I could tell she was storming the antique markets,' wrote Evelyn Lincoln, Jack's personal secretary, 'when I received letters telling me that I could soon expect some shipments...'

With another presidential election in the offing, Jack supported Adlai Stevenson, the Democratic candidate who was expected to choose Senator Estes Kefauver as his running mate. There was much speculation about alternative vice-presidential candidates and Jack was frequently mentioned as one of the dark horses. With or without his knowledge or encouragement, associates exploited his popularity to press his claim against Kefauver.

Fascinating as the political constellation was, Jackie's attention was diverted when she became pregnant again: she was confident that this time there would be a baby. Sensing how desperately Jack wanted to win the vice-presidential nomination she encouraged him to work for it and while, in the tradition of American politics, he did not at this stage put himself forward as a candidate, he did not dissociate himself either from the public speculation around his name.

The backstage manoeuvrings came to a head when the Democratic Convention assembled in Chicago to choose the candidates. In an advanced stage of pregnancy and extremely uncomfortable, Jackie travelled with Jack to Chicago where he took a suite at the Conrad Hilton Hotel while she went to stay with Eunice and Sargent Shriver. It was an unhappy time for her. She was unwell and missed Jack who was locked in perpetual conferences with his associates in the proverbial smoke-filled rooms from early morning to deep into the night. They did not get together once throughout the week.

By this time, Jack was supremely confident that he would win the nomination by simply announcing his candidature. His growing popularity seemed to justify his optimism but he soon encountered a two-pronged anti-Kennedy campaign which came as a total surprise to him. Some liberals rejected him because of his failure to denounce McCarthy, and the right-wingers warned Stevenson against naming a Catholic as his running mate. Jack battled on but was pipped at the post. He was shocked and hurt when the convention chose Senator Kefauver after all. His only consolation was that Stevenson might lose the election and he would not be saddled with the stigma of defeat. This is exactly what happened.

Throughout the political drama, Jackie felt ill and isolated and did not even get an opportunity to tell her husband how much she shared his disappointment. The convention over, she only saw him for a brief moment when he came to say goodbye before taking off for Europe to visit his father on the French Riviera and join him on a brief Mediterranean cruise. Jackie went to stay with her mother in Newport to await the arrival of her baby. For once her despondency was written all over her face but she did not complain because she realised how much Jack needed his wily father's counsel before deciding on his future course. Joseph Kennedy had been against his son's candidature from the beginning and had been proved right by events.

Father and son talked and talked under the Riviera sun and mapped out Jack's political strategy. They only broke off for a day when Jack received a message from Aristotle Onassis who was lording it in Monte Carlo where he had a big stake in the company controlling the bank. Winston Churchill was with him aboard his yacht *Christina* which was anchored in Monte Carlo harbour. Onassis's message was that Winston wanted very much to talk to the Senator from Massachusetts – the suggestion actually originated from Onassis who thought such a meeting would please his distinguished friend. Jack had met the Golden Greek before but never seen his fabulous yacht, the most luxurious in the world. He greatly admired Winston Churchill and was eager to meet him.

Receiving him with open arms aboard *Christina*, Onassis took Jack to Winston who was in a deckchair in his favourite corner on deck. Without much ado, Churchill asked Jack about his presidential prospects in the future. 'It's difficult,' Jack replied a little mournfully. 'You know I am a Catholic.' 'You can always change your religion,' Churchill quipped. They talked until the grand old man tired. Onassis showed the Senator over the yacht and introduced him to his other guests. After a few hours, Jack returned to his father's villa. The next day they set out on their cruise.

In Newport in the meantime a dramatic climax was at hand. Jackie's baby was not due for another month when she suddenly went into labour and had to be rushed to hospital where she underwent a caesarean operation. It was of no avail – her baby girl was born dead. Bobby and Ethel Kennedy hurried to her bedside and found her in a critical condition. She was asking for Jack but he was at sea and could not immediately be contacted. Psychologically as well as physically she was at a lower ebb than ever before.

Not until he stepped ashore at Cannes did Jack Kennedy receive the tragic message from Newport. Within hours, he was on his way back to the States. From the airport, he went straight to the hospital and stayed with Jackie until the worst was over. They were both desolate, gloomy, withdrawn, silent as if afraid that conversation would deepen the wound. In her frame of mind, Jackie did not want to go to Hickory Hill, not without a baby. She had planned the house with a child in mind, its emptiness could only echo her sadness and disappointment. Jack also found fault with it, the distance from Washington, the effort of commuting, particularly in winter. They decided to sell and quickly found a buyer, Bobby, whose family was growing by a baby a year. Jackie went looking for another house and settled on one in Georgetown which was close to their friends and to movie theatres which they liked to visit whenever they had a free evening. They rented it and moved in at once.

It would have been miraculous had Jack's precarious health and Jackie's unsuccessful pregnancies not affected their marriage. They did what they could for each other but memories of the misery were not conducive to a normal married life. As often in times of stress, their differences in outlook, interests and manner became more obtrusive. Jack's main topic of conversation was politics which did not interest Jackie; Jackie was always talking about art and artists which bored Jack – on one occasion he simply left the table in the middle of a small dinner party and went to bed.

Food was a bugbear. Jack was a meat and veg man, she favoured delicate hors d'œuvres, sauces and chocolate eclairs. (Once, when they cruised in the Kennedy yacht *Victura*, Jackie, Lee and her husband sat in the stern washing down *œufs en gêlée* with claret while the Kennedys in the bow munched peanut butter sandwiches and drank Coke.) Jackie read four or five novels a week but Jack's expression went blank when she mentioned them.

'It was all wrong,' she said later. It remained no secret that all was not well with their marriage and rumours about an impending divorce crept into the gossip columns. Such rumours recurred and one of them suggested that, just before the 1960 presidential election, Joe Kennedy offered Jackie a million dollars if she did not divorce his son. But the couple's closest friends were optimistic because they both showed restraint and a resolve to make their marriage work again.

Had the harsh realities of professional politics not made excessive demands on them, the damage would have been repaired more quickly and easily. Much as they wanted to be together, there was always something to keep them apart. Without hiding his bitterness about his defeat in Chicago, Jack took to the road to campaign for Stevenson.

Travelling up and down the country, he made strong speeches, hitting the headlines and enjoying nationwide recognition. He would not have been a Kennedy if failure had not spurred his ambition. Once the election was over and, though Adlai Stevenson lost – because he lost – Jack raised his sights: 'I had so little time and so few helpers,' he told Jackie, 'yet I came so close to winning in Chicago. Now I have four years ahead of me, with hard work and a bigger organisation, I ought to do better in 1960.' Jackie knew what he meant. He had made up his mind to aim for the highest office in the land. He had also set the pattern of their future.

The Senator's adrenalin seemed to flow more freely, he was inspired with a new vigour, his home life was transformed. Jackie's response was strong. If he could rise over his political setback, there was no reason why she should brood over her misfortunes. Neither she nor Jack were prepared to defer hope for a child of their own for long. 1957 was only a few months old when Jackie was expecting once more. She changed her routine, rested as much as possible, reduced her social life to a minimum. Her mother and the whole Auchincloss connection were most helpful, the Bouviers fussed over her and the Kennedys treated her as if she were the fountain of the family's future. All who helped and feared with her touched wood and whispered: 'Third time lucky.' She planned to spend the summer in Hyannis Port.

When the signs were too obvious to remain hidden, Jack confided the secret of his wife's condition to a political aide who, forever on the alert to boost the Kennedy bandwagon, promptly told reporters that Senator John F. Kennedy and

Mrs Jacqueline Kennedy were looking forward to a happy event before the end of the year. The news was published before Jackie had thought of informing her father. That reporters had been told before him, that he had to read about it in the newspapers hurt Jack Bouvier who took it as further proof that his favourite daughter had forgotten and forsaken him. He complained bitterly but did not let her know that his health was very poor. Thus, when she was told that her father had been admitted to hospital in New York (on 27 July 1957) it came as a complete surprise to her.

He was, in fact, a very sick man but did not know that he was suffering from cancer of the liver. Jackie went to see him but (to quote Evelyn Lincoln – I could just as well be quoting reports eighteen years later about Jackie in the last week of Aristotle Onassis's life) 'thinking that he was much better', decided to spend her birthday with her mother in Newport where Jack joined her. She still thought her father would be all right; he himself, as John Davis said, 'was totally unprepared for the final torment' from which death released him on August 3. Jackie, whom he had loved with fanatical intensity, was not there to comfort him in his last hour. A telephone call informed Jack that the sixty-six-years-old lonely, frustrated and bitter one-time *bon vivant* had come to the end of the road. Jackie, at a critical stage of her pregnancy, was deeply upset and borne down by remorse. It was obvious that she reproached herself for having neglected her father and was distressed, as wayward children often are when it is too late, that she could not ever make it up to him. She looked grim and downcast as she took charge of the arrangements which a death in the family demanded.

'She surprised her family,' John Davis said, 'with the decisive, detailed way she handled everything from the obituary to the funeral.' Like everybody else, Jack came under orders. She sent him to select a casket but went herself to see one of her father's woman friends who owned a photograph of him she thought the most suitable for publication, then sat down and composed the obituary. Briskly, she asked Jack to take text and photograph to the *New York Times* with specific instructions to hand it personally to the managing editor.

Every detail of the funeral service at St Patrick's Church bore the stamp of her idiosyncratic taste. Instead of the traditional crosses of lilies and wreaths of chrysanthemums, she chose bright summer flowers in white wicker baskets: 'I want everything to look like a summer garden, like Lasata in August,' she said. If she could not keep her father alive, she wanted at least to preserve his memory as a lively, debonair man-about-town; she could not bear to think of him dead. He was buried in the Bouviers' home ground, at the churchyard of St Philomena Church, East Hampton, where he and Janet were married. The Bouviers were there in strength to mourn with Jackie but only a handful of friends bothered to attend the funeral. Jackie was tense but tearless and, on the surface, composed. According to one member of the family, though, her phenomenal self-control would have failed her had she not managed to turn her thoughts from the death of her father to the life of the child she was carrying.

In his will, Jack Bouvier had made a number of small bequests to his nephews and nieces and a token provision for his grandchildren as yet to be born. He left his desk to Jackie and a painting of Arabian horses to Lee. The residue of his estate, much smaller than expected, was equally divided between Jackie and Lee who each received around $80,000.

With a child on the way Jack and Jackie wanted a permanent home, gave up the rented house and bought an attractive, if narrow, three-storey red-brick mansion at 3307 N Street, Georgetown. In spite of her condition, Jackie organised the decoration and furnishing as energetically and methodically as she did all things. Every shade of colour was noted in a little book, every piece of furniture listed. She studied hundreds of samples before choosing carpets and curtains and spent hours sketching designs for the nursery. There was a place for all the antiques she had been collecting. Everything was done to schedule to put the house into perfect shape by the time they would move in, with the baby. Jack watched progress indulgently but would obviously have preferred a few old pieces of furniture, chairs over which he could sling his legs, and carpets not so precious that he could not drop cigarette ash with impunity.

But he did not interfere with Jackie's arrangements nor dampen her euphoria. Not for a moment did she consider the possibility that anything might go wrong again. She was utterly confident that she would be a mother before long, never mind the doctors' warnings that it would not be easy, and most likely another caesarian birth. Jack was tender and constantly mindful of Jackie's precarious condition. She still insisted on riding with him to the airport whenever he set off on his speaking tours and, though he loved driving fast, he kept down the speed for her sake.

A life for a life: on 27 November 1957, four months after Jack Bouvier was struck down by his fatal illness, Jackie gave birth to a perfectly healthy baby girl. The child would bear the Bouviers' traditional name for a girl: Caroline – Caroline Bouvier Kennedy. For the parents, her arrival was something of a triumph. Jackie was ecstatic and Jack, having blamed himself for his wife's previous failures, was reassured and relieved. If he had secretly hoped for a son, he welcomed a daughter so enthusiastically that it would be utterly wrong to suggest that he was disappointed. Plenty of time to have a son – or more than one.

'The prettiest baby I ever saw!' Jack cooed. But great as was his excitement, the birth did not rate more than two or three lines in the public press. 'Child to the John Kennedys' reported the *New York Times* (November 28) on page 58. 'A daughter, their first child, was born to United States Senator and Mrs Kennedy at Lying In Hospital here yesterday.' The *Washington Post* reported that the baby weighed 7 lbs 2 ozs and that mother and child were doing well. An English nanny, Maude Shaw, was standing by to take charge of the third-floor nursery in the new Kennedy home.

Baby Caroline was three weeks old when Jackie draped her in the precious Bouvier robe she had worn at her own christening and, with the beaming father in attendance, took her to St Patrick's Church, N.Y.C., to be baptised by Cardinal Cushing, the Kennedys' family priest. For Jackie, from this time, being a mother superseded all other interests. In families as large as the Bouviers and the Kennedys, happy or, for that matter, sad, events rarely come alone. About the same time

Jack's sister Jean Smith had a baby boy, Stephen, who became Caroline's favourite playmate. 'Sometime they may elope together and cause a scandal,' Jackie joked to Mary Thayer a little later when no breath of scandal had as yet touched the Kennedy name.

While Jackie wanted to encourage a sense of family in the child at a very tender age, she was not so sure about herself. While seeking the embrace of the Kennedys, she valued her individuality and independence, a dichotomy which troubled her throughout her married life. For the child's sake, though, she welcomed Jack's decision to set up a second home in the Kennedy compound in Hyannis Port, a beehive of Kennedy children of all ages, shapes and sizes. She developed a genuine affection for Rose Kennedy, the archetypal matriarch, whom, with her penchant for French, she dubbed *Belle Mère*. As in-law relations go, theirs was harmonious but not without an undercurrent of rivalry for Jack's soul.

The Kennedys were public figures who fed on publicity which contrasted with Jackie's need to be alone and to preserve her privacy. When Jack, already deeply involved in his campaign for re-election in Massachusetts (which he hoped to win with the biggest ever majority) agreed to admit a *Life* photographer to baby Caroline's nursery, she put up a valiant fight against such intrusion and only gave in because Jack convinced her that the publicity would advance his political prospects. Much of the time, she had to reluctantly share Jack with his political associates, some of whom, like Ted Sorenson, became her friends. She had a great deal of respect for Bobby Kennedy, a constant companion during her courtship, but felt closer to Jack's younger brother Ted who, though still at law school, acted as his campaign manager and was in many ways, a more youthful, more robust version of her husband.

Having spent the summer of 1958 with his family at Hyannis Port, Jackie suggested it was her turn now and asked Jack to take her to France for a holiday on their own. It was unusual for a Senator to travel abroad in election year but Jack sensed how important it was for her and was, anyway, so supremely confident of re-election that he agreed. He sent Jackie ahead and promised to follow soon. A few days behind schedule, he joined her in Paris where she was in her element taking Jack to all the landmarks of her student days including the well-stacked antique shops on the Left Bank. She spent much time in *haute couture* salons inspecting collections and liberally choosing gowns, coats, costumes.

Then it was back to the States and headlong into the election campaign. Jackie accompanied Jack on part of his final tour of his big constituency. They spent their wedding anniversary in Omaha. Jack's charm was enhanced by his boyish untidiness, his total indifference to his appearance. Jackie struggled to keep him up to scratch and when constituents wrote criticising his hairstyle, or the lack of it, Jackie and, if she was not around, his secretary produced a comb before his appearances on platforms or before the television camera.

Jackie was a tremendous attraction in her own right. Democratic politicians jostled to have their photograph taken alongside her: 'She was cheerful and obliging, never complaining,' recalled Kenneth P. O'Donnell, one of Jack's aides, 'a very refreshing change from the usual campaigning candidate's wife because she did not bother to put on a phoney show of enthusiasm about everything she saw and every local politician whom she met. The crowds sensed that and it impressed them . . .' When Jackie travelled with the Kennedy bandwagon, the crowds were twice as big.

On one occasion she saw O'Donnell noting down Jack's instructions: 'I never see you looking at your notes afterwards,' she said. 'Do you ever do anything about all these things he tells you to do?' she asked. The answer was 'Never. I wait until he calms down and then I rip these notes off the pad and throw them away.' Jackie laughed, and Jack said: 'You son of a bitch, I bet that's exactly what you do.'

The result of the election was predictable. By midnight on polling day when Jack and Jackie arrived at his campaign headquarters in Boston, it was evident that he had achieved his target – the final results gave him a majority of 874,608 or 73.6 per cent of the votes cast, bigger than any other senator, a record for the state and a signal which the party bosses could not overlook.

CHAPTER SEVEN

'All this is completely confidential between you and me . . .'

Jacqueline Kennedy in a letter to Pamela Turnure, published by
Mary Van Rensselaer Thayer

Jackie's woman of the world manner never suggested domesti-
city but, in her elevated fashion and in spite of her jet-set
reputation, she had always been a homebody at heart. Nothing mattered as much to her as a house. It was almost patho-
logical, and dated back to her childhood when she was
constantly shuttled from one residence to another – from town
to country, from her father's apartment to her mother's – and
not allowed to take roots. Her passion for houses, for decorating and furnishing them, for moving in and out and starting
on another, persisted for years. Not until, in the middle sixties,
she found a haven for herself at 1040 Fifth Avenue, New York,
a fifteen-room apartment so personal and private that she even
resented intrusion by her second husband, did she settle down
in any real sense, and even then, though Onassis ran half a
dozen houses, her quest for new abodes did not cease.

The house in N Street, Washington, into which she moved
with Jack Kennedy in 1957, was a mirror of her personality. To
the cost, $82,000, was added the expense of structural altera-
tions which brought the total up to $100,000, not including
the expensive furniture. The hub of the house was a sitting
room with two ornamental fireplaces, wooden floors in a white-
green pattern, Louis XVI chairs to match, French period porce-
lain, delicate carpets, a galaxy of small tables, bric-a-brac
ashtrays, old clocks, all French, a few paintings by minor
French artists and a stereotype collection of coffee-table books
on such masters as El Greco (it so happened that Onassis's
most prized possession was an El Greco with whom he identified in some curious way) and Picasso, one of whose works
Onassis bought her in the passage of time. It was all very
Jackie.

For the very first time in her life she felt really at home and talked dreamily about evenings she and Jack spent alone together in the house, though there were few of those. They entertained friends for dinner, never more than six or eight, but not all of them appreciated Jackie's French cuisine. Neither did Jack who said: 'She is very good at French cooking but can't make a decent cup of chocolate.' Since Jack's associations were almost exclusively political, uninhibited social gatherings without a definite purpose were rare.

The focus of real family life was little Caroline, a lively, attractive child, and she, too, had to fit into Jackie's French design. From earliest childhood, Caroline was indoctrinated with French impressions. Pleasing herself as much as her little girl, Jackie imaginatively substituted French historical figures, her eighteenth-century idols, for popular fairy-tale characters until Caroline was more familiar with the wondrous lives of the kings and queens of France than with Aladdin or Snow White. As Jackie's interests advanced to contemporary French leaders, the distinction between Charles de Gaulle and Jack (and the Beanstalk) became blurred in the child's mind.

Too often, though, mother was not there to read her fairy stories. From the beginning, and much against Jackie's grain, even motherhood had to take second place to Jack's career (which is why ever since Jackie has been frantically making up lost ground and all but smothered Caroline with affection). Routine was upset by the constant call of politics. Life was one unending succession of forays into the political arena, tours to test the political temperature, to show his and his wife's face and impress them on the mind of the voters. It was a successful strategy and success generated increasing demand. Such was Jack's fame after the spectacular Massachusetts result that invitations to speak all over the country poured in by the thousand.

His travels covered the length and breadth of the United States and turned him into one of the best-informed American politicians. Many nights and most weekends were spent studying local issues in areas on his itinerary and notes of his experiences. Even when he and Jackie were together, his mind raced ahead to his next assignment. He saw only one of Jackie's

96

relatives, the most distant of them, Gore Vidal; bright, sharp-tongued, he was a rarity among the Auchinclosses, a Democrat with political ambitions. Vidal's own campaign was perhaps too clever to generate the kind of popular appeal which Jack had in such great measure.

Whenever Jack wanted Jackie to take a hand at canvassing or come along on his tours, she obliged without great enthusiasm but, once she agreed to go with him, no outsider could have guessed how little she cared for these ventures. Her sense of duty more than her love for Jack enabled her to perform almost to perfection. She rarely travelled without a large wardrobe, mostly French couture, but an American politician's wife could only dress too well at her peril. Her elegance was not yet at issue, as it became at the peak of Jack's campaign for the 1960 presidential nomination – the target was the Democratic primaries and the National Convention in Los Angeles – but there was already a risk that she might attract envy rather than admiration among female voters attuned to less glamorous candidates' wives. Once this became evident, particularly in rural regions, she adjusted her outfits and travelled light contenting herself with a neat, severe, tailored suit, one or two simple dresses and a couple of jackets.

The slightest scratch and her French connection came to the surface. At Wisconsin where they arrived on a hard winter's day, Jackie brought a glow of pride to the cheeks of a French-American couple whom she told: *'Moi aussi, je suis d'origine Française!'* Her command of the French language never ceased to impress the reporters. Hopelessly infected by his wife's Franco-mania, Jack developed a totally uncritical admiration for Charles de Gaulle and could quote long passages from the General's grand orations in English translation. Applied to America, they expressed his own feelings: 'All my life,' he would recite, 'I have had a certain idea of France inspired by sentiment as much as by reason . . .' France pledged to an eminent and exceptional destiny . . . Jackie echoed him in the original and more melodious French.

This was the spirit in which Jack Kennedy campaigned for the presidential nomination and which soon inspired Jackie. The tours which had started as an ordeal became a sacred mission for her. No effort was too great until she developed a campaigning style of her own which ideally complemented Jack's efforts. Even when campaigning in different parts of a locality, they were in harness as if the common ambition welded them closer together. However intense their double act on the political trapeze, there was always time for a very intimate interlude, a whispered word, a squeeze of the hand, even a sexual innuendo.

Jack's assistant, David F. Powers, recalled the couple's visit to Fort Atkinson where, according to Powers, the wife of the local parson was waiting with her thirteen children to shake the Senator's hand. Jack posed for photographs with her and the children, then asked Powers to call Jackie who was canvassing on the other side of the street. Jack introduced her to the minister's wife: 'Shake hands with this lady,' he told Jackie and, pointing to the large brood, added, 'maybe it will rub off on you!' The date of this encounter was 15 February 1960, and Powers suggests by implication that Jackie took Jack's hint literally and promptly because nine months later, give or take a week, little John Kennedy was born. (The less romantic truth is that Jackie's second baby was indeed born on November 25 but the birth was one month premature.)

But Jackie, despite being pregnant again, insisted on carrying on to help Jack for a while as yet. In Jack's private plane, *Caroline*, she flew to key points forever devising new ideas on how to woo the crowds. She tried to lead one gathering waiting for the candidate's arrival, in a song, a marching tune of the South Boston Irish, which alas, they did not know. Instead of a chorus there was great hilarity. When she appeared before a crowd of Puerto Ricans, she easily slipped into Spanish: 'Buenos dias, mes amigos,' she greeted them and continued to address them in their own language. An Italian gathering was treated to a perfectly enunciated little speech in Italian.

In Virginia, Jackie visited miners' wives in their humble homes, handed out Kennedy labels in shopping centres and joined a gang of railway workers for a chat by the roadside. Franklin D. Roosevelt Jr (who later chaperoned Jackie on her first cruise with Onassis) campaigned alongside her: 'You know why I speak for Kennedy?' he asked rhetorically. 'Because Jack and I fought side by side in the Pacific!' Cardinal Cushing entered the fray. There were six possibles for the Democratic nomination but the campaign soon crystallised into a fight between Jack Kennedy and Lyndon B. Johnson.

As Jackie's condition forced her to drop out, as reluctantly as she had entered the campaign, the Kennedy clan rallied to the cause. Bobby was the brains behind the strategy, an untiring advocate of his brother's claim, adept at wheeling and dealing at every political level. While staying in the background, in the face of ugly suggestions that he was buying the presidency for Jack, Joe Kennedy threw the weight of his experience and influence behind his son, sister Pat recruited her popular husband Peter Lawford, and Jean Smith and Eunice Schreiber and their husbands worked energetically. They visited Jackie regularly at Hyannis Port to report on progress.

Of her husband she saw next to nothing. His schedule was so tight that he could not snatch more than a few minutes now and then to see her and Caroline. He tried to shield Jackie from his more serious problems which mounted every day but talked to her about the lighter side of his campaign: how he dressed in his solemn dark blue suit for an important meeting with Protestant clergymen (who wanted to hear why he thought a Catholic was fit to become President of the United States) and found he only had a pair of brown shoes which did not go well with it. Jackie worried about the anti-Catholics: 'So unfair to Jack,' she said. 'He's such a poor Catholic!' She was upset when political rivals brought up the issue of Jack's health and spread a rumour that he was suffering from Addison's disease, yet she could not help wondering about the heavy drain on his physical resources.

At Hyannis Port, Rose Kennedy was at hand to lend moral support but much of Jackie's time was spent with Caroline, with Maude Shaw who looked so admirably after the child, and with Provi – Miss Providencia Paredes – the Dominican maid. With only intermittent campaign duties, Jackie could read, paint and ruminate and be alone when she felt the need to be which was frequently. While her future as well as Jack's was in the balance, she confessed that she passionately wanted Jack to be President, yet dreaded the effect his election would have on her own life. Ambition for Jack and for herself – for what woman would not want to be First Lady? – was not easily reconciled with her craving for privacy. Well, yes, Jackie, as always, wanted it both ways. The inner conflict aggravated the growing demands the expected baby made on her strength. She thought then, as she said later, that she would be a wife and mother first, then a First Lady, a pious hope.

Following the approaching climax as presented on television, she yet knew that the real issues were fought out behind the scenes but was rewarded with occasional glimpses of Jack addressing gatherings and meeting political associates. How favourably he compared with the other front runners, and not only in her judgment. He divided his time between the Biltmore Hotel, headquarters of the Democratic National Committee, Marion Davies's villa which had been put at his disposal, and a private apartment which was soon overrun by aides and reporters. Every evening, loyally, he telephoned Jackie to give her a brief rundown on developments. When he called on July 12, the eve of the Los Angeles Convention, he sounded at once nervous and confident. At long last, the TV cameras focused on the massed delegates of the Convention.

Jackie knew that, like her, Jack was watching the final stages on television, though his set briefly broke down when the electricity at Marion Davies's house became overloaded. Separated but united in thought, they saw the leaders of delegations, one after another, rising to announce their votes. Jackie's mind was on the magical figure of 761 which Jack needed to secure nomination. 750 votes had been cast for him when it was Wyoming's turn. Jackie held her breath although, whichever way Wyoming split its vote, Jack could count on sufficient support in the remaining states to give him victory. Jackie's agony was mercifully brief. All Wyoming's fifteen votes went to Jack. He was now the official Democratic candidate. Only the nomination for Vice President remained to be decided but Jackie cared little whether or not it went to Lyndon B. Johnson as indeed it did.

Was it the end or was it a beginning? Jackie could at least expect her husband to join her in Hyannis Port for a few days of rest and recuperation. Their time together was all the more precious since, in the years to come, there might not be many more such days. They were both relaxed and Caroline blossomed in the happy climate of their affection. They went swimming and sailing, oblivious of the prying eyes, private and professional, which observed their every move but it was a different matter when their photographs were published. That Jackie's short shocking-pink pants and orange sweater would raise a few eyebrows was predictable but she certainly did not expect the august *New York Times* to comment that the world was witnessing something of 'possibly vast political consequence', a future First Lady with a youthful, modern, personal style of her own.

Jack was back in the political fray by the time the Republicans selected Richard Milhous Nixon as their candidate to oppose him in the race for the White House. The ensuing battle for such a high prize was bound to make the campaign for nomination appear like a minor skirmish. The question was whether Jackie's condition would allow her to campaign as actively as was expected of the candidate's wife. She decided to do as much as John Walsh, her obstetrician permitted although some of Jack's advisers hinted that she might create problems rather than help him win friends and influence people.

They seemed confirmed in their view when a news story appeared stating that Mrs Kennedy was spending $30,000 a year on her wardrobe, most of it Paris *haute couture*. The Republicans seized on the report and harped on Jackie's extravagant clothes and her extravagant hairstyle. The newspapers hammered away at the subject: who spent more on clothes, Mrs Kennedy or Mrs Nixon? For the first time Jackie was under public attack: 'I've lived in Paris and I have gone to Europe to see my sister whenever I could,' she replied by way of explanation. She had never bought more than one suit or one coat from Balenciaga or Givenchy: 'I'd have to wear sable underwear to spend $30,000 a year on clothes!'

Powerful voices rallied to her defence. President Harry S. Truman spoke up: 'What the women in the families of men in public life wear or spend is no concern to others!' A New York couturier, Adolf Klein, who supplied Jackie with American designs, said there was no reason why political personalities should have to look 'like they came straight from the poor-house'. Even before Jack told her not to worry, Jackie reacted like an old trouper. When she emerged from a New York hair-dresser and reporters badgered her with the same kind of ques-tion she told them boldly: 'I can't see what my hair-do has to do with my husband's ability to be President.'

Still, she made a point of buying her maternity dresses off the peg (at Lord and Taylor) and, in the presence of a gaggle of women writers, showed off her new silk tea dress which, she said, had cost $34.95. The nine-day wonder of the 'great clothes hassle' brought the anti-Jackie undercurrent to the surface until it fizzled away in the mainstream of adulation of the cleverest, handsomest, most unusual young woman ever to knock at the door of the White House.

Worrying news came from London where Jackie's sister seemed to be having a difficult pregnancy. Early in August, Lee Radziwill's first baby was born prematurely; not a good omen for Jackie who was herself five months pregnant. She pushed all worries into the background by taking a more active part in Jack's campaign. One of her contributions was a regular column under the heading *Campaign Wife* which was addressed to women voters. She told them how frustrated she was when she could not campaign with her husband, and how disappointed at missing the Los Angeles Convention. In another column she opened a door on to her private life describing the day a hurri-cane came close to Hyannis Port and Caroline was as much concerned for her father (who was in storm-free Texas) as for her pets, Tom Kitten and Charlie.

Although it required some effort, Jackie joined her husband on his tour of New York which developed into one of those fantastic ticker tape parades. She sat with him atop the back seat of his car and was soon snowed under in a glittering downpour of paper. It was an exhilarating experience but as it went on and the crowds surged ever closer, she became appre-hensive. When the car stopped, she slipped away and, some-how, managed to remain unrecognised. Accompanied by Bill Walton, the artist-turned campaign aide and close friend of Jack's (as also of Hemingway's) she reached Madison Avenue. While Jack and his entourage continued on their triumphal tour, she persuaded Bill to escort her to one or two art galleries. Her friends – and Jack – marvelled, but could never really understand, how she managed to detach herself totally from the most momentous occasions to pursue her own foibles.

It did not mean that she neglected her duties or spared herself. With television playing a major role in the campaign, she organised Listening (Viewing) Parties for Democratic committee women at Hyannis Port. They were there when John F. Kennedy and Richard M. Nixon confronted each other in the first of their four televised debates. It was reassuring to see the familiar face emanating resolve and hear Jack's voice, thinner and less sonorous than Nixon's, yet infinitely more confident and persuasive, suggesting a stronger intellect and greater integrity. Jack's contempt for Nixon came through. A few days later he told Jackie jokingly, not so much of a joke either, that he owed it to the country to keep Nixon out of the White House.

Presently Jackie admitted the television cameras to her house to record a three-cornered conversation between herself, Jack, who was in California, and Henry Fonda who spoke from New York. Caroline came into the picture and hugely enjoyed seeing herself on the little screen. On 2 November Jackie went to Merrywood to preside over a Washington Ladies Viewing Party and the following day turned up at the Democratic HQ to thank 'all those people who have worked so hard for my husband'. And so back to Hyannis Port for three days' rest without losing sight of Jack on the last leg of the campaign, a *tour de force* which took him from one end of the country to the other ending up at Boston where they were due to meet on polling day in the Bowdoin Street apartment, their registered residence.

Jackie left Cape Cod at the crack of dawn to join Jack who took her straight to the polling station where a huge crowd awaited the presidential candidate. Jackie, in the eighth month of her pregnancy, bore herself well as Jack walked ahead of her with outstretched arms to protect her from the crush. Having cast their vote, they drove straight to the airport and flew back to Cape Cod. Jack's entourage set up shop at Bobby's house which was more spacious than his own and had the advantage of keeping people away from Jackie.

With her unique self-control, so often mistaken for insensitivity, Jackie arranged her day and her evening so as to relieve Jack of all preoccupation with her. She asked Bill Walton to join them for dinner. In the meantime, Jack went across the road to Bobby's to show himself to the faithful and garner news of the state of play before returning home to dine with Jackie and Bill. When Jackie was tiring around ten p.m., he sent her upstairs and returned to Bobby's house. By three a.m. he was still eight electoral votes short of the 269 required for election but went home without waiting to find out whether he had made it. Jackie was fast asleep.

The result remained in the balance for some time but when Jack rose at seven a.m. he was told that, though he had lost California, he had won the election with the smallest ever margin of popular votes (his majority was 118,550 out of a total of 68,832,818 votes cast). He embraced Jackie. Looking out of the window they saw a Secret Service detail in position around the house guarding the next President of the United States. They had a family breakfast but were so deeply moved they hardly spoke. Only Caroline's baby patter broke the heavy silence.

It was time for Jack to join his aides. Jackie watched him leaving with measured steps obviously deep in thought. 'There was a change in his manner and bearing,' noted O'Donnell and Powers in their fascinating account of John F. Kennedy's political progress. Their salute ushered in a new era: 'Good morning, Mr President,' they greeted him for the first time.

With Jackie and his aides, the President-elect drove to the U.S. Armoury at Hyannis where reporters, photographers and television crews were assembled. His first television address after the election was a fond bow in the direction of Jackie: 'Now my wife and I', he said, 'prepare for a new administration and a new baby.'

For Jackie the new era started with a new separation: 'I'm going to Palm Beach to think and work and talk with the boys,' Jack announced. She would have to face the final weeks of her confinement alone but Jack reassured her: 'I'll be back long before the baby arrives.' They had calculated the event would be in the second week of December. 'As a matter of fact, I'll be with you on Thanksgiving Day,' the last Thursday of November.

They flew off together in *Caroline* which set down in Washington where a car collected Jackie and took her to the house in Georgetown. Uncomfortable and apprehensive, she clung to her little daughter, the living, lively, lovely testimonial to successful motherhood. Jack telephoned her every evening from Palm Beach and she could tell from the sound of his voice that, in spite of the momentous experience ahead of him, he was deeply unhappy to be away from her in these critical days. Trying, not very successfully, to sound casual, he told her about his visit to Lyndon Johnson's ranch, they were not the world's most congenial companions; about his dinner with the wives of his aides, that would have been her job; and his courtesy call on the loser, Richard Nixon. No shortage of topics to divert Jackie.

With her obsessional application to detail, she fussed about the preparations for the new baby's arrival; the doctors, the nursery, the food, the clothes, and about Louella Hennesy who had assisted in the production of all Kennedy offspring and was standing by to await the little newcomer. Jackie was coming to terms with the prospect of another caesarian birth – no woman could have more than three, she was told – gave up smoking, a big sacrifice, and, haunted by fear that she might lose the baby, rested as much as her restless mind allowed her.

Following tradition the encumbent First Lady, Mamie Eisenhower, invited her to inspect the living quarters of the White House but, anxious as she was to see where she would be living for the next few years, her doctors warned her not to undertake such strenuous exercise. Her new secretary, Letitia (Tish) Baldrige, a statuesque, level-headed graduate of Miss Porter's who had served with the American embassies in Paris and Rome and worked for Tiffany's, the jewellers, as PRO, informed the White House that Mrs Kennedy would take up the invitation immediately after her baby's birth.

After a fortnight's absence, Jack returned to Washington for a round of talks, cabinet-making, putting the final touches on his administration, discussing his programme and inaugural address with Ted Sorenson, his friend and closest adviser. Thanksgiving dinner with Jackie and Caroline was pleasant, simple and brief – just too brief. After dinner Jack drove to the airport where his aircraft was waiting to take him and his aides to Palm Beach with the press following in a chartered DC6. The President, according to his companions, was in a happy relaxed mood.

The *Caroline* was about halfway to its destination when the co-pilot passed on an urgent radio message to the President: 'Mrs Kennedy has been rushed to hospital . . .' Jack was desolate: 'I'm never there when she needs me,' he sighed. The baby had not been expected for another three weeks but with Jackie's medical history a premature birth was always on the cards. It was little consolation to know how well she had disciplined herself to cope with problems on her own, quite in contrast to the popular notion that she could not function without a man and leaned heavily on her two husbands and her numerous (male) friends.

Speeding away from her at three hundred miles an hour when he wanted to be near her, there was nothing to be done but to proceed to Florida and take the faster press plane back to Washington. At Palm Beach, Jack hurried to a telephone and asked to be put through to Dr Walsh at the hospital. 'She is in the operating room to have caesarian surgery,' the doctor told him.

The press plane had hardly taken off for the return trip when the President entered the cockpit and grabbed the earphones to catch the next radio message. There was nothing further to report until one a.m. when he was told that there appeared to be no problems. He heaved a sigh of relief and a quarter of an hour later – at 01.17 hours – the news came through that Jackie had been safely delivered of a baby boy. Pierre Salinger, Jack's press secretary, broadcast the news over the plane's intercom. The reporters stood and cheered and the President took a handsome bow.

Recovering consciousness, Jackie dismissed the pain and the discomfort and asked to see the baby which had been placed in an incubator. She was being wheeled from the operating theatre when a photographer burst from a closet in the corridor and pointed his camera at her. As the shutter clicked she cried out: 'Oh no, no! No!' Secret Service agents pounced on the intruder and confiscated the film.

Arriving at the hospital, the President found Jackie ill and exhausted. She begged him to stay but the doctors waved him away and ordered her to rest. For a long time, he stood before the incubator looking at his tiny (6lbs 3ozs) baby boy with his blue eyes and shock of brown hair. Like most premature babies, it would need diligent care to sustain life. Jack prayed for the son he had long hoped for, then went home, bathed and changed and had breakfast with Caroline whom he told all about her new brother. After breakfast it was back to the hospital. Jackie's condition was precarious and the doctors still struggled to keep the baby alive.

That morning, as Jack took Caroline to church, an army of photographers focused their massed cameras on the little girl. She was getting agitated and the President put his foot down: 'It's time for Caroline to retire from the limelight,' he announced. He refused further facilities but was defeated by the press who besieged his house the next day to photograph and, yes, interview the tiny tots who arrived at N Street for Caroline's third birthday party.

Jackie lived from one of Jack's visits to the next – he went to the hospital three times a day – but did not burden him with her agonising thoughts which were only reflected in what she told Rose Kennedy about her baby later on: 'I nearly lost him, as I had lost our first little girl . . .' The baby was suffering from a lung infection (such as, three years later, killed her third baby, Patrick) and she was ill: 'I had a close shave myself,' she recalled. Both recovered sufficiently for little John to be christened at the hospital chapel. Unable to walk, Jackie was pushed to the chapel in a wheelchair.

After a fortnight, she was anxious to go home but the doctors agreed only reluctantly to discharge her and the baby. Jack reminded her of her White House appointment: 'I don't feel up to it,' Jackie moaned. 'You'd better go,' he told her. It seemed so important to him that she could hardly refuse. Mrs Hennessy warned her that the effort could damage her health still further. There would be a big commotion, reporters, photographers, crowds. It was more than she should ask of herself. 'I'll go!' Jackie decided and asked that the White House have a wheelchair ready for her.

Looking weak and drawn, she drove from the hospital to her home and, after a quick change of clothes, slipped out by the back door to go to the White House for her meeting with Mrs Eisenhower. Recording the dramatic encounter, reporters depicted Jackie as a heroic figure and waxed lyrical about her refusing a wheelchair. 'When I arrived,' Jackie recalled, 'there was no wheelchair!' A few weeks later she reproached J.B. West, Chief Usher of the White House: 'Why was there no wheelchair?' 'I had one ready in case you asked for it,' was the reply. According to Mr West, Jackie giggled and said that she was too scared to ask Mrs Eisenhower for it.

Be that as it may, she was given a relentless full tour of the White House ('including all those stairs') without the benefit of a wheelchair and, summoning up her last strength, posed with Mamie for the photographers. The brave face she put on was deceptive: she was on the verge of collapse. All she wanted was to get away from Washington and could not wait to escape to the peace and calm of Palm Beach – she might have known better! Having made certain that the baby would get adequate medical attention in Florida, she joined Jack, Caroline, Mrs Hennessy, Maude Shaw, Provi and Tish Baldrige on the flight to Palm Beach.

For the first five days she was too exhausted to leave her bed and her only concern was the baby's well-being, nay, survival: 'He was going downhill,' she told her mother-in-law. (It is one of the peculiarities of the massive Jackie literature that the baby's near-fatal illness was not mentioned, not a word about it in Mary Thayer's authorised story, until she told Rose Kennedy about it. Yet, it was one of the ordeals which hardened her and made her impervious to the many trials still in store for her.)

The first Sunday, she and Caroline went to church with the President and saved his life but knew nothing about it. She was not told that a madman had been lying in wait to blow up the President with seven sticks of dynamite but could not bring himself to do it before the eyes of Jackie and the child. The police were tipped off about him and arrested him a few days later. Undaunted, the President continued his routine, working on his inaugural address and his programme, snatching a couple of hours now and then to play a round of golf. Jackie, when she was well enough to get about, found her hope of tranquillity rudely disappointed. Jack's aides and advisers, secretaries and visitors were swarming all over the place. Pierre Salinger was giving a press conference in her bedroom and Jackie, looking for a corner to hide, was relegated to the bathroom, her only refuge. Her nerves were taut and she could not keep her food down. No, she could not face the women reporters who arrived to interview the new First Lady; would Jack please stand in for her and see them.

She repaired to her bed but was far from idle. As she has been doing almost every day ever since, she scribbled away furiously on her writing pads covering page after page with her bold hand-writing, diary notes, memoranda, instructions to staff, suppliers, architects, decorators, couturiers, one thought tumbling over the next, in staccato language, lots of dashes but few other punctuations, imperious in some passages, wheedling and pleading in others, cunningly clothing strict orders in the guise of humble suggestions, explaining away devious procedures which she favoured. Over the years Jackie has written millions of words in this manner, probably more than any other woman.

Typical of the memoranda she composed in these days were her instructions to Pamela Turnure, a twenty-three-year-old society girl she engaged as a Press Secretary ('Invent some lady-like title for yourself but I don't think it should be Press Secretary as I don't think a First Lady should have a Press Secretary.') As a blueprint for a technique of discretion, or rather evasion and duplicity ('Just smile and be evasive'), it was probably unique but also self-defeating because it created a Garbo-esque I-want-to-be-alone image of the First Lady which produced the reverse effect, the avalanche of unparalleled publicity which has engulfed Jackie ever since.

The future was closing in on her and kept her keyed up as she approached the climax in any American woman's life, the inauguration of her husband as President of the United States.

CHAPTER EIGHT

'I plan to make the White House a show piece for American art and artists.'

Jacqueline Kennedy, 1960

The first bold designs for Camelot took shape while Jackie was in her bed in the Kennedys' Palm Beach mansion. Chief Usher Bernard West, veteran guardian of the White House, sent her albums of elaborately annotated photographs showing the principal White House rooms under the last three administrations which she studied and analysed until she was familiar with every detail. There was a great deal she did not like, much that would have to be discarded and replaced with more tasteful pieces or patterns.

Mrs Henry Parish, the New York interior decorator, arrived armed with ideas and bales of samples of furnishings and wallpaper. For days on end, the two women were closeted in Jackie's quarters breaking off only for brief snacks ('Is Jackie getting out of bed today?' her mother-in-law asked hopefully most days but the answer was always in the negative) before returning to their drawing boards to map out the coming revolution in the White House.

Downstairs Jack Kennedy and his aides were discussing the first appointments of his new administration – Dean Rusk as Secretary of State, Bobby Kennedy as Attorney General, if he could be persuaded to serve, Adlai Stevenson as Ambassador to the U.N. Upstairs Caroline was waiting for her mother to come and read her stories and little John to be cradled in her arms. Important as the children were, they had for once to share her attention with the job in hand – remodelling the White House. Jackie attached scribbled instructions to each photograph, had them transcribed and assembled (with samples of material attached) in a bound volume, the first of many which recorded not only designs, materials, furniture and carpets but also knick-knacks, ashtrays, vases, objets d'art and paintings which were allocated places in her scheme.

Mr West at the receiving end of all these instructions, replied with counter suggestions and more information. Requests went out for materials – some rare fabrics, others simply copies to be made of her Georgetown curtains in the size required for the presidential suite. The White House maintenance staff of plumbers, carpenters, upholsterers, electricians, decorators, builders was warned to prepare for the hurricane which would sweep away the old and make way for the new. Although by tradition work for the new President was not supposed to start before inauguration day and the end of the old regime, some of it was put in hand well ahead of January 20.

Top of the list for attention were the private living quarters on the second and third floor: 'Until they are ready,' Jackie informed Mr West, 'I'll sleep in the Queen's Room.' Mamie Eisenhower was shocked because she thought the Queen's Room was literally for reigning queens only. President Kennedy would occupy the Lincoln Room for the time being but would use President Truman's four-poster bed and have his own rocking chair. A plaque in the Lincoln Room said that the great President slept there between 1861 and 1865 but it is doubtful whether he ever used it as a bedroom. According to Mary Thayer, Jackie eventually had another inscription carved which read: 'In this room lived John Fitzgerald Kennedy and his wife Jacqueline . . .'

For her own bedroom, Jackie chose the room in which Lincoln was thought to have actually slept and sketched a design with an overall white effect, bluish-white silk curtains, bedspread and chair coverings, French antique furniture and, every detail prearranged, a cluster of old prints over the fireplace, a pastel drawing of Caroline over a chest of drawers, thick white carpets and leopard-skin rugs. There were to be light-blue silk taffeta furnishings in the dressing-room next door, French-style cupboards and dressing-table, mirrors and a table for silver-framed family photographs.

The West Sitting Hall would become her office – it became her favourite room – which she planned to furnish with French antiques. President de Gaulle later contributed an attractive commode, and Jules Stein, the entertainment czar, an octagonal mahogany and satinwood desk. Pride of place was reserved for one of Jackie's prized possessions, her late father's French Empire desk. 'There are no bookshelves,' she complained. 'Doesn't any President ever read?' Caroline was allocated one of President Truman's guest rooms redecorated in a pink rosebud design, and a separate playroom.

'There certainly are going to be some changes made around here,' Mamie Eisenhower exclaimed when she was told of Jackie's sweeping plans. 'She'll redo every room in the house.' Too true! Tish Baldrige was instructed to list the contents of the N Street house, some of which were to be discarded while others were earmarked for removal to the White House ('to make the atmosphere more homely,' Jackie said). Weeks before the inauguration, Tish smuggled some of the pieces and Caroline's bigger toys into the White House where Mr West hid them away in the bowels of the storerooms as if they were contraband. Some of the Georgetown furniture was destined for Glen Ora, a house in Middleburg, Virginia, which the President had rented. Jackie was looking for a stable manager to take charge of her horses and Caroline's ponies, Macaroni and Tex.

More farflung were her plans to gather in works of art for the White House. The Smithsonian Institution was advised that the First Lady had her eye on a few choice historic items. Other art centres were informed of her interest in valuable Americana: 'I would write fifty letters to fifty museum curators if I could bring Andrew Jackson's inkwell home,' she said. She asked Mr West to search the storerooms for historic pieces, and her father-in-law for drawings and paintings from his rich collection; the Ambassador was flattered that they would hang in the White House.

Almost in the same breath she made provision for the servants. While Provi would not live in except on special nights, Jackie attended to Maude Shaw's modest needs. A book closet was to be turned into a bedroom for Caroline's nanny. Said Jackie (with a special reference to Miss Shaw's taste for bananas): 'As long as she has a wicker basket for banana skins and a place for her false teeth, she'll be all right.'

Mr West wielded the new broom on Jackie's behalf with un-shakeable composure and adroit diplomacy which prevented head-on collisions with tradition and vested White House in-terests. At her request he got rid of the 'sea-sick green' cur-tains (her description) and promised to do something about what she called 'that roller skating rink' floor of the East Room. Her demands ranged ever wider. She did not mind the Victorian decor of the Treaty Room but thought it would be enhanced by the East Room's large crystal chandelier which was duly marked down for transfer. The Lobby would have to be completely transformed to look, as she put it, 'like de Gaulle's'. As soon as she moved in, she started discarding horrors ('Off to the dungeons!' she commanded) and raising treasures from obscurity. In the process, Mr West lost the Grandma Moses in his own quarters which Jackie ('I hope you don't mind') wanted for Caroline's room; it was not unlike Jackie's own style of painting. Another American primitive and a French impressionist completed Caroline's artistic environ-ment.

Before long, Jackie required some major structural altera-tions. She ordered a more intimate private dining-room to be created and had Margaret Truman's erstwhile bedroom made into a modern kitchen and her bathroom into a pantry. But when she asked for several walls to be broken down for a passage from the White House swimming pool to the lift (as a short cut for the President from his regular midday or evening dip in the nude to his inviolable siesta upstairs), Mr West demurred because the cost was prohibitive, and Jackie had to accept a compromise solution. Time and again the Chief Usher warned her that funds were running out and, indeed, the Treasury allocation of $50,000 for the changeover (plus $25,000 for paint) was exhausted long before she had finished with the private apartments. 'The budget is too small,' she complained. Perhaps the President could ask for more funds: an extra $25,000 was made available.

Sweeping as her plans were, when they filtered through the grapevine into the public press, they were exaggerated and dis-torted. According to one report she intended to hang modern paintings everywhere. To clear the air she spelled out her intentions: 'The White House is an eighteenth- and nineteenth-century house,' she declared, 'and should be kept as a period house. Whatever one does, one does gradually to make the house a more lived-in house with beautiful things of its period.'

Dressing up the White House went hand in hand with plans for her own dresses. She ordered two outfits for the swearing-in ceremony, one black, one in red velvet, she would only make up her mind at the last minute which to wear, and the designer and an assistant flew to Palm Beach for fittings and adjustments. As a third choice, she asked Oleg Cassini, the top American couturier, to make her a fawn-coloured wool coat with a sable collar which was the one she eventually wore. Cassini was also designing her gowns for the other inaugural functions but her instructions were so detailed and so strict they left little scope for his ingenuity. He remained her favourite couturier and was understandably incensed when it was later suggested that she was not wearing his designs but using his label to camouflage creations which she had surreptitiously bought from Givenchy and Balenciaga in Paris.

After lengthy correspondence, Jackie's shoes arrived from Eugenia of Florence, who were already working on her summer footwear. She asked for her Palm Beach masseuse to be available in Washington and Jean Louis, the hair stylist, to attend to her coiffure on the morning of January 20. Her secretaries were run off their feet and things became so hectic that even Pierre Salinger was roped in to help. Tish Baldrige arranged for Tiffany's to lend the First Lady a diamond ensemble for the great day but Jackie did not think only of herself. When it occurred to her that the girls on her staff might have problems with their own outfits, she offered Mary Gallagher the splendid Empire-style gown with long gloves and handbag to match (in which she had been photographed for *Time Magazine*) to wear at the Inauguration Ball. She was adamant that none of these personal details should become known but she might have guessed that in the years to come every one of her handmaidens would produce a bestseller about her, and none so damning with bitchy praise as Mary Gallagher's.

One job to which Jackie applied herself was compiling a list of her relatives, her four families, to be invited to the official functions and to a special family party. Some of the Bouviers were out of touch, some at loggerheads with each other, others lived in distant parts of the country or abroad. The Auchincloss family was less widely dispersed but as numerous; the Lees would have to be gathered in and there were the Kennedys, altogether more than sixty close relatives. Old school friends, favoured social acquaintances, relatives of political assistants and secretaries had to be considered, hundreds of personal invitations, each a status symbol, each destined to become a prized souvenir. With each went the elaborate programme of Inauguration Day events and detailed logistic instructions on how to reach the various points. Jackie was meticulous about arrangements to collect relatives and friends from stations and airports and convey them to their hotels and to the functions, and listed those who qualified for official White House cars. Three buses were hired to take the families from their lunch to the Inaugural Parade. It was such an involved business that some of the invitations reached their destination only two days before the inauguration.

Although she had spent most of the time in bed, Jackie was worn out before the momentous proceedings began. Early on Thursday, January 19, she joined the President elect, Caroline and Maude Shaw, and baby John with his new nurse Mrs Philips for the flight from Palm Beach to Washington. Wearing a white plaid suit, striking red suede beret which showed off her bouffant hairstyle, and a large black alligator bag she looked handsome if a little pale and tense. At the airport there was a crowd to see them off; there was a crowd awaiting them at Washington, from now on there would be crowds wherever they went. A carnival greeted them at their home in Georgetown which was besieged by sightseers, wellwishers and reporters barely held in check by uniformed police. Secret Service agents were stationed all round the house.

Inside, the scene was as frantic and confused. Jackie sipped a glass of Dom Perignon before going upstairs for a bath and a massage. Fitters and seamstresses were waiting to put the final touches to her gowns, Jean Louis sneaked in by the back door to escape the reporters who were sniffing around for snippets of information. Provi's family, in town for the ceremony, squatted in the front room, and Jack's assistants were taking up so much space that, to quote O'Donnell, 'Jackie threw him out of the house' long before he was due to go to the White House for a takeover conference with President Eisenhower. Banished from his own home he went to Bill Walton's at P Street to continue his consultations.

That morning Washington was in the grip of the worst blizzard in living memory with sheets of snow cascading from dark heavens. In the gloom Jackie contemplated the inaugural round with growing trepidation. The crowded day seemed to go on for ever. Come evening, she could not eat a bite and Jack only grabbed a snack before they went out at eight p.m. to make brief appearances at a reception for Eleanor Roosevelt and another party. Mugsy O'Leary, Jack's driver, steered the car adroitly through mounds of snow to get them to the big concert in the Constitution Hall which was half empty, because hundreds of ticket holders were stuck in the unprecedented traffic jams and others had not even ventured out on the impossible journey.

Still, when they drove away from the concert, the streets were lined with people anxious to catch a glimpse of America's premier couple in the car: 'Put on the light inside,' Jack told Mugsy, 'so they can see Jackie.' It was a miracle that they made it to the Armoury for the Inauguration Gala, an all-star variety performance laid on by brother-in-law Peter Lawford and Frank Sinatra. Again, artistes and audience were held up by the weather and there was a long delay but once they got under way the performers: Harry Belafonte, Ella Fitzgerald, Bette Davis, Leonard Bernstein and Sir Laurence (now Lord) Olivier made it great entertainment. Ethel Merman, although a staunch Republican, lustily intoned 'Everything's Coming Up Roses,' and Frank Sinatra sang 'That Old Jack Magic . . .'

Jackie was visibly wilting. By midnight she excused herself and went home. Jack, who had a weak spot for stars, stayed on to the end. His day was not done. He went on to a late dinner given by his father at Paul Young's restaurant, drank champagne and had such a marvellous time that he dragged himself away only reluctantly in the small hours. It was the last time he could let his hair down in a public place.

After a restless night, Jackie woke early on Inauguration Day, Friday, 20 January. She came down in her dressing-gown to have breakfast with Jack who was already dressed. As she went back to her room, Jack, followed by a gaggle of reporters, walked to church where his mother who had arrived a little earlier was praying for her son.

The President elect was back in good time to change for his appointment with history. His things were laid out but when he tried to fix his stiff white collar it was too tight because he had put on more than ten pounds in the last few months. He sent a secretary to his father's house to borrow a bigger collar but it did not fit either. In the end George Thomas discovered a suitable one in his own wardrobe. Despite the delay, Jack was good and ready when, at the appointed hour, ten-forty a.m., the bubble-top presidential Lincoln limousine with his cere-monial escorts of the Inauguration Committee, Speaker Sam Rayburn and Senator John Sparkman, drew up at the house.

As they made their way to the door, Jack called out to Jackie who was still upstairs dithering with her pillbox hats. She could not decide which to wear and every time she took one off her hair had to be put in place before she tried another: 'Jackie, for Heaven's sake!' Jack shouted. His exasperation dissolved when she appeared at the top of the stairs (with the fawn-coloured pillbox) looking glamorous yet dignified, her outfit striking in its simplicity. Provi patted her coat down more to reassure herself than to smooth out non-existent creases, George Thomas held the door open, reporters surged forward and the crowd cheered as Jack and Jackie settled in the car and drove off.

A little behind schedule they reached the North Portico of the White House to pick up President and Mrs Eisenhower. Eisenhower sent word that he expected his successor and the new First Lady to come up for a cup of coffee. He had probably forgotten that eight years earlier he had angrily turned down a similar invitation from his predecessor, President Truman, who had attacked him in the election campaign. Jack Kennedy had no reason to refuse and went upstairs with Jackie to join Eisenhower's party, outgoing Vice-President Nixon and his wife, incoming Vice-President Johnson and his wife, Senator

Bridges and other members of the Inaugural Committee. Never good at small talk, Jackie was ill at ease, not in the mood to exchange fatuities and not happy either when she found herself sitting next to Pat Nixon who did not turn to her once and remained throughout in deedy conversation with Senator Bridges. It was not a convivial gathering. For Jackie it was a very long and uncomfortable half hour.

In the freezing cold, President Eisenhower and his successor, followed by Mamie Eisenhower and Jackie in another car, drove to the Capitol for the swearing-in ceremony. It occurred to Jackie that, though Jack had read out odd paragraphs of his inaugural address to her while working on it, she had never heard it from beginning to end. All eyes were on her as she took her seat in the stand between Mamie Eisenhower and Lady Bird Johnson. Around her was a sea of familiar Bouvier faces, a mirror of her own background. They looked at her in wonderment, some with pride, some with not a little envy. Was it possible that the shy young girl they had known since childhood was now the First Lady in the land? Come to think of it, some of them had expected her to become just that when they learned that she was marrying John F. Kennedy.

Jackie watched the proceedings as if in a dream, Jack materialising and discarding his overcoat in spite of the cold, Robert Frost's halting, faltering delivery of his poem which caused delay and embarrassment, Cardinal Cushing intoning his prayers and the Chief Rabbi his benediction, Chief Justice Earl Warren administering the oath and the President responding in a firm voice which betrayed no sign of strain. His stature grew, and not only in Jackie's eyes, with every sentence of his inspiring recitation. The impact was tremendous, generating patriotic fervour and giving deeper meaning to the national anthem which concluded the ceremony. The President turned to Jackie whose eyes were moist. She rose, stepped forward and gently stroked his cheek: 'You were so wonderful,' she whispered. That was as far as she would allow emotion to show in public. Later she said: 'I could not kiss him in front of all these people.' She was certain the address would go down in history as one of the most moving speeches ever uttered

118

'with Pericles's Funeral Oration and the Gettysburg Address,' she said and was not far wrong.

The ceremony ended fully twenty minutes behind schedule and was hardly over when the select band of official guests including four former First Ladies (Mrs Woodrow Wilson, Eleanor Roosevelt, Bess Truman and Mamie Eisenhower) were whisked away with unceremonial haste to the Inaugural Luncheon at the Old Supreme Court Chamber. By the time they got there, the timetable was totally out of gear and the grand parade was almost due to start. Jackie could only just inspect the menu – tomato soup with crabmeat, stuffed lobster, ribs of beef, grapefruit and avocados, and hot garlic bread, before it was time to move on while plates heaped with food remained untouched. Spritely and grinning, President Truman rushed over and asked Jack to sign the menu; the young President was moved by the great little man's simple homage. Then he and the First Lady left for the Inaugural Parade.

Meanwhile, their families blinded by flashbulbs and Klieg lights, pursued by photographers and television crews, made their way to the Mayflower Hotel for a lunch given by Ambassador Kennedy. Rose Kennedy made the honours, assisted by Janet Auchincloss who introduced the distant and disparate relatives to each other. Among her own kin, Jackie was the principal topic of conversation – 'So lovely, so simple, so composed' – but the highly political Kennedys were more interested in the President's inaugural address. Three buses were waiting to take all of them to the parade: 'Which bus for the Bouviers?' one of Jackie's cousins asked. 'Who're the Bouviers?' a policeman retorted. Jackie's Bouvier past was far behind her.

She has never given more than vague hints of what went through her mind in these historic hours, and it is by no means certain that, as has been related, she said she had felt like the men who had reached the top of Everest, though this is probably as good a comparison as any. To close friends she confided, not that her confidences were respected, that her feeling was one of deep humility, humility vis-a-vis her husband. This was Jack's achievement, his finest hour. She did not want to attract any of the limelight. Yet, a cousin deduced from one of her remarks that she was acutely conscious of undergoing a metamorphosis, of a mysterious psychological chemistry which elevation to supreme height produces, and which was so evident in Jack, an automatic reaction to unbridled adulation and homage. Nobody who experienced the sensation could ever completely shake off the effect. Even if she had wanted to remain herself, the world would never again let her be 'just Jackie'.

Perhaps there was a grain of truth in what one of the Bouviers said, that it was really the other way round and that Jackie's new status had simply caught up with her state of mind which had always been attuned to life at the top. Whichever it was, she was remarkably in character. Refusing to drain the cup of glory, she decided on her own priority which was to save herself for the grand finale of the day. Actually, she felt rotten but those who knew her well were convinced that she would not have acted differently if she had been in perfect health. She only waited for the parade to unfold in Pennsylvania Avenue, then rose abruptly, whispered her apologies to Mamie and Lady Bird and tapped Jack lightly on the shoulder. Absorbed by the spectacle of the parade he hardly noticed. As the clock struck three-thirty, she was gone with the now obligatory military aide (Air Force Colonel McHugh) in hot pursuit. Protocol or no, she went home; home to the White House.

Her instinct was to do what every woman does when she moves into a new home, check her bedroom, her dressing-table, her personal effects. She was too tired. One glance at her big ball-gown which was still in its plastic cover as Provi had taken it into the White House at the precise moment the President was sworn in, and she flopped on to her bed, closed her eyes and tried to shut off her mind.

She found no rest. Her head and her legs hurt. 'Call my doctor!' she demanded. Dr Janet Travell diagnosed total exhaustion and cramp in the legs, gave her a Dexedrine and told her to stay in bed as long as possible. Five hours remained before the Inaugural Ball, long enough for her to recover but it meant missing the first White House function of the new reign, the reception for the families of the President and Mrs Kennedy which was scheduled to begin almost at once.

The Bouviers were looking forward to having Jackie to themselves away from the increasingly madding crowd. Escaping the icy wind sweeping the stand, they left the parade before the end and made for the White House. By five p.m. they were gathered in the unprepossessing State Dining Room with its 'sea-sick' green walls, dark mahogany furniture and Abraham Lincoln's portrait looking down on them. They reached for the hot tea or coffee, the punch, the cocktails, anything to thaw out the numbness. The Lees arrived in a group followed by the Auchincloss clan and the hardy Kennedys who had held out longest, and huddled together away from the Jackie brigade whom they knew to be Republicans to a man (and woman) although some of them had voted for Jack.

Taking a jaundiced view of the Democratic victory, Jackie's people looked around for chinks in the presidential habitat. They were quick to seize, in every sense, on the big silver bowl brimful with Molossol caviar. John Davis heard one of them say that, at five dollars an ounce, there was at least a thousand dollars' worth of it: 'Wonder how many tons of this they serve in a year?' a Bouvier voice piped up. 'Maybe it's a gift from Kruschev!' sneered another.

Food and drink mellowed the mood but by six p.m. they were getting restless when there was still no sign of the President or the First Lady. Pat Lawford and Jean Smith ambled off to explore the White House, others followed until groups were milling around inspecting the furniture and the paintings on the silk-lined walls of the East Room, Green Room, Blue Room and the Red Room with the big mirror crowned by a golden eagle. Everybody was asking: 'Where is Jackie? Where is the President?'

Janet Auchincloss went to investigate. The Secret Service guard let her go upstairs where she found her daughter half asleep. 'Please look after things,' Jackie mumbled. Returning to the party, the First Lady's mother reported: 'She's in the Queen's Room resting.' She did not mention Jackie's indisposition. Unaware of the minor drama upstairs, the family still clamoured for Jackie and the President.

It was six-thirty when the President arrived looking so well and vigorous it was hard to believe he had been up since six a.m. and spent the most gruelling and emotional day of his life.

He smiled broadly, shook hands that reached out towards him but his eyes strayed over his partners' shoulders and searched the room: 'Where's Jackie?' he asked. When he was told that she was resting, he shrugged his shoulders in a gesture of resignation ('with a faint look of incomprehension', it seemed to John Davis), and excused himself: 'I'd better get ready,' he said and disappeared.

Although Jackie was recovering, he agreed that she should stay in bed but suggested she let the folks downstairs know that she would not be turning up. She sent for Michel, her favourite Bouvier, greeted him fondly and told him: 'It is important for me to be at my best tonight.' Television cameras would be trained on her, the whole nation would be watching, she could not let the people down. When Michel passed on her apologies, there was some muttering: 'She could have come down for a second,' one Bouvier said. 'You can't blame her,' another retorted. Ah well, said a third, Jackie had always been ill at ease with her relatives and would find it less arduous to face the nation than the family.

The President showered and changed, kissed Jackie goodbye and went to the pre-ball dinner at George Wheeler's to discharge a promise to a loyal campaign helper. Once more time was so short that it was another meal at which nobody had a chance to eat. The guests rose when the President left to return to the White House where his Vice-President and Lady Bird were already waiting in the Red Room. A minute or two later, Jackie floated through the door in a rustle of chiffon, the spectacular white, silver and diamante-studded ballgown loosely covered by a fine-webbed cape reaching down to her ankles (it later went to the Smithsonian's collection of First Lady gowns). She looked gorgeous. The President raised his glass: 'Your dress is beautiful,' he said. 'You've never looked lovelier.'

This was also the reaction of the people who filled the ballroom of the Mayflower Hotel for the first of the night's five inaugural balls. They cheered Jackie to the roof. It was no different when they arrived at the Statler Hotel for the second ball. Jackie settled in the presidential box with Lyndon and Lady Bird Johnson but the President was nowhere to be seen.

Jackie seemed extremely irritated: did she guess where he was? Upstairs, she knew, Frank Sinatra was playing host to the performers of the previous night's gala; Jack had slipped away to join the stars. Kenny O'Donnell noted: 'When he finally returned to Jackie and the Johnsons looking rather sheepish and carrying a *Washington Post* under his arm as if he had just gone outside to pick up the newspaper, his knowing wife gave him a chilly look.'

The silent marital scene was unique only in that it involved a First Lady and a President on his first day in office. It was not so unusual in the context of their married life. Jack had always had an eye for pretty girls and was as susceptible to film stars as the next virile young man and, by virtue of his looks, wealth and position, had found them rather more responsive than they were to lesser admirers.

How far he had carried his amorous excursions during his marriage was a matter of keen speculation and juicy gossip in Boston and Washington but whether Jackie was suspicious or not it was beneath her dignity or contrary to her ostrich nature to reproach him except when he upset her social routine, when he arrived flushed and late for her dinner parties, when he preferred evenings out with 'the boys' – or were they girls? – to her sedate gatherings or disappeared without plausible explanation. These little contretemps did not seriously affect their harmony and when he went on doing much the same things, only less frequently, as President, Jackie never admitted the existence of a problem even after his death – except with a little wink when the subject cropped up in conversation with her second husband: 'Jack was a naughty boy,' Onassis remarked on one occasion.

The presidential couple's third appearance that evening was at the National Guard Armoury where a thousand guests gave Jackie a frenetic ovation: Rose Kennedy spoke of a wave of love and admiration which engulfed the President and the First Lady. Her admirers did not notice, and neither did Jack, that the smile with which Jackie acknowledged the cheers was forced and fixed. She looked so ravishing, so regal, it would have been difficult to believe, if she had told anybody, that she was once more on the verge of collapse. Will-power kept her going until an aide suggested that it was time to move on to the next function. It was midnight when Jackie told the President: 'You go on . . . I'll have to go home.'

The President was in the thick of the fourth major festivity when Jackie reached the Queen's Room: 'She could not have gotten out of that ballgown by herself if her life depended on it,' said the White House maid who had waited up for her, 'I'm sure glad I was here – she'd have had to sleep in it!' Jackie was so weary she could have slept in a suit of armour.

CHAPTER NINE

'This is a girl with a lot of savvy!'

Newsvendor in St Louis, 1961

'It's like Lubianka!' the new First Lady exclaimed when she surveyed the seven rooms of her private quarters in the White House on her first day in residence. The Eisenhowers had removed their furniture and paintings, her own had not yet arrived from N Street. The emptiness was depressing and the workmen with their tools, paints and ladders did not improve the atmosphere. The First Lady turned her back on the chaos, and, with Dr Travell in attendance, fled to the Queen's Room and retired to bed. She did not expect visitors and was taken aback when there was a knock at the door and Jack ushered in Harry Truman to say hello. Seeing the First Lady in bed, the old President gave her a wave and withdrew hurriedly. Jack evaded his wife's reproachful glance.

Though still showing signs of stress, Jackie was too impatient to rest for long. She called Tish Baldrige and asked her to invite her first White House guests, the Franklin Roosevelts, Bill Walton and columnist Joseph Alsop for dinner on Sunday; and her mother and stepfather and the Bartletts for lunch the following day. Mercifully, no official engagements were scheduled until the end of the week. Within a couple of days, Jackie was out and about the house. Mr J. B. West, her prim and proper upstairs-downstairs expert, was surprised and charmed when she turned up casually dressed in slacks and blouse, her hair falling over her face. As they talked, she settled down on the floor and kicked off her shoes. 'A daily delight,' he commented. Yet for all her uninhibited behaviour she never dropped her guard and, as Mr West put it, 'drew a line against familiarity which could not be crossed'. She had one foot on firm ground, the other on a pedestal fit for Amriki Rani (the American Queen) as an Indian newspaper called her.

In these early days the First Lady investigated every one of the White House's 132 rooms with their closets and cupboards as well, listed the silver, china, everything used by previous occupants. Every detail that caught her eye was recorded in her notebook or dictated to her secretary and presently spawned a barrage of messages addressed to Mr West. She wanted the marble busts of American historical figures (which she discovered in a Men's Room) restored and put in the public area. Could Mr West trace President Monroe's French furniture? One bookcase needed a new panel, one secretaire ought to be sent back to the dealer in exchange for something more useful and, top priority, the East Room curtains would have to be replaced. She allocated new places for the brass and glass ashtrays, demanded a rug for the Blue Room . . . And there was a tear in the rug in the West Sitting Hall by the round wooden table where the telephone was – 'Could it be fixed maybe when we are gone for a week at Easter.'

Jackie lost no time initiating some high-level White House entertainment. With a series of ballet displays in mind, she asked Georges Ballantine, director of the New York City ballet to come and see her ('She looked like a pussycat', he said afterwards) and sent an invitation to Greta Garbo to visit her as soon as possible. Two of her most ambitious long-term projects were to get Pablo Casals to come and play at the White House and have Margot Fonteyn and Nureyev perform for her guests. Her youthful energy, her youth, was such a novelty and in such striking contrast with the three previous First Ladies, people assumed that she was the youngest First Lady ever although she was only third in the youth league; Frances Glover was twenty-two when she moved into the White House and the wife of John Tyler, the tenth President, was twenty-four.

When the President said that there were too many servants and quipped 'They stand around even when I'm showering and shaving!' Jackie decided to review the White House staff, there were twenty-four people. She asked the Chief Usher to call them all together but he disabused her of the idea and organised a rota. When she engaged a French chef, Réné Verdon, and an assistant chef, Julius Spessot, her faithful old cook, the voluminous Pearl Nelson became redundant but the First Lady did not have the courage to sack her: 'Will you please fire Pearl for me,' she implored the Chief Usher. On the other hand, there were so many Italians and Spaniards in the kitchens that the President ordered citizenship papers for the chef and his assistant to be speeded up. No sooner had Julius Spessot become an American citizen than Jackie had him eased out too: 'What we need is a pastry cook,' she told Mr West. Every maid came under her scrutiny: Gloria, she should be assigned to the second floor; Cordenia, she could help Provi; Wilma, wasn't she getting on a bit? Lucinda, 'good maid for guests'. She had no time to teach the girls but Provi could train a ladies' maid.

Every member of the staff leaving, every new member coming in increased the risk of leaks, one of Jackie's obsessions. She instructed the Chief Usher to ask all employees to sign a pledge of absolute secrecy. The news promptly leaked out: 'President Muzzles Staff' ran the headlines. The President did not want Jackie involved in the row and approached the Chief Usher: 'Would you mind taking the blame?' Mr West obliged. Looking over his shoulder at public reaction, the President was getting increasingly troubled by Jackie's innovations. He started to take an interest in all departures from tradition and echoes of his forceful comments and Jackie's plaintive explanations were picked up by alert ears.

Had Jackie not occupied herself so compulsively with every minute detail of the refurbishing she would not have been so desperately busy. Her secretaries were driven to distraction taking dictation of letters, instructions, diary notes, and typing unending memoranda and inventories. Photographers were called in to record every room – before and after; one whole volume of photographs showed the step-by-step development of her new design for the White House rose garden. Jackie crowded more and more activity into every hour so as to leave herself plenty of time for the children whom she was determined to bring up like any other children. Yet, as Mr West noted sadly, they never ran up and down the State Halls by themselves, never slid down the banisters. There were always nannies and nurses around, chauffeurs and valets and a butler who served hamburgers on a silver tray. Occasionally Caroline escaped and stormed into the President's office to hide playfully under his desk but such fun soon had to be stopped.

Jackie often pushed baby John, John-John as he came to call himself and was called by the family, around the grounds in his pram. She went with Caroline for sleigh rides on the snow-covered White House lawn and played hide-and-seek with her behind the new high fence she had had erected, 'Too high,' grumbled the President. In the centre of the little girl's playground, designed by her indefatigable mother, was a mysterious tunnel; there was also a swing and a slide. Working to another Jackie design, carpenters installed hutches for rabbits and guineapigs and a sand box in Caroline's third-floor playroom which the servants often found in a shocking mess in the morning. 'Mrs Kennedy and the children come and play here at night,' a maid confided to a friend. Jackie enjoyed the games as much as the children; in spite of her sophistication she gave the impression that she had never really grown up.

Caroline was treated to private filmshows and received her first lessons from Betsy Boyd (ex-Miss Porter's) at a White House kindergarten she shared with carefully selected little playmates but at least one youngster proved too boisterous for such exclusive company and had to be relegated to a more conventional establishment. Most evenings Jackie sat with the children while they had their meal. The President looked in when he could spare the time; on his very first day in office he collected the silver-framed photograph of the children which remained on his desk to the end.

Most days, the First Lady woke up between nine and nine-thirty a.m. by which time the President was already in his office. She had breakfast in bed served on a tray by Provi, read the newspapers, then rang for Mary Gallagher who brought her personal letters which had been separated from the stacks of mail delivered to Tish Baldrige's office. Only calls from privileged relatives and close friends were put through to her bedroom. Whether talking to them or to her staff, she was brisk and impatient: 'Keep it short!' she demanded when she thought people were rambling on and on. Around ten-thirty, still in bed, she started dictating or scribbling away on her big pads, sometimes signing with her initials JBK. She said, inci-

1 (*above*) Janet and 'Black Jack' Bouvier in 1936 (*Popperfoto*)

2 (*below right*) Young Jackie with her favourite horse, Danseuse (*Popperfoto*)

3 (*above left*) Jacqueline Bouvier, 'Inquiring Photographer' on *Times-Herald* in 1952 (*Popperfoto*)

4 (*below*) New York debutante, Miss Jacqueline Lee Bouvier, marries Mr John F Kennedy, future Senator from Massachusetts, 1953 (*Popperfoto*)

5 (*above*) Senator John
Kennedy with his wife and
daughter Caroline
(*Camera Press*)

6 (*below right*) Jackie
walking to watch the
inaugural parade, arm in
arm with Jack who has
just been made 35th
President of the United
States; in the background,
the White House
(*Popperfoto*)

7 (*above*) Jackie is a
fine horsewoman; this
photograph of her was
taken in Seville
(*Popperfoto*)

8 (*right*) Pictured
between her two
brothers-in-law, Bobby
(left) and Teddy
(right), Jackie attends
her husband's funeral
in Washington
following his
assassination,
November 1963
(*Camera Press*)

9 (*above*) Five years later, Jackie is the bride of Aristotle Onassis,
the Greek shipping millionaire (*Camera Press*)

10 (*below*) An English Christmas for Jackie and her family in 1969.
From left to right: John-John, aged 8, Anthony Radziwill, Caroline,
aged 12, Jackie, and her sister Princess Lee Radziwill, photographed
near Henley on Thames (*Popperfoto*)

11 (*above*) Jackie and Ari visited a shipyard in Belfast, Northern Ireland where Jackie responded with unusual warmth to the enthusiastic reception she received (*Popperfoto*)

12 (*below*) Jackie and Ari dining out in a Paris bistro (*Camera Press*)

13 (*above*) Jackie, on the arm of her son John, walking with other mourners to her husband's funeral on the island of Skorpios in March 1975

14 (*right*) Jackie takes a turn on the wheel of a New York ferry in 1976 (*Popperfoto*)

15 (*above*) Jackie takes delight in tossing the dice in one of the newest games in town, 'Counterstrike', with its inventor Roger Tuckerman (*Popperfoto*)

16 In September 1975, Jackie started work as a consulting editor for Viking Press, the American publishing house. Here, with book designer Bryan Holme, she checks one of the photographs for her book *In the Russian Style* which was published in January 1977 (*Popperfoto*) dentally, that she did not like being referred to as the First Lady preferring to remain known simply as Mrs Kennedy.

As she got to know her staff better, Jackie could sense what was being said behind her back. Sometimes she tried to smooth ruffled feathers, Mary Gallagher's for one, but this was the exception. She asked Mr West to discourage backstairs talk about the President and herself but this did not stop the sergeant-majorish housekeeper Mabel Walker making snide remarks about her innovations: 'How could she tell what she was looking at,' Mr West heard Mabel Walker say after one of Jackie's inspections, 'with all that hair falling over her face!' 'And Mabel,' he noted, 'was the first to go.' She was succeeded by the more amiable Anne Lincoln.

As Jackie's plans for the White House matured, the annual budget of $500,000 which covered the pay of servants and maintenance staff as well, was strained to the limit. When it was suggested that, perhaps, the President might chip in with funds from his private purse, Jackie said pointedly: 'We have far less money than you read in the papers.' Still, the cost for the first month's private entertaining (which came out of the President's pocket), caviar, champagne, five-course meals, was so sky-high that she hit the roof. She was shocked when Jack contemplated refusing his official salary, and his friend Benjamin C. Bradlee recalled hearing some heated arguments about it.

The first official White House guests, the American 'spy-plane' airmen just released by the Soviets, presented no problem. It was a different story when the President persuaded his father to visit him. Preparations occupied the respective secretaries for many days. Tish Baldrige passed on Jackie's message that the President would be delighted if the Ambassador would have lunch with him alone at one p.m. and dinner with him and the Attorney General (Bobby Kennedy) at seven-thirty p.m. The First Lady was in two minds whether to join them or stay in the background and, as usual, suggested a compromise: 'Jackie asked,' the Ambassador's secretary reported, 'if she could possibly sit quietly in the corner and be included for dinner.'

From the first day of her reign, public curiosity about the

First Lady was acute. What was she doing? What was she thinking? Rumours about her grandiose designs for Camelot, King Arthur's mythical eighth-century court proliferated. Shrewd publishers satisfied this curiosity with a rich diet of one-shot magazines with mostly apocryphal stories about her clothes, home, family, sayings and loftier thoughts for which a Wykagyl publication (*Jacqueline Kennedy*, 7 February 1961) set the pattern. The trend was towards a full filmstar treatment as in *Jacqueline Kennedy, Beauty in the White House* which marked the entry of the fan magazines into this new lucrative market.

TV Star Parade and Modern Screen (May 1961) popularised the 'Jackie Look', her clothes, hair-style, jewellery: 'There's no question,' the magazine stated, 'it's the look women the world over will be copying for the next few years . . . relaxed, casual and very American . . . Instead of dressing more-so than the women in the street, she dresses less-so, and on her it looks great . . . One look at her wardrobe and you know she's a well-organised shopper . . . Though she is tall and inclined to thinness, Jackie Kennedy does not give the effect of having figure problems.' American women were encouraged to copy Jackie, it was good American citizenship to do as Jackie did. The children too: it was reported that John-John's coat was being copied by Bond Street and worn by Princess Margaret's son. Six hundred newspapers published the self-evident assertion about Caroline that 'Not since Shirley Temple . . . has an American child received so much international coverage in so short a time.' Gazing into her crystal ball, one writer predicted that a whole new Kennedy look might be expected in 1977 when Caroline would come of age.

Jackie was variously described as 'The Modest but Envied First Lady' and 'The Glamorous Political Figure who Does Not Neglect her Children.' *Photoplay* proudly presented 'Jacqueline Kennedy, America's Newest Star – All the World Salutes Jackie Kennedy.' Alongside revelations about Eddie Fisher's love-life, readers were told about '10 Ways Jack Kennedy is Romantic to Jackie.'

As yet unpublicised, the President's romantic inclination occupied the mind of an inner circle who thought that his elevation had not slowed down his pursuit of glamour. When he and Bobby spent a day in New York, it was hinted that the hidden reason for his trip was an assignation with Marilyn Monroe, at the Carlyle Hotel, of all places, where he did not remain unobserved for a minute, although the rumourmongers could not make up their minds whether it was the President or the Attorney General who was supposed to be enjoying Marilyn's favour. A year later when Marilyn Monroe led a show-biz tribute to the President in Madison Square Gardens (admittance cost three to a thousand dollars) to celebrate his forty-fifth birthday, and sang: 'Happy Birthday, Dear Mr President, Happy Birthday to you!' imagination really ran riot. Marilyn wore a revealing, body-clinging gown and looked suggestively in the President's direction; there could only be one explanation and that was a clandestine association between him and the Hollywood sex bomb. Once foreign magazines published the rumour about Marilyn and Jack, it never died down, and after Marilyn's tragic death the names of Jack and Bobby Kennedy were bandied about with even more fantastic implications. She had killed herself because Jack had left her – or was it Bobby?

More reliable evidence suggests that relations between Jack and Jackie were never better than in their first year in the White House. The President introduced a novel touch of family life into the sombre atmosphere. Caroline's shouts could be heard as she walked her father from his bedroom to the Oval Office: 'Must you go Daddy?' she asked. 'I'm afraid so,' he replied. 'I have to work to earn money for Mummy and you – and to pay Miss Shaw.' As with the children, so with Jackie. However busy he was, he always nipped into Jackie's apartment to tell her of some incident of personal interest, as when a man who had served with him in the war came to see him and they talked of old times while Australian Prime Minister Robert Menzies was kept waiting. Jack looked in on Jackie before going for his pre-lunch swim in the White House pool, often with one of his aides to keep him company. He hated being alone and when Jackie was at Glen Ora often asked Dave Powers to dine with him and stay on until the early hours. Dave called himself 'John's other wife'.

Although the President enjoyed a good film, it was Jackie who persuaded him to visit the theatre more frequently. When she took her in-laws to a show, Jack promised to join them as soon as possible but lingered at the White House to watch a heavyweight fight on TV and caught up with them during the second act. The end of the show was not the end of their evening. With the Ambassador and Rose Kennedy, they went on to a supper party at the British Embassy given by one of Jack's oldest friends, David Ormsby-Gore, recently appointed British Ambassador in Washington. They were roughly the same age, had first met when Jack was in London with his father. David had been close to Jack's sister Kick (Kathleen) who had married his cousin Bill (Marquess of) Hartington, and Rose Kennedy had seen a great deal of David and his wife whenever she visited London.

A former Minister of State at the Foreign Office, David Ormsby-Gore (later Lord Harlech) was the same timbre as Jack, worldly, amusing, with a sharp brain and considerable experience in diplomacy on which Jack drew freely. What fascinated David about Jackie were not only her obvious attractions but her subtle wit, social dexterity and irreverence which she could indulge in his discreet company. There was a strong bond between them long before the President's death and before their names became romantically linked. The evening went well. The President and Jackie stayed till two-thirty a.m. which made it a nineteen-hour day for the Chief Executive who was up bright and early the next morning while Jackie slept till noon. Ormsby-Gore saw so much of the President that he was described as an honorary member of the Kennedy administration. His direct access to the White House displeased the French Ambassador who demanded a similar privilege – request granted.

Considering Jackie's dread of the press, she gave a stunning performance when, a few weeks later, she entertained two hundred women reporters to lunch at the White House. She immediately won them over by having them admitted by the Southwest Gate which was normally reserved for state occasions, and had a word for every one of them. 'How nice to meet you at last,' she said to the lady from the *Herald Tribune* who could not wait to write her eulogy of the First Lady. The chef excelled himself with a buffet of patés, hams, lobster thermidor and Hungarian goulash. In a brave little speech, Jackie defused the controversy about her White House restoration: 'I'm terribly grateful that people are so interested,' she said blandly. 'The White House, of course, belongs to all the people.'

The following week, she played host at the traditional reception to introduce congressmen to cabinet ministers. At her suggestion, the old-fashioned, dreary reception line was scrapped and guests were encouraged to spread themselves over the redecorated lower floor, she and the President mingling freely with them. There was liquor galore but when people began to drink too much at White House functions, Jackie, with memories of excessive drinking in her own family, rationed drink – a move which was quite falsely interpreted as parsimony. She also lifted the old ban on smoking at White House functions but did not herself light up in public. Although the big party for congressmen and ministers was essentially political it became Jackie's party for the President was called away to deal with the first and biggest crisis of his term, the Bay of Pigs disaster – the C.I.A.-sponsored invasion of Cuba by anti-Castro Cubans which had been prepared under Eisenhower and was going grievously wrong.

Without dispelling the popular notion that she was non-political at heart, Jackie took a growing interest in Jack's problems. Almost every day she sent to the Library of Congress for new material, reference books, historical tomes, documents and newspaper cuttings to acquaint herself with the background of political events and soon came up with ideas and suggestions which surprised the President. It was her way of encouraging him to share his thoughts and discuss his troubles with her; indeed he had more troubles than he had bargained for. The Russians trumped America's man-in-space project, and Laos threatened to go down the Communist drain. The Bay of Pigs was like a millstone round his neck and even Jackie could not lighten his burden though later in the year she went with him to a rally of frustrated Cuban exiles at the Orange Ball in Miami and bravely addressed them in Spanish.

All through she showed the world a radiant smile which

glowed in the political darkness. It charmed the American people and delighted the President's eminent visitors. She made an impression on British Premier Harold Macmillan who spent a day on the presidential yacht *Honey Fitz*, named after Jack's grandfather, and entertained Lady Dorothy Macmillan to a decorous English tea. Instinctively or deliberately, impossible to tell, she worked her charms on the President's brainstrusters until they became ardent Jackie fans to a man: Arthur Schlesinger, Ted Sorenson, McGeorge Bundy, Walt Rostow, Ken O'Donnell, Dave Powers and Larry O'Brien who repaid her with life-long loyalty. None of them came, and remained, closer to her than Deputy Defence Secretary Roswell Gilpatric to whom she wrote those affectionate yet strangely innocuous letters whose unauthorised publication later shocked her deeply.

The only defector from her intimate fan club was Gore Vidal. Having failed to get into Congress, Vidal concentrated on his writing, spent much time abroad but was still welcome at the White House until he had a row with Bobby Kennedy. Accounts differ. The row was either political, which seems to be borne out by Vidal's campaign against Bobby a few years later, or it was private. According to the latter version Vidal exceeded the strict White House ration of liquor and was turned out by Bobby, an unlikely story. But the erstwhile friend and courtier at Camelot turned into a bitter enemy of the First Lady.

Keeping these men sweet was a public duty privately performed which left her less time than ever before for her family except for her mother who visited her at the White House or played hostess to Jackie and the President at Hammersmith Farm. Her young half-sister, Janet Auchincloss, and cousin Michel Bouvier were frequent lunch guests but her most regular companion was Lee Radziwill who came from London with her husband Stas (Prince Stanislaus), a boon for Jackie who had missed her younger sister's company. The White House dinner for the Radziwills was a gastronomic event, but then most of Jackie's dinner parties were outstanding which disposes of Mary Gallagher's gratuitous sneer that 'perhaps she could not help showing off for her sister'. In April, the Secret Service got wind of a plot to kidnap Caroline. Though it was quickly scotched, it was the kind of danger the President and his family had to live with. He and Jackie often talked about crackpots and fanatics who were forever lurking in the shadows. The danger of assassination was a recurring subject.

As early as March Jack told his wife that he was trying to arrange a personal meeting with Kruschev to clear the air between Soviet Russia and the United States and let the Soviet leader see what kind of man he was dealing with. His own staff and the State Department prepared the ground for an East-West summit. Vienna was chosen as a neutral meeting place and, as the project took definite shape, the President decided to stop over in Paris for talks with General de Gaulle and, before returning to Washington, to visit London under some innocuous pretence to give Harold Macmillan an account of his conversations.

Jackie looked forward to these big diplomatic events as an exciting adventure. She laughed heartily when Kenny O'Donnell returning from a reconnaissance trip to Europe told her that the French expected her to spend most of her time in Paris promoting their *haute couture* industry. It gave her an idea. Dismissing a passing thought that she was liable to incur the wrath of the Buy American lobby, the Ladies Garment Workers Union and *Women's Wear Daily* she wrote to Hubert de Givenchy suggesting that he make her a gown for one of the Paris functions, and sent him a sheaf of sketches to show what she had in mind. She asked Oleg Cassini to design a Greek-style toga which should be something quite out of the ordinary. With Provi's help she checked her wardrobe and made a list of the kind of clothes she would need, four or five changes for every day of the trip, each involving nine major items from hats to underwear. The list grew into a voluminous ledger in which every function, every dress, every handbag, every pair of shoes was entered.

Functions at home were crowding in on Jackie. She went to great trouble to cater to the individual taste of each visiting statesman and chose suitable presents: ancient volumes, historical documents of common interest or objets d'art with national associations. After Macmillan came the starchy old German Chancellor Konrad Adenauer, followed by the suave Greek Premier Karamanlis. King Ibn Saud had hardly left when it was the turn of President Sukarno of Indonesia, a notorious ladies' man not averse to a little flirtation with his hostess. President Bourghiba of Tunisia, Prince Bernhard of the Netherlands and Jackie's old friends, Prince Rainer and Princess Grace of Monaco, appeared in quick succession.

These visits were overshadowed by the prospect of the President's first state visit – to Canada – which Jackie looked upon as a dry run for her big Continental tour. Staff work, schedules, wardrobe were easier to manage for a hop just across the border. It enabled Jackie's secretaries and personal assistants to learn . . . The visit went well until the President planted a ceremonial tree in Ottawa and wielded the shovel with such vigour that he damaged his vulnerable spine. He spent the rest of the trip in agony and had to use crutches again when he returned home, though not in public view.

After the Canadian 'dress rehearsal' Jackie concentrated her mind on her début on the international stage. Her first contribution was to provide Jack and the State Department with a perfect excuse for the detour to London, the christening of her sister's baby girl, born in August 1960, who was to be named Anna Christina. The President was delighted and agreed to be one of the baby's godfathers. To emphasise the private character of the visit, he and Jackie could invite themselves to the Radziwill town house just around the corner from Buckingham Palace. Jackie could stay on a couple of days longer than the President and, perhaps, take Lee on a short vacation to Greece. The transatlantic telephone lines were kept busy as Jackie outlined the plan to her sister and to Stas. Jackie in turn asked Lee to come to Paris and attend some of the official functions as her guest. Jack wanted his mother and sister Eunice (Shriver) to join them in the French capital.

While official preparations went ahead covering literally every single minute of the trip, Jackie's own arrangements were hardly less detailed. Tish Baldrige went ahead to Paris, Vienna and London to check on conditions, staff, doctors, friends, and relatives – one of them, Michel Bouvier, had just taken up a business appointment in Paris. Jackie was amused when told that the U.S. Embassy in Paris had been inundated with requests from French Bouviers claiming to be her blood relatives and asking for invitations and appointments to meet their famous cousin.

When Tish Baldrige added up the matters she had to deal with, they amounted to 439 items including the presidential couple's personal baggage – eventually there were two truckloads – presents of silverware, engraved silver pens and pencils, signed photographs by the dozen . . . There were lists of places the First Lady wanted to visit and lists of things her hosts wanted her to see. There were the 'special supplies' such as bottles of American water to guard against foreign bugs, medicines, a board for the President's bed. Tish made sure that the right breakfast food would be available for the First Lady and made notes of the temperature in the respective bedrooms. Alexandre, Washington's leading hair-stylist, was invited to come on the trip. Jackie discussed with him her coiffure for each occasion and gave him a lock of her hair to study and prepare the necessary hair pieces. Nathalie, the European make-up artist, was engaged to attend the First Lady in Paris and Vienna.

While dealing with these technical problems, Jackie also prepared material for a television interview she had agreed to give. The subject: her restoration of the White House. She devoted much time to thinking up questions and framing her answers. Some time later, these notes served as raw material for her guide book of the White House and her celebrated grand tour of the Executive Mansion for American television viewers. Not forgetting the children, she wrote a dozen postcards with 'love from Mummy' for Caroline and John-John to be handed to them on each day of her absence.

The prospect of returning to Paris as First Lady galvanised Jackie. She had read advance notices in the French press which made much play with her French descent and assured her of an enthusiastic welcome, but not in her wildest dreams could she expect the triumph that awaited her. After the tremendous effort and the pent-up emotion that she had put into the preparations, the day of departure, May 30, came upon her with alarming suddenness. She found little sleep on the night flight and was tense as she stepped from the the presidential aircraft at Orly Airport on the morning of May 31.

After the formal reception, President de Gaulle, not much of a linguist and happy to speak to someone who knew idiomatic French, turned to Jackie and engaged her in conversation (at Jack's expense) rather longer than their first official encounter warranted. In the spirit of his remark after his visit to Washington a year earlier ('if there were anything I could take back with me to France, it would be Mrs Kennedy') he seemed delighted that his compatriots had a chance to see her. The airport interlude was only a hint of what was in store when Jackie, riding with Madame de Gaulle, emerged from Orly and when the cavalcade reached the centre of Paris. Over 500,000 Parisians – some put the figure nearer one million – lined the route and received the First Lady with their most rapturous applause: '*Charmante!*' they cried. '*Ravissante!*' Their shouts of '*Vive Jacqui! Vive Jacqui!*' drowned the noise of the motorcade. Jackie was overwhelmed.

As a gesture to her the cavalcade went along the Boulevard St Michel, the cobble-stoned artery of the university quarter, which Jackie had trodden so often in her days at the Sorbonne. The cheers merged with a 101-gun salute when it passed the Place de la Concorde and rose to a new crescendo when it turned into the Quai d'Orsay where the Kennnedys were taken to the Palais des Affaires Etrangéres, their Paris residence. The President was conducted to the King's Chamber and Jackie to the Queen's Chamber which had recently been occupied by Queen Fabiola of Belgium and Queen Elizabeth of England. Weary after the long flight, Jack could not wait to shed his clothes and soothe his aching back in the bath, a huge gold-plated tub. 'We ought to have one like that in the White House!' He gloated when Jackie told him that her's was only silver-plated.

There was not much time to linger. While Jack discussed final points with his aides, Jackie had her hair fixed by Alexandre and her face made up by Nathalie and only just managed to make contact with Rose Kennedy and Eunice Shriver. Lee Radziwill was the only visitor admitted and stayed with her sister while she dressed – in a narrow pink-and-white straw lace gown – for the first official function, lunch at the Elysee. The select group awaiting the arrival of the guests was carefully checked by security guards; so rigorous was the control that Michel Bouvier had difficulty in gaining admittance.

Jackie took her place by the side of President de Gaulle who turned the lunch into a twosome with the First Lady. He forgot to eat as he listened to her expounding her views on French history: 'Your wife knows more about French history than any French woman,' he told President Kennedy. 'Then,' O'Donnell recalls, 'he turned back to Jackie and did not take his eyes off her for the rest of the meal'; even put on his glasses to study her although he did not normally use them in public. Madame Herve Alphand, the French Ambassador's wife, felt upstaged and looked miserable. De Gaulle was visibly sorry when it was time to break up, and unusually mellow during his afternoon talks with the U.S. President who felt they had got on so well 'probably because I have such a charming wife'.

Leaving her apartment that evening for the big banquet in the Hall of Mirrors at Versailles, she looked so stunning in her Givenchy ensemble and her sweeping fourteenth-century hairdo with topknot and diadem that Jack exclaimed: 'Well, I'm dazzled!' As effective as her regal appearance was her skilful personal diplomacy. Taking over the function of the official interpreter, she brought the two Presidents together for an informal chat. De Gaulle was relaxed and outgoing as never before with a foreign statesman and Jack complimented his wife who, he said, was not only helping him to establish a useful relationship with the President but was creating much goodwill for America.

Escorted by André Malraux, the French Minister of Culture, she went to an exhibition of Impressionist paintings – her favourite was *Olympia*, the reclining nude by Manet – visited a children's hospital where she told photographers how much Caroline hated flashbulbs, and drove to Malmaison to inspect the Empire furniture. Her television interview was a big success. In spite of the rain, crowds were so dense that they brought her car to a standstill several times. President Kennedy adroitly summed up the First Lady's impact at his press conference at the Palais Chaillot the following morning when he told the assembled newsmen: 'I do not think it entirely in-appropriate to introduce myself to this audience,' and continued with a straight face; 'I am the man who accompanied Jacqueline Kennedy to Paris – and I have enjoyed it!' His listeners did not know what to make of it but when he broke into a broad grin they burst into laughter. Kennedy intimates thought they detected a slight edge of jealousy in the President's humorous remark.

The Kennedy-Krushchev meeting in Vienna was less convivial: the political differences were too great to be overcome in these brief discussions. The President's spine hurt and he was treated with pain-killing drugs which, it was said years later, included some rather dangerous amphetamines (popularly known as 'speed'). Jackie, too, was supposed to have been treated by a Dr Max Jacobson who was known to specialise in elaborate mixtures of hormones, vitamins and enzymes but there was no suggestion that she ever needed stimulants.

What stimulated her in Vienna was her enthusiastic welcome by the Viennese who turned out for her in much greater numbers than for Nina Kruschev. In spite of the language barrier and the lack of common interest, Jackie talked brightly to Kruschev at the state dinner at Castle Schoenbrunn, Vienna's Versailles and once the residence of Napoleon. With the Soviet space programme in mind she asked him, with the help of an interpreter, about the dog the Russians had sent into space in the second Sputnik. 'She's very well,' Kruschev said with a twinkle in his eye. 'She has become a mother . . .' Jackie thought no more about it until some time after her return to Washington when the President stormed into her room with a little dog: 'It's a gift from Kruschev,' he said. 'It's called Pushinka and is an offspring of the Russian space dog Strelka . . .' He looked at Jackie quizzically: 'Do you know anything about this?' Jackie blushed: 'I was only trying to make conversation,' she pleaded. Pushinka was accepted into the household and joined the Kennedys' other pets.

There were a few nostalgic moments when Jackie toured Vienna and passed landmarks she had seen when visiting the Danube city 'on the cheap' in her student days. She accompanied the President to mass at St Stephen's Cathedral and to lunch at the Soviet Embassy. While she enjoyed Vienna, the virtual failure of the President's mission, no agreement on Berlin, no agreement on nuclear testing, dampened spirits in the American camp. Rather than dwell on the problems, she cast her mind ahead to London and her reunion with Lee. She and Jack went to stay at the Radziwill house where they enjoyed more privacy than they had had for some time. The sisters had a lot to talk about. There was the christening of Lee's baby and lunch at Buckingham Palace, her last official function of the trip. She longed for a respite and, as Jack returned to Washington, spent two days resting with a little antique hunting in Chelsea and Kensington.

Next stop Greece. It was not easy to recognise the handsome woman, bare-legged in a casual sleeveless dress, her hair falling over her face, as the celebrated, couture-gowned First Lady who only a few days earlier had had Paris and Vienna at her feet and dined with the Queen in Buckingham Palace. Stepping ashore from a small yacht at the village of Epidaurus, near Athens, Jackie had left the glitter of state occasions behind to enjoy a private holiday uninhibited by protocol. She had flown to Athens at the invitation of Greek Prime Minister Constantine Karamanlis who, unable to offer her the hospitality of his own modest apartment, installed her in the beachside villa of his friend Markos Nomikos, a wealthy shipowner and Member of Parliament. Her party included the Radziwills and an American public affairs officer and his wife.

The Greek Navy patrolled off-shore to protect Jackie from intruders while she swam in the emerald sea and sunned herself on the beach. Markos Nomikos put his yacht, *North Wind*, at her disposal and mapped out a cruise to the Aegean Islands which took her to Delos, birthplace of Apollo, Mykonos with its 333 churches aad Hydra where Jackie drank retsina in a taverna and joined some islanders dancing the Kalamatianos. The *North Wind* took her to Epidaurus to see a National Theatre cast performing an emotional scene from Sophocles' *Electra* at the local amphitheatre.

'I don't speak Greek,' Jackie said, 'but I know *Electra* and other Greek tragedies very well from studying them at school.' Wide-eyed and gripped by the classic, Jackie was happily free from any premonition that her next visit to Greece would be in the wake of a sad personal drama, that fate would cast her as the central figure in a tragedy which was Sophoclean in its dimension, and that she would, less than a decade later, share her life with a latter-day Greek Croesus whose wealth would not protect him against a series of doom-laden family feuds, violent deaths and grief such as served Sophocles as his theme. When Markos Nomikos casually mentioned his friend and fellow shipowner Aristotle Onassis, whose name cropped up sooner or later in most conversations in Greece, Jackie countered that she knew Ari, that the President had a very high opinion of him . . .

Unburdened by any foreboding, Jackie relaxed in the Aegean sun and quickly recovered from the strain of her European tour. Crown Prince Constantine called on her and took her for a ride in his Mercedes through the Greek countryside. A message from Washington mentioned her husband's spine trouble but when she telephoned to ask if she ought to break off her holiday, Jack told her to stick to her schedule. In high spirits, she flew from Greece to Morocco to stay with King Hassan II for a few days before returning to Washington and the White House.

CHAPTER TEN

'Whether she chooses to expose herself or keep her veil of misty secrecy . . . Jacqueline Bouvier Kennedy Onassis will always remain the wide-eyed and winsome Queen of Camelot to me.'

Catherine Harvey

The President was staying at his father's house in Palm Beach, sleeping a lot, catching up on his reading, swimming gently in the sea and, with Dr Janet Travell's help, nursing his damaged and painful spine. At one point, his pain was so acute that another operation seemed the only remedy but the President improved and even ventured out to look over houses to accommodate the vast communications apparatus which kept him in touch with Washington.

After three weeks' separation, he and Jackie were reunited at the White House but were soon off for their out-of-town weekends; Fridays they went either to Glen Ora where Jackie could roam and ride undisturbed in the rolling Virginia hunt country, or to Hyannis Port, which was too family-bound for her liking, or to Hammersmith Farm to which the President became greatly attached. Since they rarely returned to Washington before Monday, Jack became known as the 'Four-day President'.

Jackie was still restoring relentlessly. Her appeals for historic paintings, furniture and memorabilia were so successful that the total value of gifts reached two million dollars. Rich donors, among them Henry Ford II and Jackie's close friend Bunny Mellon, wife of multi-millionaire Paul Mellon, as well as humble patriots contributed generously. Jackie was not particular how funds were raised as long as they furthered her purpose. She allowed *Life* magazine to produce an illustrated feature about the new White House on condition that they made a financial contribution to the restoration fund. Her own family came up with an interesting item when Aunts Maude and Michelle celebrated their first invitation to a White House function with the gift of a tattered civil war flag which they had rescued from Lasata. One choice prize reaching Jackie was two chairs made by an ancestor, cabinet-maker Michel Bouvier, around 1820. A paintings committee, chaired by her, obtained a Cézanne which nestled modestly among American *objets d'art*.

The typewriter on which Woodrow Wilson had tapped out his Fourteen Points for ending the First World War was located by Jackie and brought home. Supplementing presents and discoveries, she commissioned new-old things such as copies of a tapestry by nineteenth-century French designer Zuber which she had seen in a house in Maryland. The cost, some $12,000, raised awkward questions in Congress about extravagance. Golden draperies she ordered for the East Room would take two years or more to weave; they were not completed until some time after Jackie had left the White House. Her private abodes were refurbished with equal abandon. When she received a bill for $10,000 for work carried out at Glen Ora, she wondered whether the amount could be charged to the government: 'Absolutely not!' replied the Chief Usher citing several precedents.

To protect her handiwork, Jackie campaigned to have the White House declared a national monument and asked Clinton T. Anderson, the Senator from New Mexico, to initiate the necessary legislation. The Senator was not keen until she lured him to the White House for an informal talk and was so persuasive that he declared himself 'a reluctant convert'. No risk to her treasures, however small, found her unprepared. She gave instructions for the blinds to be kept drawn in the state rooms lest the sun faded the curtains, and was as definite about the White House lawn which was not green enough for her liking: 'Wherever I have lived, we always managed to keep the grass green!' she declared and went into a long discussion about the kind of sprinklers to be used. The White House crystal was not up to standard: she ordered it to be replaced. The linen was a disgrace . . . Scrapbooks listing old and new grew apace with her innovations.

Foreign statesmen beating a path to Washington admired her taste: seventy-four of them visited the White House in the first two years of the Kennedy administration. Each involved the First Lady in an orgy of planning and endless consultations with Chief of Protocol, Angier Biddle Duke, who was so overworked that he fell asleep during one state dinner. White House chef Verdon no longer needed to be told how to cater for the private tastes of the President and the First Lady but spent hours with her composing menus for official dinners. She supervised the shopping lists and, while the menus grew more ambitious, gradually cut down on the quantities of liquor until they settled at around one case of Dom Perignon for each twenty guests with spirits kept within narrower bounds. 'No drunkenness at the White House!' was her motto.

It was a matter of intense pride to her when Pablo Casals agreed to play his violoncello at the White House. The distinguished gathering to hear him play included the world's leading composers and musicians, Bernstein, Stokovsky and Gian-Carlo Menotti among them. Questions of etiquette had to be settled, one of them Rose Kennedy's rating in the official pecking order. Though relations between Jackie and her mother-in-law were not as cordial as appearances suggested, she insisted on Rose being given top status behind the President and herself.

For Pakistan's President Ayub Khan, Jackie went completely overboard. To give his Washington visit an unusual aura, she staged the banquet in his honour not at the White House but at Mount Vernon, home of George Washington. The guests were taken fifteen miles down the Potomac in the *Honey Fitz* and two naval vessels, and Chef Verdon's offerings had to make the same trip from the White House kitchens. Not everybody appreciated the First Lady's ingenuity as much as her guests. Dubbing her Cleopatra of the Potomac commentators asked why it was necessary to go to all the trouble of ferrying *Poulet Chasseur Couronne de Riz Clamart* and *Framboises à la Creme Chantilly* down the Potomac when steak and ice-cream could have been served in the White House just as well. By way of contrast India's Prime Minister Nehru, later in the year, was entertained at Hammersmith Farm. 'Anywhere but Palm Beach,' Jack said. 'It would give him a wrong idea of America.'

People on the fringe of Jackie's court put it about that she had changed. Where she used to be tense and restless, she was now serene and stable, living up, as it were, to the popular craving for a goddess in the White House who was perfection personified, had infallible taste and inexhaustible knowledge and was equal to every demand and superior to her peers in other parts of the world. This idealised version of Jackie was too good to be true – and it was not true. Once the novelty of her exalted position began to wear off, she reverted to her old ways of restlessly flitting from one diversion to another, looking for new hobbies to squeeze into overcrowded leisure schedules. In Hyannis Port, she took tennis lessons. 'Keep your hair out of your eyes and your eyes on the ball!' her coach yelled at her: she was no sooner able to clear the net than she switched to golf at Hammersmith Farm, addressing the ball with the concentration, if not the skill, of a Gary Player. Next it was water-skiing at Cape Cod and, of course, long lonely rides at Glen Ora.

Because life at the White House was rather frantic, Jackie kept the children out of Washington as much as possible. They were shuttled between Glen Ora, Newport and Palm Beach but were brought back after almost four months' absence for a joint birthday party, Caroline's fourth, John's first, with Susie, an educated woolly black monkey, as star attraction. For once the sombre halls of the White House reverberated with the sound of children tricycling in the corridors. Presently there was more family togetherness at Hyannis Port with scores of other Kennedy children.

Then the President and the First Lady were off for another official tour, this time to South America, where Jackie drew crowds of many hundreds of thousands and made several pretty little speeches in Spanish. She was impressed by the palace of the Colombian President in Bogotá where the furnishings and works of art reflected the country's history, and her own ideas for the White House. On the way back she and the President went to Palm Beach where the children were staying with their grandfather. Jackie remained with them but the President was due back in Washington. His father and Caroline accompanied him to the airport, then Joe Kennedy went to the golf course where he played a vigorous round; too vigorous for a man of seventy-three. He was taken ill and driven home but tried to stop Jackie calling a doctor: 'It's nothing to worry about!' he said. There was a great deal to worry about. The doctor diagnosed a stroke and ordered the old gentleman's immediate removal to hospital.

Jackie telephoned the President who was severely shaken by the news. He had a busy day ahead, was due to meet Harold Macmillan in Bermuda two days later, but cancelled all appointments and called Bobby and Jean (Smith). Within the hour the three were aboard Air Force One, the presidential plane, and heading for Palm Beach. By the time they arrived, their father was being given the last rites, Cardinal Cushing was on his way to see his favourite parishioner for the last time, and obituaries were being circulated by the wire services. But will-power carried the patient over the crisis. In the shadow of his illness, the Christmas holiday was a muted affair.

For Jackie it was back to Washington for a day, then on to Glen Ora for a day's riding to hounds on her horse Rufus. She had got rid of an irreverent bay gelding which had tossed her over a fence at a previous outing. The following day she was back in Washington to preside over a musical soirée in honour of Igor Stravinsky, but the old Russian-born composer did not stay long. His place at the piano was taken by Pierre Salinger, a musical child prodigy-manqué who treated the guests to one of his early compositions.

The big event of early 1962 was Jackie's TV Show, her invitation to the American people to view the White House through the lens of C.B.S. television cameras. She had been working on her commentary for some time and knew her lines by heart. Her bra was fitted with a tiny microphone and transmitter supplied by the same electronics expert who performed a similar service for the lady best known (by the title of her book) as 'the Happy Hooker'. In case anything went wrong with the transmitter, Pamela Turnure stood by to make the necessary adjustments: 'We couldn't have a technician fiddling with the First Lady's person,' said Charles Collingwood, the C.B.S. interviewer. Jackie, who refused the services of a TV make-up artist, looked as if she did not need them. She was in complete command of the situation, untroubled by the crew of forty-five who trundled two tons of electronic equipment behind her, and gave her commentary in her familiar whisper with astonishing expertise making only one small mistake requiring a retake.

A few weeks later, along with some fifty million Americans, she watched her own performance, an erudite seminar on artists, craftsmen and their work interspersed with choice bits of intimate White House history: how Jefferson introduced macaroni to the United States, how Woodrow Wilson hated Theodore Roosevelt's stuffed animal heads, how much most Presidents loved the Lincoln Room. So complete was her performance, it left little scope for Charles Collingwood who, at one point, trying to get a word in edgeways, spoke up as they moved from the Red Room to the Blue Room: 'This has a very different feeling from the Red Room,' he said. 'Yes, it's blue!' Jackie replied. A George Washington portrait and bust dominated the Blue Room while the Green Room's outstanding painting was the often-copied portrait of Abraham Lincoln by a Scottish artist, a gift from publisher Walter H. Annenberg, later U.S. Ambassador in London (where he refurbished his residence in the Jackie Kennedy manner). Mrs Theodore Roosevelt's portrait was the centrepiece of a tasteful arrangement of paintings. Dwelling on each, Jackie spoke in an even tone but in her eyes was pride in her achievement. She played her role superbly. There was no place for her, though, a few days later at the state dinner for King Saud of Saudi Arabia, an all-male function. Instead, she flew off to New York with Lee Radziwill.

There was some doubt in the State Department when Jackie eagerly accepted an invitation from President Ayub Khan for a private visit to Pakistan. A First Lady's private visits being subject to political considerations as much as official tours, it was pointed out to her that, if she went to Pakistan at all, she would have to go to India as well. Jackie was glad to go and Nehru was more than willing to have her. She went one better still and suggested that the trip offered a golden opportunity for her to meet the Head of the Church, Pope John XXIII, on the way. Rome was included in her itinerary. Preparations involved lengthy correspondence about such details as a special elephant-mounting platform, arrangements for the transport of presents she agreed in advance to accept: two tiger cubs from Nehru, a gelding from Ayub Khan . . . So complicated were the negotiations with the First Lady's hosts that the trip had to be postponed. Then Jackie developed sinus trouble which caused further delay. Schedules were changed and changed again – forty-seven times altogether. Worried about public reaction to the lone trip, the President's advisers were hoping that it would have to be abandoned. Jackie went ahead. She had six injections without the slightest ill-effect, supervised the packing of trunk after trunk with her new wardrobe from Oleg Cassini, Chez Ninon and Tassel with the odd Balenciaga dress thrown in. She was not to be denied. She and Lee were going – and that was that!

They made a handsome pair: Lee, if anything, more elegant, more attractive and certainly less inhibited than her sister who enjoyed her puckish, stimulating comments which took them back to their first trip together. But the First Lady was the undisputed star when they arrived in New Delhi to be greeted effusively by Nehru who seemed as captivated by her as de Gaulle had been. Her guide and mentor in India was Kenneth Galbraith, the brilliant economist. Serving a spell as U.S. Ambassador in New Delhi, he smoothed her path, briefed her, amused her; the beginning of a close friendship that has survived all changes in their respective fortunes. Her only regret on the trip was the reporters' exaggerated interest in her clothes: 'Mrs Kennedy does not regard this trip as a fashion show!' a stern American official rebuked them. It was to no avail. Everything she wore was scrutinised and described in minute detail. One correspondent even inspected her shoes when she exchanged them for a pair of satin slippers before entering a mosque: 'I can state with absolute authority,' reported the *Chicago Daily News*, 'that she wears 10A and not 10AA.' Every one of her comments, however trite, was quoted. Jackie's private visit – with Lee panting to keep up with her – turned into a triumph for the beautiful *Amriki Rani*. It was the same in Pakistan. Accompanying Lee back to London, Jackie found an invitation for lunch at Buckingham Palace waiting for her. When she emerged from the Palace, she was quick to nip embarrassing comparisons in the bud: 'I thought the Queen's clothes were lovely,' she said.

J.—8

On her return to Washington after three weeks abroad, Jackie looked tired. Her temper was not improved by the public grumbles about her trip. Again she tried to disarm her critics: 'I've missed the family,' she declared. 'If people were kind to me, it was because I was the wife of the President.' But there was no mistaking the resentment of American housewives who did not approve of a First Lady travelling alone to distant parts.

If public criticism or Jack's occasional reproaches persuaded Jackie to take a closer look at herself and at what she was doing, she rarely revealed her feelings: 'My natural tendency is to be rather introverted and solitary and to brood too much,' she told Rose Kennedy. She did not say what she was brooding about and there was nothing to suggest that she thought deep thoughts. Apart from Jack and the children, the raw material of her thinking process was the books she read, the people she met, the works of art she saw. The books satisfied her curiosity about the past, the people she liked best were those who lobbed new ideas in her direction but the works of art, though she never admitted it in so many words, brought out her acquisitive streak.

There was less tension in her life with Jack but the complexity of his political concerns made it virtually impossible for him to discuss them intelligently with his wife or, for that matter, with anyone outside the circle of his informed aides. On the domestic front, Jackie acquired a knack of defusing explosive situations which sometimes developed from silly issues. Her preoccupation with the rose garden and the green grass became so irritating that Jack reacted violently – she ceremoniously gave him a basket of green grass as a birthday present. There seemed to be an unspoken agreement that Jack could go his own way if he felt like it without incurring Jackie's silent wrath when his excursions took him into forbidden associations. Yet, as 1962 was drawing to a close, his entourage became aware of a new intimacy between President and First Lady.

Lee Radziwill came closest to being Jackie's confidante. A mutual friend said that Lee would have loved to have been First Lady, as much as the First Lady craved for Lee's freedom from etiquette and restraint which restricted her own life. Jackie enjoyed Lee's gossip and her anecdotes about the world outside. But even Lee did not come up with much when she tried to plumb the depths of Jackie's personality. Perhaps, one of their cousins concluded, there was not much depth. Jackie's asset was her position, illuminated by her surroundings and official encounters. Her great quality, rare at her level, was to be a very good listener, receptive and understanding, which appealed to the great men who sought her company. There was no need to make a contribution of her own, and, apart from her White House duties, her lifestyle was simply that of a very wealthy American woman whose interests revolved around horses, antiques, books, travel, clothes, parties, famous personalities, playing hostess, organising and running things, and people. Only the best people though. Rudely intolerant of second-raters, she refused to attend a reception for a minor South American diplomat; she was 'too tired'. The diplomat was not amused to see photographs of her water-skiing at Cape Cod that same day.

The following weekend she went to Glen Ora to ride to hounds, mostly out of public view, yet well protected by the Secret Service men discreetly hiding in the bushes. Meanwhile Caroline was enjoying an outing with the Middleburg Pony Club and Jack splashing about in the big pool in the grounds. But there was trouble with the Glen Ora owner, a dispute over payment for major renovations. As the lease was running out, Jack decided to give up the place and build a house of his own in the neighbourhood. He even chose a name for the new place, Atoka, and work on it was already in progress when he and Jackie spent a weekend at Camp David, the official retreat available to Presidents. He loved it so much that he told Jackie: 'I don't know why we are building Atoka when we have a wonderful place like this for free.' Camp David had everything, stables for Jackie's and Caroline's horses, even a golf course. It had a perfect security and communications system and the President could go to mass in the Military Mess Hall which was inaccessible to the public and to photographers.

Photographers of the Italian species known as *paparazzi* were much on Jackie's mind when she decided to join Lee and

Stas Radziwill at their rented summer house in Southern Italy, Villa Sangro, a 900-year-old, nine-room palazzo in Ravello, a thousand feet above the glorious Bay of Salerno. The notorious paparazzi would have to be endured . . . Jackie parked little John with her mother in Newport but took Caroline along on her first trip abroad for a week of Italian sunshine, swimming, water skiing, a new ambience.

The road from Amalfi was lined with cheering crowds as Jackie drove up to the hilltop holiday villa. That same afternoon she was water-skiing, giving Caroline a ride on her skis, plunging into the sea with happy shrieks, bravely facing the paparazzi in her demure swimsuit. At the week's end, she was revelling so much in the free and easy atmosphere, she extended the holiday for another week. Fiat heir Gianni Agnelli, exceptionally handsome and fabulously rich, a brilliant business brain with the lifestyle of an international playboy, put his yacht at her disposal and acted as her guide to the simple pleasures which were rare luxuries for a First Lady. They gave the leech-like White House security detail the slip and, among other diversions, turned up at a roadside café at one a.m. to drink the local wine, next day took the yacht on a mystery tour accompanied by a crooner and a five-man mandolin band who serenaded them all the way to Capri.

Such romantic excursions in the company of such a personable escort could not but encourage rumours of a closer association. They persisted or re-surfaced whenever the two met again. More visits to cafés and shops (from which Jackie took away an armful of silk blouses), dancing under the dark blue sky, music, wine, cruises . . . Caroline entertained local children and was taken to an ice-cream parlour, an unaccustomed treat. And there were still the delights of the fireworks on the Feast of St Pantaleone to come. Jackie stayed on for a third week and a fourth.

The usual round of functions awaited her in Washington but nothing caused her greater anxiety than a visit from her father-in-law, his first major outing after his near-fatal stroke. Overawed by the Ambassador as by no other man, Jackie was almost sick with worry lest the slightest hitch should disturb the ailing old man's stay at the White House. Her memos and verbal instructions to the staff covered every conceivable aspect and her attention to detail was worthy of a military operation. The Chief Usher was instructed to find out whether the Ambassador needed a hospital bed and a medical lift in the bathroom, and where to get it and how to install it. 'I will meet him at the plane – in a convertible as he can only sit in the front seat,' one of Jackie's memos specified. 'He will be staying in the Lincoln Room, his three nurses on the third floor – they will eat in the mess to avoid troubling the household . . . They can sign "JFK" – we will pay for the meals . . .' The nurses should have a TV set – 'so they can watch at nite.' For the Ambassador's room she ordered: 'Tray – with gin and tonic – coke – ginger ale, rum, Scotch, ice, cocktail shaker – lemon juice – sugar syrup in a jar . . .' The Ambassador would want to spend as much time as possible with the children; Jackie asked for them to be brought back from Glen Ora ahead of his arrival. The visit, as most things Jackie organised, went smoothly.

Washington was not a good place to have secrets, and prying eyes scrutinised the First Lady as ruthlessly as the paparazzis' cameras in Italy. People put two and two together or, in the case of Jackie's couture, counted the clothes she wore, two or three models every week, adding up to a hundred and fifty or more over the year. Her extravagance was a recurring theme, as were her bulging wardrobes, spawning all manner of rumours. It was said – and later publicised by Mary Gallagher – that, while the First Lady gave away some of her old, or rather once-used clothes, she secretly sold others, the proceeds going via her secretary's account into her own. Jackie, of course, did not want her discarded gowns to become collectors' items, neither did she cherish the thought of a hundred women going around boasting that they were wearing the empress's clothes. Still, the charge of extravagance was paradoxically coupled with the new accusation of parsimony. Talk about Jackie's personal expenditure stimulated curiosity about the President's private fortune.

Though the Kennedys kept their financial cards close to their chests, their position was, to say the least, a healthy one. Long before his grave illness, the elder Kennedy had set aside many of his millions in trust funds for his children. As the eldest surviving son Jack received the income from a five million dollar stake and another five million after his forty-fifth birthday. He had not accepted any official salary since he was first elected to office in 1947 foregoing some $400,000 – not a great sacrifice as it would seem since his trust income put him in the ninety percent tax bracket. His presidential salary was $100,000 plus $50,000 expenses bringing his total income to around half a million dollars a year (apart from book royalties and proceeds from sound investments). Part of his assets were set aside for the children and Jackie controlled around one million dollars but drew freely on her checking account.

While his personal finances were never much on his mind, at this particular time the President certainly had weightier matters to ponder. Relations between the U.S.A. and the U.S.S.R. deteriorated and Jackie watched her husband's growing anxiety and his exasperation with the Soviets and with Kruschev. Matters were coming to a head. She was one of the small circle who knew that aerial intelligence photographs of Cuba had revealed the presence of Soviet nuclear missiles and launching pads in firing positions. Confronted with this intolerable menace, the President decided to demand the removal of the missiles and ordered a naval blockade of Cuba.

Arriving at Glen Ora with Caroline and John at the critical weekend, Jackie received a call from Jack who asked her to return to Washington immediately with the children so they could be together if there was a sudden emergency. She found Jack tense and nervous as rarely before. Dave Powers recalled that the President, while taking his usual evening swim, talked about the threat of war: 'I keep thinking about the children whose lives would be wiped out,' he said. Later he clutched Caroline to himself. It was an emotional moment. Powers added: 'I got out of there as fast as I could. I was all choked up!'

Once the American ultimatum was delivered there was no saying what the Soviet reaction might be. They might retaliate in another area as they often did, in Berlin, for instance; they might – everything was possible – attack Washington with nuclear missiles. 'You and the children will have to go,' the President told Jackie. He wanted them out of the capital and close to the underground shelter which had been assigned to them. Jackie flatly refused to be parted from him. If there was danger she wanted them to share it. From the sidelines she watched the crisis growing and reaching a climax when Soviet warships and submarines were spotted heading for Cuba on a collision course with the U.S. Navy. Did they think the President was bluffing? Were they trying to break the blockade? Would they risk a conflagration? The confrontation was a severe test of nerves – until U.S. naval intelligence reported that the Soviet fleet was halting and some of the vessels turning back. The President had defeated the threat. Diplomacy took over from the mailed fist.

Early in 1963, Jackie confided to Lee that she was expecting another baby later in the year but would carry on her routine for as long as possible. She went to the French Embassy to attend a dinner for her friend André Malraux who had brought with him (or rather sent ahead by sea) another glamorous lady, the *Mona Lisa*, on her first trip abroad, fulfilling Jackie's ambition to give the American people a chance to see the unique smile of *La Giaconda*.

In April, Pierre Salinger called a press conference in Palm Beach. 'Was it to announce the President's trip to Ireland?' a reporter asked Ted Kennedy. 'No, it's sexier than that,' was the reply and Jackie's pregnancy became public knowledge. Her inclination was to cut down her public duties to an absolute minimum and rest so as to give the baby a chance. But she would not miss the state dinner for the King of Morocco who had played host to her two years earlier. As a Moslem, the King would not allow his wife to appear in public and Jackie invited his sister, Lalla Aisha, instead.

When the Grand Duchess of Luxembourg was due to visit Washington, the First Lady was determined to entertain her in style. Having been advised that the Grand Duchess was an ardent Shakespeare fan, Jackie wanted her to hear the best recitation of St Crispin's speech (from *Henry V*) America could offer, and listened for hours to tapes of well-known actors rendering the speech before deciding that Basil Rathbone had the ideal voice. To cap it all, Jackie arranged for a performance of sixteenth- and seventeenth-century tunes on authentic

Shakespearean instruments. As her doctor thought it might be too strenuous for her to attend the reception for the Grand Duchess on the White House lawn, she asked sister-in-law Eunice Shriver to act as hostess and watched from an upstairs window. Having rested all day she was able to attend the state dinner and the Shakespearean offering.

Jackie's condition made life for the staff difficult. The less she could do herself, the more precise her instructions and the more difficult to carry them out to her satisfaction. The First Lady, intolerant of lapses at all times, was harder to live with than ever. Battered by constant badgering in the slow, deliberate whisper which hardened so readily into a hiss, Tish Baldrige threw in the towel. That anybody should wish to leave her services was a blow to Jackie's pride although she had hardly bothered to conceal her irritation with her social secretary's independence and popularity, and had treated her less well than a loyal servant deserved.

Nobody could have guessed at such undercurrents when Jackie threw a farewell party for 'dear Tish' who was shunted off to one of Joe Kennedy's enterprises in Chicago. Standing modestly in the wings was her successor, yet another ex-room-mate of Jackie's at Miss Porter's, Nancy Tuckerman, who had been working as a travel consultant in Manhattan. Here was the kind of girl Jackie appreciated, shy and retiring as she herself had been, the perfect lady, a model of discretion; a dozen years later and all the fantastic, unpredictable upheavals in Jackie's life notwithstanding, Nancy was still with her.

Jackie was in the seventh month of her pregnancy and there was no question of her joining Jack on his next trip abroad to Naples (for a N.A.T.O. meeting), Ireland (for no other reason except, as he said, that he wanted to go to Ireland) and Berlin. The Berlin visit would be an international event because the President planned to make a declaration of deep commitment to the defence of the city against the Soviets, to pay tribute to Berlin's stout heart in the face of constant Soviet harassment, and to say, in German for greater emphasis, that it was a proud boast indeed if a man could declare: 'Ich bin ein Berliner!' The four German words did not flow as fluently from his tongue as Jackie's essays in French or Spanish, nor would he let her advise him on pronunciation: it was no secret in the White House that he was a little envious of Jackie's linguistic talents. In the event, addressing a huge crowd of Berliners from the balcony of the Rahaus, he made a magnificent speech culminating in the perfectly pronounced German words which Berlin has echoed ever since. After a visit to the Pope and to his ancestral Ireland, the President returned to Washington.

At the end of June, after months of agonising political in-fighting and consultations with Bobby and Lyndon Johnson, he sent a package of sweeping, controversial, explosive civil rights legislation to Capitol Hill and pledged himself to fight for equal rights for blacks over the whole spectrum of human activities. He was aware of the powerful opposition which might not shrink from violence. Exhausted by the struggle and his deep emotional commitment to the cause, he was in need of a rest. On July 3, he flew to Cape Cod to spend Independence Day, and another three or four days, with Jackie and the children. From their rented house at Squaw Island, away from the Ken-nedy compound, he went cruising on Nantucket Sound, lounged and talked and played with the children. Jackie seemed un-troubled by complications such as had marred her previous pregnancies. There was a good deal of banter about the prolific Kennedys – Bobby's wife Ethel was expecting her eighth baby later that month, and Teddy's wife Joan her third a few weeks after that. The baby would make Joe Kennedy a grandfather twenty-three times over. It would also be the first in over sixty years to be born to a First Lady and workmen in the White House were busily installing and equipping a new nursery.

All seemed well – Caroline, at five, was having a last fling before going up from kindergarten to school, little John was forming his first sentences. The President left his family fairly confident that his worries about Jackie's pregnancy were un-founded and that she would not have too bad a time. In any case, Dr John Walsh and Dr Janet Travell happened to be in Cape Cod on vacation, vacations providentially arranged by the President, and were keeping an eye on her. Jackie would be having the baby at the Walter Reed Army Hospital in Wash-ington but, another precaution, the authorities at nearby Otis Air Base had been warned to make arrangements for an emergency admission at the military hospital if the need arose and were keeping available a whole ten-room wing, redecorated and equipped with new air conditioning, fridges and dishwashers. Rumours about the extensive preparations were countered with hints that Ethel Kennedy would have her baby at Otis, which was true, but not the whole truth.

On the morning of 7 August Jackie took Caroline to her riding lesson. On her return she collapsed with acute pains. Dr Walsh was summoned. Caroline and John were despatched to Grampy Joe's place. She had just enough time to pick up her bag before being rushed away by helicopter at Otis Air Base which was put on alert and posted two hundred guards at strategic points. An airman with Jackie's A-1 Rhesus Positive blood type, one of three standing by, was giving two pints of blood for the First Lady.

The President was called from a conference and told that his wife was at Otis . . . Twenty minutes later, accompanied by White House correspondents, he was on his way to Cape Cod. Neither of the two presidential planes being available, he travelled in an eight-seater Lockheed Jet-Star, the first time the Chief Executive had flown in an aircraft not equipped with the elaborate communications installations with which he always travelled. While he was in the air, Dr Walsh at Otis, assisted by a military medical team of ten, performed a caesarian operation on Jackie and, five weeks before her time, delivered her of a 4lbs 10oz boy. The baby was so small and delicate, it was decided to have him baptised immediately by the Base chaplain. Jackie's third child was named Patrick Bouvier Kennedy.

By the time the President arrived at the hospital, his son was in an incubator. Two hours later, he was allowed to wheel the baby into Jackie's room, the first and last time the mother saw her child. Doctors told the President, but not Jackie, that little Pat was suffering from congestion of the lungs which often afflicts premature babies as he knew from his previous sad experience. It was a desperate situation. Otis was not equipped for such a contingency and there was nothing but to rush the baby by ambulance to the Children's Medical Centre in Boston, an hour away.

While doctors fought for his life, the President flew to Squaw

Island to lunch with Jackie's mother, tried to call Jackie but did not talk to her because she was asleep, and left word that he was going back to Boston. Later that day, when she was able to take his call, he told her how serious the baby's condition was. Bobby Kennedy and Dave Powers were with him when he returned to the hospital to spend the night there in an upstairs room with Bobby beside him on a camp bed. At two a.m. they were woken and told that there was little hope and that the end was near. Dave Powers recalled a poignant incident. Pacing the corridor while oxygen was being administered to the baby, the President noticed a very sick child in a ward: 'What's his mother's name?' he asked, then wrote out a note of sympathy. Unknown to each other, a mother and a father were trembling for the lives of their babies.

At five a.m. the struggle to save little Patrick was lost: 'He put up quite a fight,' the President said. 'He was a beautiful baby.' He was crying. He flew to Otis and spent an hour with Jackie alone behind closed doors. Later Jackie said that she had told him: 'There's only one thing I could not bear – if I ever lost you.' But she was made of sterner stuff than he. Her next visitor was Dave Powers wearing a suit the President had lent him ('You can't go in your crumpled suit to see Jackie!'). Dave paraded the borrowed suit before Jackie in a mock fashion-show routine: 'She clapped her hands and laughed,' Dave reported.

The funeral mass celebrated by Cardinal Cushing was attended by the Kennedys, Lee Radziwill and Jackie's half-brother and half-sister James and Janet Auchincloss. The baby's desolate father, with tears in his eyes, placed the St Christopher locket, Jackie's present, in the casket before it was buried at the Kennedy family grave at Hollyhood Cemetery. Janet Auchincloss, though looking forward to her coming-out party at Hammersmith Farm the following day, offered to cancel it but Jackie told her to go ahead.

Leaving hospital for Squaw Island a few days later, the First Lady looked deceptively composed but the President turned his back on Washington to stay with her. Both were shattered by their loss, yet misfortune shared seemed to double their sorrow; rather than bringing them closer together, the tragedy loomed like a barrier between them until the President returned to the White House while Jackie stayed behind at Squaw Island. For almost two months she seemed paralysed by gloom.

When her doctors advised that it would be better if she resumed her normal life, she returned to Washington and the White House (where the new nursery had been tactfully dismantled and the room restored to its previous state) and attended a few minor functions, but what she needed was a change of scene. It was Lee Radziwill who came to the rescue. Lee was in Athens dining with Aristotle Onassis, her jet-set friend and sparring partner; her husband was also present. Let me take up the story in the words of Aristotle Onassis who – with a few mixed-up dates and sequences – gave me a graphic account of what followed: 'I was dining with the Radziwills in Athens when Lee mentioned how depressed Mrs Kennedy was since the death of her baby. Jackie, she said, was a very introvert person who did not share her troubles with others but was very vulnerable and obviously suffering greatly . . . I immediately suggested,' Onassis continued, 'that there was no better way of getting rid of one's troubles than a cruise . . . I said I would be happy to put my yacht at Mrs Kennedy's disposal. I remembered Marcos Nomikos telling me how much she had enjoyed her previous visit to Greece . . .' Lee thought it was a splendid idea, just the thing to cure Jackie of her depression; she telephoned her sister who accepted the invitation without a moment's hesitation (Jack never told her that in the run-up to an election her cruising with a foreigner might not go down too well with some of the voters). Onassis stressed that she could regard his yacht *Christina* as her own for as long as she liked.

'When I explained that I would keep away and she could take her own friends on the cruise,' Onassis said, 'Mrs Kennedy let me know that she would only come if I went as well. The Franklin Roosevelts, who happened to be in Greece, and the Radziwills could come along, and I asked my sister Artemis to join us. Mrs Kennedy thought these arrangements were admirable.'

Jackie flew to Athens, spent a few days at the Nomikos villa, went to tea with King Paul and Queen Frederika at their summer residence in Tatoi, then boarded *Christina* and, once more her radiant self, presided over a dinner party on the yacht followed by a midnight dance on the ingenious mosaic dancefloor-cum-swimming pool on deck. Next morning, *Christina*, decorated with red roses and gladioli, carrying a crew of sixty including a band and two hair-stylists, weighed anchor and steamed into the Aegean en route to Istanbul.

First stop was Lesbos, the island of Sappho, queen of the Lesbians, which Jackie and her party explored while Onassis stayed discreetly aboard. Did he know there was some doubt in Washington about the First Lady's wisdom in cruising with him? He would not say. 'When we sailed on,' he told me, 'Franklin Roosevelt came to me and said the First Lady could not understand why I had hidden myself away. She insisted that I join her whenever she went ashore . . .' They reached Crete where Jackie and Lee clambered over the Minoan ruins . . . When they went back aboard there was a call from the President on *Christina*'s radio telephone. The cruise was doing wonders for her, Jackie told him, she was feeling much better. But the radio telephone was not what it was cracked up to be, connections became difficult and when Jack phoned again everybody could hear what they were saying. Jackie all but gave up, instead sat down in her stateroom every evening to write ten-page letters to him about her day, ending up with 'Wish you could enjoy the Mediterranean calm with me.'

Onassis smothered his guests with comfort and luxury making Jackie feel at home. She occupied Chios, one of the nine staterooms, each named after a Greek island, whose previous occupants had included Winston Churchill and Greta Garbo. They were furnished with a hint of eastern splendour, the bathrooms with solid marble tubs. Two chefs relied on larders stacked with caviar, foie gras, lobsters – every delicacy under the sun. Dom Perignon was the staple drink at the *Christina*'s colourful bar where the stools were covered with the tender skin of whales' testicles.

Jackie was fascinated by Ari's fund of anecdotes, his animated accounts of life in ancient Smyrna, the city of his birth, and of grandmother Gethsemane who had imparted much of her native wisdom to him. She talked about her own grand-father who had exerted such a strong influence on her in her formative years. Many a time they sat together on the poop deck under a theatrically starlit sky long after the others had retired. The days were cloudless, the velvety sea unruffled. In this rarefied atmosphere they became friends. They visited Ithaca, the island of Odysseus, which Onassis had adopted and which had adopted him, and Jackie became aware that he thought of himself as a modern Odysseus forever roaming the oceans. She found him a splendid guide and diverting com-panion with a deep sense of Greek history, stimulating, roman-tic. His up-to-date interpretations of mythological events put the emphasis on basic emotions and reactions which time had not changed. The loves, the feuds, the tragedies were the same still. Ari, though uneducated by her standards, revealed great wisdom and deep understanding of human nature.

As Onassis recalled the cruise in conversation with me, his eyes glowed and a flush of excitement deepened his swarthy complexion. There could have been as yet no hint of involve-ment, not with the President alive and well, but his account reproduced the atmosphere on *Christina*, the instinctive under-standing across the gap between two utterly disparate back-grounds, his reaction to the close proximity of an exceptionally handsome young woman with a latent, passive sexuality, and the intoxicating sea air which enveloped all aboard in an Elysian euphoria.

Reliving the cherished memories, it was obvious that, during this cruise, the aging tycoon had fallen in love with the First Lady. For the first time in the past four years, his paramour Maria Callas was excluded from his life, and replaced in his affection; the reason why, though his association with her went on for some time, he would not marry her.

In the early seventies when we discussed a new edition of his biography to include his life with Jackie, possibly a full bio-graphy of her, to show her as he knew her and repudiate the silly rumours about their relationship, I asked him point blank whether he had been in love with his future wife while her first husband was still alive: 'I suppose so,' he replied in his casual manner, 'but I did not admit it to myself, not for a long time after Jack's tragic death.' Two of his friends later told me that they guessed that he had fallen hopelessly in love with Jackie. (There had already been another President's lady, Eva Peron, who had not been impervious to his attractions.) In retrospect, it became clear that he began to nurse an 'impossible dream'.

She, too, made no secret of her strong feeling for Onassis, though they were not feelings of love, when she said after his death: 'Aristotle meant a lot to me,' adding a sentence whose significance escaped the uninitiated: 'He rescued me at a moment when my life was engulfed in shadows' – a reference to 1963 – 'He brought me into a world where one could find both happiness and love . . . I will be eternally grateful to him.' She responded to his comforting solicitude, his profound admiration for and total enchantment with her, with gratitude and affection which can forge a bond between a young woman and an older man as strong as love between two more conventionally matched partners.

In the wake of the cruise, some nasty flotsam was swept up and hurled at Onassis, rudely rousing him from his dream. With malice and ignorance, it was suggested that he had invited the First Lady so as to get even with his ex-brother-in-law and rival, Stavros Niarchos, who had scored by entertaining Princess Margaret and other royals on his yacht. Maria Callas's husband, still smarting from her defection, fed the fires of speculation by saying publicly that Onassis had abandoned Maria in favour of Lee Radziwill. Two congressmen in Washington said the First Lady should not have consorted with a foreigner who, moreover, had been under indictment in the United States, a reference to a brush between the U.S. Maritime Commission and several Greek shipowners, including Onassis, in the course of which Onassis was briefly arrested and fingerprinted and, no criminal charges involved, fined for technical breaches of American maritime laws. It was a sensitive point. While Onassis glossed over the incident with a few laughs, arrest and fingerprinting were no joke to the Kennedys.

Aware of the delicate situation, O'Donnell did not mention Onassis in connection with the First Lady's cruise in his Ken-

nedy biography, while her cousin, John Davis, wrote that
Onassis was quite heavily in debt in the United States which
was quite untrue. President Kennedy went out of his way to
thank Onassis for the hospitality so kindly given to his wife
but, according to his friend Benjamin C. Bradlee, insisted that
Onassis should not come to the United States until after 1964.
Did the President think Jackie's trip had damaged him politically? Bradlee says the President noted that 'Jackie's guilt
feelings' – no other evidence of such feelings – might work to
his advantage. He quotes him as telling Jackie with a smile:
'Maybe you'll come with us to Texas now next month' to
which Jackie is supposed to have replied: 'Sure I will, Jack.'
To Texas – and death.

CHAPTER ELEVEN

Tragedies cast their shadows ahead, but it is hindsight which sheds an ominous light on what goes before them. Jack and Jackie spending their tenth wedding anniversary, their last, at Hammersmith Farm and sailing in Narragansett Bay; looking over their new estate next door, a summer White House they would never occupy. The President driving through Manhattan without his motorcycle escort and being 'shot' at a traffic stop by a woman firing her camera's flashbulb straight at him, and a New York police officer shuddering: 'She might well have been an assassin!' Taking his small son with him to Arlington Cemetery on Veterans' Day barely a week before the boy would return to stand by his father's grave . . .

To get the election campaign off to a flying start, the President's visit to Texas had been planned six weeks before; Texas Governor John Connally hoped it would swing a few votes and unite the warring local Democrats who had won the state by a whisker. The President hoped to overcome opposition to his stand on civil rights although he was told that feelings on this issue were running high. Altogether it was an important mission. Jackie, who had only recently said that 'It's the President's job to win votes, mine is to look after the family and the home,' had agreed, much to his surprise and delight, to accompany him on the tour. Her pregnancy, her depression, her trip abroad, whatever she thought about their division of duties, gave her a need to integrate her life with Jack's and if this meant campaigning with him that's what she wanted to do.

The President thought Jackie would melt some stony Texan hearts, that she would be a tremendous asset. It would be a hard grind for her as well as for him: parades, meetings, banquets, speeches in dangerous territory, political enemy country; San Antonio, Houston, Fort Worth, Dallas, but with Texas congressmen to support them and the Texan Vice-President to welcome them. They would be surrounded by his faithful praetorian guard, his Irish Mafia of O'Brien, O'Donnell and Powers, his large personal staff and a small army of Secret Service guards.

The presidential helicopter was revving up on the White House lawn to ferry him and the First Lady to Andrews Field where Air Force One was waiting. Jackie was much on his mind. Minutes before they were due to leave she was standing before the mirror putting on her hat when the telephone rang. Provi lifted up the receiver – it was the President: 'Tell Mrs Kennedy that it is very warm in Texas,' he said. 'Make sure that she has enough light clothes.' It was the last time Provi would hear the President's voice.

The flight was uneventful. Jackie read a magazine while the President went over his first speech. Both were wondering what to expect at San Antonio. Leaving the aircraft a step behind the President, Jackie smiled her most dazzling smile. There was a fair-sized crowd, hustle, noise, the volatile Texan temperament. The first thing she could make out was a woman shouting: 'Jackie! Jackie!' and the cry being taken up by hundreds. The Vice-President and Lady Bird Johnson were there to greet them. The First Lady had just time to glance at a poster with big bold letters, 'Jackie – come waterski in Texas!' when another woman lurched forward trying to touch her. She was taken aback, her smile looked forced. 'I have touched her, I have touched her!' the woman shrieked.

Jackie abandoned herself to the cheers of the crowds which accompanied them all the way. The visit was brief and brisk and reassuring, their reception much better than the President had dared to hope. 'How big is the crowd at Houston?' he asked on the way to their second stop. His staff was in radio contact with the city. 'As big as on your previous visit,' was the answer, 'but a hundred thousand more to see Jackie.' Once more they shook hands with the Vice-President who had gone ahead as he would at Fort Worth and Dallas. Again the crowds, the noise, the cheers, mostly for Jackie. In the hotel, she ran through the last few sentences of the President's speech to a Spanish-speaking audience which she would repeat in Spanish. It had all been so easy in South America but this time she was struggling. Was her memory failing, was it the shock of last

August's tragedy? 'You'll be all right,' the President reassured her. She spoke her lines well and the audience rewarded her with a rousing 'Olé!'

The pace was hotting up. Aides, officials, politicians, police, reporters, secret service agents. At Fort Worth the press wanted a statement from the First Lady. She asked Pam Turnure to tell the reporters that it had been a wonderful day: 'Texas friendliness was everything I'd heard it to be.' In her apartment she found a stack of messages. Where was Mary Gallagher? The President was annoyed: 'She has no business in the motorcade,' he grumbled. 'She should have been here to help Mrs Kennedy.' Jack was as tired as Jackie: 'Don't get up with me,' he told her after they had nibbled at the caviar and the foie gras and sipped a glass of Dom Perignon before retiring. He had to make a speech very early but she could join him for breakfast at nine-fifteen. She laid out her outfit for the next day: pink suit and pillbox hat, navy blue blouse and handbag, low-heeled shoes.

There was a drizzle next morning which threatened to keep people away but the President was mainly concerned about what the rain would do to Jackie. Her crowd appeal was turning the tour into a major success and it was vital that she looked her best. She was late for breakfast; it took time to make herself look as beautiful and elegant as Jack expected her to be. Then, unexpectedly, there was an hour to spare and she noticed for the first time the Picassos, Monets, van Goghs which the hotel manager had borrowed from the local museum as a gesture to her. She was delighted. A catalogue listed the names of the sponsors of this private art show and the President impetuously called one of them, Mrs J. Lee Johnson, wife of a Fort Worth newspaper executive, and thanked her profusely. It was his last telephone conversation. Then Jackie spoke to her: 'We are both touched,' she said. 'They are going to have a dreadful time getting me out of here.' When the First Lady appeared at the big banquet she did not disappoint the guests or the President: 'Two years ago,' he told them, 'I introduced myself in Paris by saying I was the man who accompanied Jackie Kennedy . . .' He could only repeat what he had said.

The President had no time to linger. He was busy sorting out conflicts among the local Democrats who were at sixes and sevens. Senator Yarborough was at loggerheads with Governor Connally and would not ride with him in the same car; there were arguments who should or should not sit at top tables. Tempers flared easily hereabouts among friends and foes, only the previous month Adlai Stevenson had been roughed up at a public meeting. As if this was not bad enough, the President, while trying to knock reluctant heads together, was shown a copy of the *Dallas Morning News* which carried a vicious, slanderous, provocative full-page anti-Kennedy advertisement with an ominous deep black border, an incitement to violent opposition if not physical violence. He read it out to Jackie who grew pale and felt acutely sick as if hit by a low punch: 'We are heading into nut country,' he told her, adding with a flash of frightening premonition: 'you know, last night would have been a hell of a night to assassinate a President.' At Dallas, the local radio station was running a programme about the assassination of Abraham Lincoln.

The rain forecast for Dallas held off, the sun was shining brightly. If the weather stayed fine, the bubble-top of the President's car could be left off. But the mood in Air Force One was subdued. As the aircraft taxied in at Love Field, Dallas, it was easy to see the extensive security arrangements, police stationed at the tarmac, controlling crowds at the perimeter and watching from rooftops. Vice-President Johnson was there to shake hands with the President and Jackie for the fourth time in twenty-four hours, Jackie good-humouredly returning his apologetic smile and accepting a big bouquet of roses from a local lady. Following the President to the perimeter she shook hands which reached out for her and chided him gently when he lagged behind. Unaware of sudden confusion in the entourage and a scramble for places in the official cars behind her, she took her seat in the presidential Lincoln by the side of the President, followed by Governor Connally and his wife Nellie who took the flap seats, Sam King, the Secret Service driver, and his colleague Roy Kellerman. Four police motorcyclists, two on either side, flanked the car as it moved away from the airfield to the sound of cheers from supporters, and angry insults from hostile youngsters.

Jackie's eye fell on one of the big posters which proclaimed (ungrammatically): 'YOUR A TRAITOR!' and others crudely inscribed, 'Yankee, go home!' They passed a group of children carrying a placard which pleaded more amiably: 'Mr President, please stop and shake our hands!' and the President stopped the car, got out and shook hands with his young well-wishers. There were more cheers as the crowd thickened but they could not dispel the menace, the threat, the violence in the air. It was uncanny, a terrific strain, and Jackie, unlike the roses on the seat beside her, was wilting. The atmosphere was heavy and the sun bright. She waved weakly and put on her dark glasses. 'Jackie, over here!' shouted the crowd, anxious to see the First Lady. 'You can't say that Dallas is not friendly to you today,' said Nellie Connally to the President, but there were blocks of people glowering in sullen silence.

'Five more minutes and we'll have him there,' said the police officer in charge as the cavalcade passed the seven-storey Texas School Book Depository building: five minutes to the Trade Mart where the President was scheduled to make his speech. Dave Powers, riding with Ken O'Donnell and two Secret Service men in the follow-up car, looked at his watch and worked out that they were five minutes behind schedule. Abraham Zapruder, a local dress manufacturer, who had joined the crowd to make a film of the occasion, let his camera roll. Jackie was exhausted but the President continued to acknowledge the cheers. Out of the blue and above the noise she heard Governor Connally exclaim: 'My God, they are going to kill us all!' 'Why is he screaming?' she thought to herself. There was a short, sharp sound but she thought it was a motorcycle back-firing. Suddenly Jack fell forward: 'My God,' he said, 'I'm hit!' She turned towards him and saw a quizzical look in his eyes which she had seen often before. Then it dawned on her: 'Jack! Oh no! No!' she cried out.

There was another cracking noise, no doubt about it this time, a shot which ripped into the President's skull. She saw his hand reaching for his head and the gaping hole. He slumped towards her, what remained of his head coming to rest in her lap. Blood spurted over her hand, her blouse, her skirt and her stockings. She was not aware that John Connally was also hit but heard driver King shouting: 'Let's get the hell out of here.' He was trying to carry out emergency procedure and detach himself from the cavalcade which was scrambling up in confusion.

Deep in shock, Jackie could not remember what she had been doing in these agonising seconds, but every one of her moves has been recorded. For a moment she sank to the floor which was soaked with blood, then rose from her knees and, as if accusing the crowd, turned towards the pavement and cried out: 'My God, what are they doing? My God, they've killed Jack, they've killed my husband. Jack! Jack!' Mingled with the blood on her clothes were spatters of the President's brains . . . From the pavement came shouts echoing her cries. It was Zapruder whose camera was still turning as he screamed: 'They've killed him! They've killed him!'

Nellie Connally heard Jackie sobbing: 'He's dead – Oh Jack, oh Jack – I love you!' The driver put his foot down and the Lincoln jerked forward just when Clint Hill, Jackie's own Secret Service guard, jumped from the follow-up car on to the back of the Lincoln to protect her, lost his foothold and slipped. Instinctively clambering over the rear of the Lincoln, Jackie grabbed his hand, held on and saved him from falling under the follow-up car and being crushed. Later, when examining Zapruder's film, the only photographic record of the assassination, Jackie did not remember the incident at all and felt as though the frames showed another woman.

She did not hear agent Kellerman signalling an alert over the car radio, was barely aware that the car was taking her towards Parkland Memorial Hospital, some four miles away. With her husband's body sprawling on the floor, she hugged his head, seemingly anxious to hide his grisly wound, the cruel gaping hole in his skull. Her hat fell over her face and she whipped it off so violently that the hairpin caught a big tuft of hair and tore it out. She was wailing faintly, a humming sound that came from the back of her throat. She was still wailing when the car came to a standstill at the hospital. Two stretchers appeared and Governor Connally was carried in but Jackie held on to Jack and would not let him go. Catching up with the Lincoln, O'Donnell and Powers arrived as yet unaware of the full extent of the tragedy. Seeing his chief's staring eyes, Dave Powers broke into tears, O'Donnell stood quite still as deeply in shock as Jackie. In the tradition of 'The King is dead, long live the King!' one of the Secret Service agents stepped forward to see with his own eyes that President Kennedy was dead, then told a colleague: 'I'm going to Johnson.' His job was to guard the President of the United States, not a corpse.

All eyes were on Jackie but she did not move. As if trying to hide, she turned away holding her husband's face to her. She was weeping. An agent touched her lightly but still she did not move. Hanging on to Jack's body she was fighting a battle to conquer her agony, sobbed out aloud, a last sob, before gaining control of herself – her incredible, iron self-control. Her face, when she showed it, was still, without expression. According to William Manchester's masterly, deeply moving account (*Death of a President*) Clint Hill mumbled: 'Please, Mrs Kennedy! We must get the President to a doctor.' Jackie later told friends – and the official investigators into the assassination (The Warren Commission) – how she reacted, and repeated her account to Manchester. 'I'm not going to let him go, Mr Hill,' she replied. 'You know he's dead. Leave me alone.'

She remembered Hill giving her his coat, wrapping it round the wound, and keeping it in place when it threatened to slip. Then she allowed the President's body to be eased out of the car and put on a stretcher which Dave Powers helped to carry inside while she kept her hand on Jack's heart hoping against hope to coax a glimmer of a beat from it.

For the first time since the fatal moment Jackie was seen to be covered in blood, her blouse, her skirt, her gloves stained dark red. Like wildfire the rumours spread: 'Jackie's been shot!' But Jackie's wound was deep in her heart and did not bleed. Entering the hospital she collapsed into a chair in the corridor while the President's body was taken into an Emergency Room where neuro-surgeon Dr Kemp Clark examined the wounds. Nine doctors joined the battle for his life, gave him oxygen, performed a tracheotomy, fed fluids intravenously into his body, gave him a blood transfusion and massaged his heart but the electrocardiograph recorded no contractions, no heart beat.

Outside, Jackie waited with a look in her eyes, as one observer remarked, 'like that of an animal that had been trapped.' Among the voices from the Emergency Room she seemed to hear the word 'resuscitation' – did this mean, was it possible, that he was still alive? 'I'm going in there,' she said firmly. One of the doctors turned to her and said: 'Your husband has sustained a fatal wound.'

'I know,' she answered.

She moved forward to take Jack's hand. Summoned from the nearest church, two priests, Fathers Huber and Thompson, appeared on the scene, administered the last rites and tried to comfort Jackie. 'Thank you for taking care of the President,' she said. 'Please pray for him.'

Evelyn Lincoln came up to her. 'Oh, Evelyn . . . He's gone,' was all Jackie could get out. Mary Gallagher had retrieved Jackie's handbag and hat with the hair caught by the pin. Seeing Jackie covered with blood she asked whether she did not want to take her stained gloves off: 'No, thank you.' She refused all offers of help. 'I'm all right.' She looked frail and lonely, no longer the proud First Lady but a pathetic widow stricken with grief. Yet she was surrounded by friends, by her dead husband's closest collaborators whose loyalty had survived his death, who would do anything to comfort her and whose affection gently washed over her consciousness. Only they could know at this moment what she had lost. Larry O'Brien, whom Jack had held in such high regard, the austere Ken O'Donnell, man of few words but deep feeling, the more volatile Dave Powers whose world seemed to have died with the President. They saw Jackie rising slowly, swaying as if about to faint, collecting herself. Was there anything they could do, anything at all? Silently she shook her head. The routine of death took over. A bronze casket was brought and taken into the Trauma Room. 'Get me in there before they close it,' Jackie pleaded with O'Donnell. She wanted to see Jack again and give him something of her's to take away with him. They tried to stop her: 'I've seen my husband die,' she flared up, 'shot in my arms. His blood is all over me. How can I see anything worse?'

She could have added that nothing, nothing that could ever happen to her could be worse than the two hours she had lived through. Shattered by the tragedy, she seemed yet hardened by the ordeal and girded herself to face what could not be changed. She felt an upsurge of anger and hate such as she had not known before. She was a widow, no longer a wife, and what she gave her dead husband was the symbol of their marriage and their life together – her wedding ring. She went to the casket and a medical orderly helped her to push the ring on her husband's finger.

Back in the corridor she sank into a chair. They wanted her to go, to leave the hospital where she could do no more for her husband. No, she would not leave without Jack. 'Why not go back to the plane?' She shook her head. Her cup was not yet drained. There was an ugly incident when an eccentric priest slipped through the cordon of guards and, however well-intentioned, pestered the tragic widow; there was the Dallas coroner intent on following regulations governing a violent death.

Dreading the moment of her final parting from Jack, Jackie did not dwell on the assassin – or assassins. She had no means of knowing, though the police did, of the existence of the shiftless Lee Harvey Oswald, disgraced ex-Marine Corp private and would-be revolutionary, who had spent eighteen unhappy months in the Soviet Union and married a Russian girl, had tried but failed to get into Cuba, had made an abortive attempt to murder a general and was currently employed at the Texas School Book Depository from which the shots had apparently been fired. Within minutes of the shooting (according to Chief Justice Earl Warren's Commission which investigated the crime in depth) one of the presidential police motorcycle escorts tracing the origin of the shots had entered the Depository and passed Oswald on the second floor but failed to arrest him. On the sixth floor, near a window at which the assassin had been seen, police found the rifle which had just been fired, and established that it belonged to Oswald.

It appeared that after the shooting Oswald had slipped away, walked a few yards, boarded a bus and switched to a taxi which drove him to his rooming house. By this time his description, based on an eyewitness account, was being broadcast. Oswald changed, picked up a revolver and went out. On the corner of 10th Street and Patton Avenue he was seen by Police Officer J. B. Tippit who called him to his squad car. They spoke briefly before Tippit got out and walked to the front of the car. At this point, Oswald pulled his revolver and shot him four times. The officer was killed instantly. One of the people who watched the incident heard the murderer say 'Poor damn cop' or 'Poor dumb cop', saw him diving into a doorway, emerging and running into the Texas Theater where he passed the cash desk without buying a ticket. Alerted by the cashier, the police, with sirens wailing were already on their way. They entered the cinema, had the lights switched on and discovered Oswald in a seat near the back. He was arrested but denied that he was the man who had killed the President and the police officer.

Police inquiries were far from complete when, two days later, Oswald, while being escorted by two police officers, was shot at point blank range and killed by one Jack Ruby, a character in his own way as way-out as Oswald himself. The death of the killer left many vital questions unanswered and raised a host of new ones, none of which were or could ever be answered conclusively. Although the Warren Commission devoted much attention to all the speculation and rumours which circulated in the wake of the assassination, its findings had never been completely accepted and new revelations or theories continue to be offered. Doubts remain about many cardinal factors. Was the assassination the act of a lone wolf or the culmination of an evil conspiracy? Were the guilty men, if any besides Oswald, foreign communists or home-grown reactionaries? Was Ruby hired to kill the assassin to protect his accomplices? Was he perhaps one of them? Were all the shots fired from the Texas School Book Depository?

The Commission dismissed the rumours and brought the crime home to Lee Harvey Oswald but without determining his motive. Their theory was that the man had suffered from a combination of personal and political frustrations. He had been at odds with his Russian-born wife who accused him of failing to provide for her and of being sexually inadequate. His love affair with Communism had been equally disappointing. Bitter and disillusioned, he had wanted to prove himself – and hang the consequences. In this frame of mind he had planned and carried out his deed. It was no more than a theory but the Chief Justice and his team put it forward as a plausible explanation. They severely criticised the F.B.I. for not keeping tabs on Oswald; the Dallas police for the security breakdown which led to Oswald's death before the facts could be established beyond doubt; and, most severely, the Secret Service for neglecting to check the Depository and not even knowing that Oswald worked there.

For a few minutes it looked as if the dignity of his victim's death would be violated by the unseemly row between an obstinate, narrow-minded Dallas coroner who would not release the body, even posted guards to prevent it being taken away, and the Secret Service agents who were trying to get the coffin and Jackie back on Air Force One. Victory did not go to them until, fighting like tigers, they shouldered their way through the throng and pushed past the police guard with the coffin. Jackie put her hand on the bronze cover and did not remove it until it was lifted into the waiting ambulance. She climbed into the vehicle followed by Dr Buckley, the late President's personal physician. Agents Kellerman and Greer joined the ambulance driver in the front seat and ordered 'Love Field.' Faster than any hearse ever, the ambulance sped away at the head of three cars carrying Evelyn Lincoln, Mary Gallagher, Press Secretary Mac Kilduff and the rest of the staff.

A hush fell over the airfield as the sad procession stopped by the side of Air Force One. Jackie watched the Secret Service men manipulating the heavy coffin clumsily up the steps of the aircraft helped by Dave Powers, then, with head bowed and faltering steps but looking strangely beautiful, followed it inside. The time was two-twenty p.m., less than two hours since Oswald's bullets had hit their target. The coffin was placed in the rear passenger compartment and Jackie remained with it.

The atmosphere was stifling, physical discomfort heightened by the tension among the people around her. If she sensed the schism between her husband's staff and Johnson's acolytes, she

175

gave no sign of it. Accustomed to the aircraft taking off within seconds of the President entering, Jack's people were impatient to take off as if he were the only rightful occupant of the presidential plane. But now it was a matter for the new Chief Executive to give the signal and his aides were only concerned with the constitutional process which demanded that the new President be sworn in as quickly as possible, right here on the aircraft. They were waiting for a lady judge, Sarah T. Hughes, a friend of Lyndon Johnson, who had been summoned to administer the oath.

Lyndon Johnson was at work in the plane's sleeping quarters which Jackie had occupied with her husband on the way out. He came out struggling for words to comfort her. Lady Bird solicitously asked whether she would not care to take off her stained gloves. Jackie shook her head. 'Lyndon . . .' she started saying, then corrected herself: 'I mean, Mr President . . .' No, no, Johnson protested; he hoped he would always be Lyndon to her. Then it was Mary Gallagher's turn to press Jackie to change her clothes. She was adamant. O'Donnell thought she needed a drink and offered her a whisky. 'I've never tasted whisky in my life,' she answered but took a little gulp.

After what seemed like hours, Judge Hughes arrived and prepared to perform the swearing-in ceremony. In the sweltering heat, twenty-seven people crowded into the plane's main compartment and grouped themselves in some order. Perched up high, a photographer was wondering how to take his historic picture in the confined space, how to avoid focusing on the dark stains on Jackie's costume. Standing to the left of the new President, she was closer to the camera than Lady Bird Johnson who was on his right . . . The noise of the engine all but drowned the words of the aging Lady Judge pronouncing the oath which Johnson, one hand raised, the other on President Kennedy's Bible, repeated in a strong voice: 'I do solemnly swear that I will faithfully execute the office of the President of the United States . . .'

The President kissed Lady Bird. He took Jackie's hand and told her: 'The whole nation mourns your husband.' Jackie shuddered. Police Chief J. E. Curry stepped forward. 'God 'bless you, little lady,' he said, 'but you ought to go back and lie down.'

'No thanks,' Jackie replied. 'I'm fine.'

As if suddenly realising that he was the President – which he had actually become the moment President Kennedy died – Johnson issued his first command: 'Now let's get this thing airborne.' Still anxious to comfort Jackie, he turned to her but realised that all she wanted was to remain with the coffin. Powers, O'Brien, O'Donnell and McHugh sat with her.

President Johnson called Rose Kennedy over the radio telephone: 'I wish to God,' he said, groping for words, 'that there was something I could do . . .' Rose did not tell her husband, deciding to wait for the morning when he would be stronger to withstand the shock. Ted Kennedy already knew: the news had reached him in the Senate building. Bobby Kennedy went out walking with his dog for a full hour trying to come to terms with the fateful blow before making his way to Andrews Field. Dr John Walsh was asked to meet Jackie on the tarmac.

The terror of the last few hours was etched deeply in the faces of the men with Jackie whose self-control slipped for a brief moment, tears filling her eyes and rolling down her cheeks. Deeply moved by her distress, one after another they sank to their knees before her. She pulled herself together and rose, the bloodstains on her outfit looking like a badge of undying loyalty, a symbol of suffering and witness to the crime that had robbed her of her husband. Did she not, after all, want to put on a fresh dress? 'Let them see what they have done!' she hissed defiantly. There would have to be an autopsy: did she want the body to be taken to Walter Reed Hospital or to Bethesda Naval Hospital? 'The President was in the Navy,' Dr Buckley ventured. 'Bethesda,' Jackie answered. Instructions went out for a military ambulance to await the plane's arrival.

The radio link was humming. President Johnson was asking leaders of Congress to meet him. He was told that the White House was being made ready for him; at this moment secretaries were clearing President Kennedy's desk, removing his war mementoes, his silver calendar marking the date of the Cuban missile confrontation and the silver-framed photograph of Jackie and the children. (In the event, President Johnson decided to work for the time being in his vice-presidential suite in the Executive Office building.) Jackie, too, her disciplined mind shutting out the pain to concentrate on what had to be done, went to the telephone and called Bill Walton: 'Take charge of the arrangements,' she asked him. 'Get in touch with Mr West . . .' Mr West recorded his reaction to Walter's call: 'It told me that Mrs Kennedy, even in her shock, knew what to do.' She was quite specific: she wanted the house to be just what it was when Lincoln lay in state. If necessary, Sargent – Sargent Shriver – could help.

The aircraft was approaching Andrews Field. Would Mrs Kennedy prefer to leave by a door out of public view? No, she would leave by the main door. Her eyes would not leave the coffin, not until the aircraft landed and Bobby Kennedy came aboard to embrace his brother's widow. 'Oh, Bobby . . .' she whispered. He clutched her hand and gently led her away. He was taking her back to the black White House Cadillac but she held back: she was going in the ambulance with the coffin.

At the Bethesda Hospital, Jackie at long last agreed to be separated from Jack. After the autopsy he was embalmed: in spite of the huge hole in his skull his face (contrary to rumours) had remained undamaged. Jackie stayed close to Bobby who was a pillar of strength in comforting his sister-in-law and looking after the thousand and one things that needed attention. Other members of the family arrived, each greeting, each embrace, each commiseration another painful tug at Jackie's taut nerves. Janet and Hugh Auchincloss were among the first followed by Jack's sister Jean and brother Ted. Doctors Buckley and Walsh fussed over Jackie, implored her to change and to rest but she had no intention of doing either. Lee Radziwill, who heard the news in London, telephoned to say that she was catching the next plane to Washington. Rose Kennedy was on her way and Cardinal Cushing was coming to perform the funeral rites. In every capital, leaders were preparing to fly to Washington . . .

Jackie's shock was entering a secondary phase, a strange agitation and irresistible urge to talk. Talking incessantly, often in unrelated snatches, she cornered Bobby and relived the tragedy from the very beginning, every tiny detail that returned to her tortured mind, the trip to Dallas, the drive from Love Field, the cheers, the shots, Connally's outcry, Jack's collapse. Bobby did not want to hear, did not want his sorrow compounded but girded himself for her sake and let the flood flow uninterrupted.

She embraced Ben and Toni Bradlee and said: 'Oh, Benny, do you want to hear what happened?' and started to tell her story all over again. Yet a little later, Bradlee says, she seemed completely detached. But when she was told about the assassin's political background, she stamped her foot and burst out angrily: 'That's absurd. He didn't even have the satisfaction of being killed for civil rights. It had to be some silly little Communist!' The hateful Dallas reactionaries were not the ones to blame after all.

When Janet Auchincloss mentioned that the children were with her and quite all right, Jackie flared up again: 'I want them back in the White House!' Their routine was not to be disturbed. Caroline, not John, would have to be told before she heard from outsiders. Janet felt that her daughter should be relieved of the awesome burden but did not want to take it on herself either. She called Maude Shaw and ordered her to break the news to the little girl. The English nurse demurred but in the end did it beautifully, telling Caroline that her father had gone to take care of little Patrick.

Jackie, lighting one cigarette after another, stubbing them out half smoked, was still talking and working the oppressive experience out of her system, repeating her account to whoever was close to her. Bobby was on the telephone organising the funeral, summoning a marine detachment to escort the casket to the White House where workmen, with the aid of an old print of Lincoln's lying-in-state, assembled the historic catafalque in the centre of the big East Room, draped and decorated it with leaves from Andrew Jackson's magnolia tree.

At Bethesda in the morgue, Bobby and Dr Buckley retrieved Jackie's ring from the dead President's finger and returned it to her. She accepted it without comment but, she said later, remembered how much she still had to tell Jack and made up her mind to write him a farewell letter and put it in his coffin. It was three thirty a.m. when the hospital released the body and the casket was carried to an ambulance. Again Jackie remained close with Bobby crouching on the floor of the ambulance beside her. Yes, of course, he would be staying the night at the White House, and Janet and Hugh would be staying too: they were only stopping over at their house to get a few things together. At the White House, the coffin was placed on the catafalque and Jackie spent a few minutes with it in thought and prayer before allowing herself to be persuaded to go up to her room. She asked Bobby to sleep in the Lincoln Room and, though they protested, Janet and Hugh to take Jack's bedroom.

It was four a.m. when Jackie at long last took off her battle-scarred clothes. Provi put them in a bag and hid them away. Dr Walsh came up and suggested she take a sleeping draft but she refused. An injection then? She felt that she would not be able to sleep and agreed in the end. The injection knocked her out completely. Dead to the cruel world, she slept for two hours, woke up and asked for coffee and fell asleep again. By eight a.m. the effects of the drug wore off and she got out of bed.

Downstairs the Chief Usher was making preparations for a short Mass to be read before the coffin was taken away. He had rows of chairs put up in the State Dining Room, a priest was standing by and family and aides were already assembled when Jackie came downstairs at ten thirty. She shook her head: she did not like the arrangements. The Mass should be held in the East Room by the coffin. The chairs were transferred and everybody gathered around the catafalque. It was time for the coffin to be taken to the Capitol Rotunda for the President to lie in state – from all over Washington and beyond people were flocking to the Capitol and already queues stretched for miles, the advance guard of a half a million or more who would pass the coffin in the next forty-eight hours.

While Air Force One roared overhead dipping its wings in a farewell salute, Jackie and Bobby knelt by the coffin and kissed the flag which covered it. Then, her head held high, she walked with him past the crowd and, with one last look towards the floodlit dome, was driven off to the White House. Later in the day, Lee Radziwill and her husband arrived from London to take over from the Auchinclosses. 'Lee will be sleeping with me in my bedroom,' Jackie announced and directed Stas Radziwill to Jack's bedroom. Jackie played with Caroline who shed a few tears for her father but was soon distracted with stories and games. John-John was a problem. 'Here comes Daddy . . .!' he shouted when the presidential helicopter landed on the White House lawn. He upset his mother by talking about his father as if he were still alive. The little boy was puzzled because his birthday party was postponed; it fell on the day of the funeral. Jackie chose two near-identical powder-blue coats for the children to wear and asked Provi to find her a veil but did not like the one she was shown and a search went on for another . . .

Every foreign leader of note let it be known that he would attend the funeral: President de Gaulle, President Luebke of Germany, Queen Frederika of Greece, King Baudouin of the Belgians, Haile Selassie, the Duke of Edinburgh. Jackie was determined that they should see the funeral worthy of one of America's great leaders. The coffin would remain closed although tradition demanded otherwise for the President of the United States and Commander-in-Chief. Jackie was adamant. Why did she still not want outsiders to see Jack? Inevitably rumours began to spread that the President's face had been disfigured probably by shots coming from the front as well as the back which suggested more than one assassin with all sorts of political implications . . .

Still in a state of high agitation, Jackie wandered around the White House handing out mementoes to members of the staff – the President's ties to his Irish friends – and talking emotionally to her own people, to 'Poor Nancy' who had been lured from her lucrative job in New York. What now? To Pam Turnure – what was she going to do? To the Chief Usher: 'Will you be my friend for life?' Suddenly she remembered her own uncertain future: 'Where am I going to live?' she asked forlornly, not expecting an answer.

Bobby Kennedy was taking care of this as of so many things. He talked to President Johnson who agreed that Jackie could stay on at the White House; a few days made no difference. Averill Harriman, the multi-millionaire diplomat, offered her his house in Georgetown at 3038 N Street, only a few blocks from where she and Jack had had their first home. A beautiful house in typical Georgetown colonial style, it was a treasure trove of van Goghs, Picassos, Matisses, Toulouse-Lautrecs, Chagalls, a house after Jackie's heart. But there was another heartbreak: what to do with the children's animals? Pushinka eventually went to the White House gardener, Charlie; the Welsh terrier to a Secret Service man; but John kept Shannon, his gentle spaniel, and Caroline her love-birds and, of course, her pony.

After checking records of previous presidents' funerals, Jackie approved the plans for a Mass at St Matthew's Cathedral and burial in a temporary grave at Arlington Cemetery. Once his final resting-place was ready on a plot nearby, his coffin would be joined by the caskets of his two babies who had not survived. Anxious not to strike a single false note when receiving the eminent foreign mourners individually, Jackie asked Mr West to remove the Cézanne from the room in which she would be seeing President de Gaulle and replace it with scenes from American history.

As strong as her grief was Jackie's resolve to impress her husband's place in world affairs on the American consciousness, to remind Americans what they had lost when he died. The funeral was one means of demonstrating his eminence in history, his links with Lincoln, Jackson, Roosevelt. She watched his coffin being placed on the gun carriage which had carried Franklin D. Roosevelt in 1945 and the riderless horse with boots reversed in their stirrups which followed it. At the entrance of St Matthew's, she was received by Cardinal Cushing and kissed his ring before entering with Caroline and John. Struggling to keep her composure, Jackie walked behind the coffin when it was taken from the cathedral to the strains of *Hail to the Chief* and gently reminded little John to salute the flag which covered it.

The ordeal was showing in her face, tears glistening in her eyes behind the veil as the procession moved to Arlington Cemetery some three miles away. The roar of fifteen jet-fighters overhead pierced her mind which had drifted back to Dallas. When the coffin was lowered into the grave, she hugged the

flag to her breast and kissed it, then lit an eternal flame –
symbol of Jack's enduring greatness – with a taper, as did
Bobby and Teddy. That evening, she returned to Arlington with
Bobby, put a small bouquet of lilies on the grave, wept, prayed
and tore herself away.

CHAPTER TWELVE

The good and the bad, the hardships, the joys, the tragedies, loves and happiness are all interwoven into one indescribable whole that is called life.

Jacqueline Kennedy Onassis

For Thanksgiving Day, Jackie took the children to Hyannis Port. If only for their sake there was no overt sign of mourning. Within days they were all back in Washington where some of the family furniture was installed in the Harriman house while the rest went into storage. Dave Powers came to lunch. Would he come every day, please, and play with the children? Of course he would; it helped him as much as it cheered them. Most afternoons Bobby and Ken O'Donnell dropped in to talk about the old days and about the future. Evenings Jackie and Bobby drove to Arlington to visit Jack's grave. Among the few people she saw were Mr West and Nancy Tuckerman who came to dinner: 'I hope you will remain with me for some time,' she told Nancy.

Congress voted Mrs Kennedy $50,000 to pay off the servants and a widow's pension of $30,000 a year for life. Bobby dealt with Jack's personal estate and his interest in the Kennedy family trust. The late President's assets were smaller than generally assumed and his share of the trust was divided between his widow and the children. Knowledgeable friends estimated that the total was well below the ten million dollars mentioned in the press – five for Jackie, five for the children – and that she received no more than a million in cash and an income of $150,000 a year while she remained unmarried. At this stage it seemed inconceivable that there would be another man in her life, a ridiculous notion considering that she was only thirty-five. Probate was granted in Boston within weeks of Jack's death.

Jackie spent an hour and a half with Lady Bird Johnson at the White House briefing her about some of the First Lady's concerns; her own secretaries were snowed under with letters and condolences from all over the world. More than 185,000 were counted in the first few weeks and a hundred volunteers were helping to answer them. But when letters kept coming in at the rate of several thousand a day, reaching a total of over a million, personal acknowledgements had to be abandoned. Instead, Jackie went on television to thank her wellwishers. It so happened that her appearance coincided with Lady Bird Johnson's first big White House dinner and there were whispers that Jackie had skilfully and maliciously set out to upstage the new First Lady. Next morning the newspapers gave much space to the broadcast but only a few lines to the dinner.

Apart from her closest friends only a few statesmen received a personal acknowledgement. One of them was Nikita Kruschev. Jackie told him how moved she was that Mrs Kruschev had burst into tears on hearing the sad news. She went on to recall one of her husband's thoughts, namely that big men needed self-control and restraint. Her gesture puzzled the State Department which nevertheless cleared the letter.

The people who most helped Jackie over this difficult period of readjustment were the Bartletts, the Bradlees, Defence Secretary Robert McNamara and his wife, Ted Sorenson, William Walton who took turns asking her out to dinner or going to her house to spend the evening with her: 'We mostly ended up reminiscing,' said one of the regulars, adding that Jackie smiled when they recalled Jack's wisecracks, listened intently when they discussed his political thoughts and looked tearful when the talk became too nostalgic.

One friend who insisted on telling her personally how deeply he felt for her was Aristotle Onassis who had heard the news of the assassination in Hamburg when about to sit down to a dinner celebrating the launching of his latest oil tanker: 'It was a terrific shock,' he recalled. 'I left immediately. I was desperately sorry for Mrs Kennedy who had so recently lost her baby and had hardly recovered.' Their recent cruise together was vivid in his mind, a big occasion in his life, a great emotional experience. It was almost intolerable for him to think of this gentle, beautiful woman under a hail of bullets, her husband killed by her side, and time had not mellowed the memory when he talked about his feelings some years later: 'This lady has suffered so much — what happened in Dallas — that one cannot do enough to make it up to her and soften the terrible blows of fate.' Though he did not say it in those exact words he gave the impression that this was what he told 'Mrs Kennedy' when he flew to the United States shortly after the assassination and went to see her. She told the story of the dreadful minutes all over again, then talked about Greece and he said he hoped she would soon come cruising with him again. Again she felt his deep compassion and devotion. After that, whenever Onassis visited the United States, he telephoned Jackie and was usually asked to dinner at her apartment but they never showed themselves together in public. It suited both of them that way; Jackie was anxious to avoid gossip and criticism; Onassis did not want more hostile comments to spoil a beautiful friendship which meant more to him than any association with a woman ever before.

One problem that worried Jackie was the children's schooling. They were continuing lessons at the White House until January but then what? Sissie (Sylvia) Ormsby-Gore came to the rescue offering the small class a temporary home at the British Embassy, a great relief to Jackie. She was facing Christmas without Jack, a melancholy thought, and decided to spend it in Palm Beach where friends lent her a house. Lalla Aisha went with her and brought a present from her brother, not the actual present but a photograph of a hundred-years-old Moorish villa near Marrakesh which King Hassan begged Jackie to accept. He hoped she would spend some time there in the near future. Disregarding the personal implication of the King who was greatly attracted to her, she accepted her most precious Christmas present to date.

Jack's death had done little to bring his widow and his mother closer together but formalities were strictly observed. Jackie went to Mass with *Belle Mère* and visited her ailing father-in-law, but she was happy not to stay under their roof. She seemed in high spirits when taking the children shopping in Worth Avenue. Alas, she was soon recognised and engulfed by a big crowd which put her and the children to flight. Unable to shop in the stores, she ordered Christmas presents by telephone, lavishly, extravagantly, to brighten the children's first Noel without their father.

Back in Washington, it was even worse. She was under permanent siege by the crowds who waited from morning till night outside her door to get a glimpse of her, followed her when she took the dog walking, John to his playgroup or Caroline to school. Mostly silent, respectful, people seemed to expect her to make a big pronouncement. One neighbour thought the mood was one of veneration as if they hoped she would take over from her husband; the press echoed these sentiments by suggesting that she should stand for Vice-President or, at the very least, be sent to France as a special ambassador. A State Department official opined that she could become the most powerful woman in the world. It was not what Jackie wanted to be. What she did want was to live where she had lived with Jack and bring up the children in Washington. Luckily one of the houses, 3017 N Street, almost opposite her temporary home, was on the market. Jackie snapped it up and started decorating it with something of her old enthusiasm. But all the while, the crowds became more intrusive, photographers dogged her every step, privacy was well-nigh impossible. She was, as she put it, becoming a Washington monument.

The Warren Commission – Michigan's Gerald Ford was one of its seven members – sent an investigator to interview her. Yet again she repeated the story of Dallas, as always with mingled feelings of agony and relief. Reminders of happier times in Georgetown did not help and the wish to get away from it all·became irresistible. For a much-needed change of scene, privacy and anonymity, Jackie went to New York for a weekend at the Carlyle, Jack's favourite hotel, with Lee Radziwill keeping her company. She came for another weekend, extended her stay, felt happier and more relaxed in New York than in Washington where everybody was obsessed with politics, particularly Bobby Kennedy who was already contemplating his brother's death in terms of his own political future. Though Jackie adopted him as an ersatz Jack, they had little in common except their grief. David and Sissie Ormsby-Gore (Lord and Lady Harlech to be) were a great comfort but they were due to leave Washington before long; Lord Harlech returned to London in 1965 and a year later Sissie was killed in a motorcar accident in Wales.

Writers, artists, actors were the kind of company she sought. She had lunch with Irwin Shaw, saw Truman Capote, dined with *New Yorker* cartoonist Charles Addams and was entertained by Mrs Leland Hayward (formerly Mrs Randolph Churchill); much more stimulating than the Washington scene. Could she not put the traumatic past behind her more easily away from the capital? Might life not be better in New York? The moment she asked herself these questions, there was little doubt about the answers.

Washington did not easily accept defeat. Trying to hang on to the celebrated widow, society ladies showered her with invitations and devoted much time and cunning to discovering where she was most likely to be found. The first invitation she accepted was to a cocktail party in her honour at the F Street Club which President Johnson had promised to attend. O'Donnell, who accompanied the President, recalls that all the guests were swarming around Jackie who was 'radiant and happy to be making her first social appearance since her husband's funeral'. Nobody was paying much attention to Johnson.

Her year of mourning was not tranquil. At Easter she took the children skiing in Vermont where she joined up with Bobby, Ted and their families. Leaving Caroline and John with their little cousins, she took off for a Caribbean holiday at Bunny Mellon's house in Antigua. Back in Washington, she went to dinner with the McNamaras and the Ormsby-Gores at a French restaurant and did not mind the newspapers reporting it but would have preferred them not to have given chapter and verse to her meal of baked oysters, foie gras and duck with oranges.

What did upset her was the furore caused by her next social excursion, a spur-of-the-moment thing which came about when Lee Radziwill (who was already being accused of 'dragging her sister into New York's showbiz world of senseless entertainment') asked film producer George Englund to join her and Jackie at Jackie's house for a chat. Englund brought along his friend, Marlon Brando, thinking, and thinking rightly, that Jackie would enjoy meeting him. Lee, Englund and Brando were going out to dinner and asked Jackie to come with them. As they were going to the Jockey Club Restaurant, which she had visited privately and unreported during her husband's term, Jackie agreed. To elude the press she and Lee went ahead, Englund and Brando following after a discreet interval. Even though the press got wind of it, the harmless assignation would not have caused such a stir had Brando and Jackie's press secretary not given different versions of the occasion, Brando denying that he had met Jackie and Pam Turnure explaining that they had only met to discuss the Kennedy Library. As a result, the intriguing twosome made headlines. 'Jackie's night out' was the story of the day. It finally decided her to leave Washington and make her home in New York. It also showed a lot of people that mourning did not become Jackie.

Though the *Washington Post* regretted that Georgetown was losing a long-time resident and tourist attraction (sic) and added that she, Jackie, 'came among us like some wildly unexpected fairy queen – and with her goes the heart of everyone who lived in this place when she did', her departure was not well received and she was accused of deserting the world of John F. Kennedy. It was a quixotic reaction. While claiming her as national property, people were at the same time cruelly critical of her. An undercurrent of inexplicable hostility brought curious complaints to the surface. Jackie was blamed for certain features of the late President's funeral arrangements: the link with Lincoln which was not so far fetched since he had after all also been assassinated; and the eternal flame which she had probably copied from the Arc de Triomphe in Paris but which was not an exaggerated tribute to the Kennedy spirit which many hoped would burn brightly for a long time.

At the other end of the scale, the movie magazines, which had exploited her as First Lady, now went to town on the handsome widow. *Inside Movie* gave 'Jackie's First Party' front-page treatment while *Motion Picture* explained 'Why Jackie's Sister is a Bad Influence on Her.' (Lee, incidentally, someone remarked, was what Jackie would have been if she had not married a Kennedy.) *Photoplay* pondered whether it was 'Too Soon for Love?' and *Movie Mirror* responded with 'Jackie in Love Again'. The mags offered unsolicited advice on how she should conduct her life and bring up the children. They asked their readers to decide whether 'Mrs Kennedy should marry again' or 'Devote her life exclusively to her children and her husband's memory'. Such blanket coverage attracted more celebrity hunters to her doorstep. To put them off the scent, she went out wearing a wig and a nurse's uniform and was triumphant when she remained unrecognised. She truly was what Bill Walton called her: 'A strong dame!'

Her move to New York not only removed her from the Washington fishbowl, it was almost a home-coming. The home she chose set the pattern of her lifestyle for the next decade and beyond. It was an elegant fifteen-room apartment in a co-op block (owned jointly by the tenants) at 1040 Fifth Avenue, corner of 85th Street, fourteen of the twenty-three windows overlooking Central Park Reservoir. She paid $200,000 for it. Service and maintenance came to $14,000 a year which has since multiplied many times. Fifth Avenue was teeming with Kennedys. Peter and Pat Lawford lived at 80th Street, Steve and Jean Smith a couple of blocks further away. Central Park South was the New York base of Joe and Rose Kennedy and, for good measure, Lee and Stas kept an apartment at Fifth Avenue and 78th Street.

It was all Kennedy. The name was immortalised all over the country with Kennedy streets, Kennedy bridges, Kennedy centres, Kennedy schools; New York's Idlewild airport became Kennedy Airport and the rocket base at Cape Canaveral was renamed Cape Kennedy. The proudest Kennedy monument would be a ten-million-dollar John F. Kennedy Memorial Library to be built in Boston. Jackie flew to the capital of 'Kennedy country' to inspect a two-acre plot by the Charles River donated by Harvard University on which the library would be built. She met Cardinal Cushing and received tremendous ovations from large crowds wherever she went. Although it was a triumphal excursion she was extremely nervous and, while dining at the elegant Stella Restaurant with Ted and Joan Kennedy, toyed with her gold cigarette case and smoked continuously – for the first time in public.

To raise funds for the library project, she organised a massive assault on the pockets of rich and poor at home and abroad, and was on the telephone for days on end soliciting contributions. She could take credit for much of the success. Without her, the French government might not have given as much as $100,000; Ted Kennedy flew to Paris to thank them; nor would corporation bosses have given as generously, among them names closely associated with Jackie's: Gianni Agnelli of Fiat ($100,000) and André Meyer of Lazar Frères ($250,000). Tactfully she refrained from asking Aristotle Onassis.

Although Bobby Kennedy and Lyndon Johnson were in open conflict over Vietnam, the President made a handsome gesture by giving a dinner for Jackie and the library trustees at the St Regis Hotel, New York, which pulled in the biggest gathering of celebrities in years. In her black sleeveless dress with the obligatory long white gloves, Jackie looked wistful, waif-like but very beautiful. Well ahead of the first anniversary of Jack's death, her social life was increasingly active. On what would have been his forty-seventh birthday, she launched an exhibition of Kennedy memorabilia including his rocking-chair, and took part in a transatlantic television birthday tribute linking up with Harold Macmillan in London, Willy Brandt in Bonn and Sean Lemas in Dublin. Then, with the children and the Radziwills, she flew to Hyannis Port to join the family.

It was not as free and easy as it looked. Intent on their future role in American affairs, the Kennedys expected Jackie to play her part so that public sympathy for her could serve the Kennedy cause and advance Bobby's and Ted's prospects. The Kennedy show must go on! It received a temporary set-back when Ted was involved in a tragic helicopter crash which cost the lives of his two fellow passengers. His spine was so badly damaged, shades of Jack, that he had to wear a corset for some time. At the same time, Jackie discovered that Caroline was walking around with a broken bone in her wrist but, loyal to the Kennedy maxim, had not let on until her hand became swollen.

One subject under discussion at Hyannis Port was the rumour about the assassination. People simply refused to accept that it was the work of a lone wolf and suspected a major conspiracy behind it. They asked whether the C.I.A. was not involved after all; or whether it was a Cuban plot to avenge

Kennedy's stand against the Soviet missiles. Whatever the Warren Commission found, the Kennedys wanted their own man to put the tragedy into perspective and chose an able young historian, William Manchester, who had written a profile of the late President which, Jackie remembered, Jack had liked very much. When Manchester accepted the commission, she promised to talk to him freely and in the event submitted to his questioning for two sessions of five hours each. An agreement vested control of the finished manuscript in the Kennedys – though this is not how it worked out.

In August, Jackie, with Bobby's wife Ethel, and the Kennedy sisters Pat, Eunice and Jean flew to the Democratic Convention in Atlantic City in the *Caroline*. 'Now there are only five or six of us left,' Bobby Kennedy said in his address moistening the eyes of family and delegates. There were tears, too, when Jackie heard Frederic March read extracts from Jack's speeches and his favourite poetry including *I have a rendezvous with death* by Alan Seeger. Having done her duty by the Kennedys and, as if to escape the emotional effect, Jackie flew off to Europe with her entourage (maid, secretary, Secret Service men) and a mountain of luggage for a Mediterranean cruise with oil millionaire Charles Wrightsman; Italy, Yugoslavia, new seas, new skies. The travel bug was difficult to control.

Back at the Carlyle Hotel in New York, Jackie called Billy Baldwin, the interior decorator who had advised her on the furnishing of Glen Ora and the house in Georgetown. They spent hours discussing every detail of the new apartment; nothing grabbed Jackie's interest as completely as decorating and furnishing a new home. In September her furniture and personal effects arrived in a convoy of vans but it took another four weeks to make the place habitable. Caroline was enrolled in the Academy of the Sacred Heart, a French convent school at 91st Street. Not many months later, St David's School welcomed a new boy in the nursery class – John F. Kennedy Jr. Jackie took the children rowing in Central Park and supervised John-John's riding lessons. Matrons cocked their ears to pick up what she said to the boy. What did they hear? 'Keep your heels down,' Jackie instructed her son. On a slightly higher equestrian level, Caroline rode her pony Macaroni at a club show in West Barnstaple, Long Island, and came sixth out of twelve competitors, some of them several years older than her.

By the time Thanksgiving and John's fourth birthday came round, 1040 Fifth Avenue was ready to receive a whole platoon of his little friends who were treated to ice-cream, cakes and games organised by Jackie with the schoolmistressy knack of keeping excitement and exuberance in check. The scene swiftly shifted to Long Island for Caroline's seventh birthday and more ice-cream, cakes and games. At the end of her year of mourning, Jackie chose a United Nations concert for Civil Rights to show herself in public in an alluring shoulder-free black crepe gown and white ermine jacket. What she wore was once more of greater interest than what she thought or said. Adlai Stevenson, U.S. Ambassador to the U.N. escorted her, and was hence invariably referred to as 'one of Jackie's escorts' until the day he died.

Admirers from many parts of the world beat a track to her door. It would have surprised the *cognoscenti* if the King of Morocco had not taken the earliest opportunity to visit her. Another exotic visitor was Emperor Haile Selassie of Abyssinia. 'When the children hear of these countries, they look them up in the atlas and we discuss them,' Jackie remarked on the educational aspect of her social life. Equally educational was the set of Winston Churchill's collected works, bound in fine leather, which his son Randolph gave her as a present: a similar set went to Aristotle Onassis who was playing host to Sir Winston on his yacht *Christina*. Reading as voraciously as ever, Jackie studied Churchill's writings systematically but it is doubtful whether Onassis ever more than flipped through them.

A certain pattern of life was emerging. Prominent friends, exclusive restaurants and night-clubs, New York, Boston, Newport, Hyannis Port, Palm Beach, Vermont and with ever quickening pace foreign trips in all directions, *La veuve s'amuse*. Was this what she wanted to do with her life? It was impossible to say and she only smiled her Mona Lisa smile and said nothing. Jackie without Jack was indeed more like Lee every day and what price the learned sociologist who predicted that JFK's widow would go great things?

A big night at the Met – unthinkable without Jackie – had

the added poignancy that the star of *Tosca* was Maria Callas who, when not performing, was the 'constant companion' of Aristotle Onassis. Intensely curious (as Onassis later remarked) Jackie availed herself of the prerogative of distinguished spectators and went backstage to confer the obligatory compliment on La Callas: 'Magnificent!' The flamboyant extrovert Callas and the retiring Jackie had nothing in common and did not meet again. Three years later Callas told David Frost that she had tried to re-establish contact with Jackie but had been rebuffed: 'It is not wanted,' she said. (By that time, of course, Jackie had separated Callas from Onassis and married him.) With less personal involvement, Jackie, a few weeks later, complimented Maurice Chevalier on his show and took him off for a night at El Morocco. But when Leonard Bernstein asked her to a late-night discotheque party, she begged to be excused because she was off on a holiday early the following morning.

No sooner was she back in New York than she gave one of her own super-supper parties. Guest of honour was her friend John Kenneth Galbraith, economist and former ambassador to India, who had coined the phrase affluent society (not with Jackie in mind). The party's twenty-seven predictable ingredients included a big helping of family (the Smiths, the Lawfords, the Bobby Kennedys), a dash of writer (Truman Capote), a soupçon of artists (Charles Addams), a sprinkling of rich ladies (Bunny Mellon) and a solid old standby (William Walton). Vetted by the Secret Service, they poured into 1040 Fifth Avenue and were topped up with daiquiris. Having put them in the mood, the hostess took them to the 'Sign of the Dove' restaurant where she asked the band to play 'the fastest music you've got', twisted and frugged – not too well, according to her partner – until one fifteen a.m. when she offered her guests a buffet which incongruously included spaghetti and goulash. She departed an hour and a half later.

That same week she flew to Boston to preside over a $150-a-head benefit for the Boston Symphony Orchestra but was so tempestuously hustled by the crowds that she almost disappeared into her Jean Patou coat. She had a smoother evening bidding farewell to Nicole Herve Alphande, her rival and runner-up in America's elegance stakes, whose husband was taking up a post in Paris.

The children's share of their mother's time was getting smaller but Maude Shaw was as dependable as ever and her little charges did not lack attention. Maude remembers Caroline coming into her room at 1040 which was only a slight improvement on her White House cubby-hole: 'Your room is very small, Miss Shaw,' Caroline said. 'It's much smaller than mine and you are much bigger than I am.' Miss Shaw assured her that she was quite content. On another occasion Caroline asked: 'Are you rich, Miss Shaw?' Now that her father was no longer there to earn money and pay the servants, she was afraid that her governess might lose out. It was Jackie herself who had to cope with a ghoulish incident when a gaggle of boys followed her and John-John in the street and shouted: 'Your father is dead! Your father is dead!' The little fellow was not easily disturbed: 'He squeezed my hand as if to reassure me,' Jackie said. His teacher told her that John-John made enemies as easily as friends and only the other day had punched a classmate on the nose.

Caroline was less ebullient and shared her mother's love of books: 'She reads so much,' Jackie said, 'she needs glasses that thick!' Fair-haired and solid with the build of a Kennedy and her mother's sensitivity, the little girl lacked the burning ambition of either; in spite of constant exhortations she was no great horse-woman and in the annual horseshow on Long Island, was easily overtaken by two of Bobby's brood, Kathleen and Mary Courtney. As the man of the family John-John was being indoctrinated with John F. Kennedy tales. Jackie said of her effort: 'I feel John is getting to know his father better.' But she did not want the children to go to Arlington Cemetery on the anniversary of Jack's death and, in the end, decided not to go herself either. She was living too much in the past as Bobby Kennedy always told her, and Maude Shaw said she ought to marry again: 'Oh, Miss Shaw,' Jackie answered, 'I couldn't – ever!'

With a touch of nostalgia she followed the fate of Merrywood. Having been sold by Hugh D. Auchincloss (for around $600,000) the pleasant meadows where she had exercised her horses were being fought over by greedy property developers. Her only remaining horse, the proud Sadar, and Caroline's ponies were installed on an estate in Long Island which she acquired for a more modest sum. Another new establishment was a four-room rented office-apartment in Park Avenue to which she transferred her voluminous personal papers, correspondence, records and her two assistants, Nancy Tuckerman and Pamela Turnure (Pamela became Mrs Timmins, wife of a Canadian millionaire, a year later).

Intermittently, the press indulged in bouts of Jackie-baiting. There were unwarranted sneers when her name was dropped from *The Social List of Washington*, the *Who's Who* in capital society, for the simple reason that she did not live there any more. She was reproached for enrolling Caroline in a Catholic rather than an open school and advised to go and live in Harlem 'as a symbol of her husband's civil rights bill'. Her critics variously accused her of shunning publicity and inviting it; as if she was responsible for her children's little faces peering from every magazine; anyway, they said, she spent too little time with the children and travelled too much. Keeping up a running commentary on her, newspapers and magazines seemed troubled that she did not fit into any category or behave as she was expected to. Constant change was the most unchanging feature of her life.

Two changes were imminent and bound to affect her deeply. The first was Lee Radziwill saying goodbye to the United States to return to Britain where her Polish prince owned a house round the corner from Buckingham Palace and a country place in Buckinghamshire. Lee gave a little farewell party for a hundred friends starring Jackie (stunning in an Yves St Laurent gown) supported by a glittering cast of great players: Leopold Stokowski, Sam Spiegel, Leonard Bernstein, Sammy Davis Jr, Maurice Chevalier and Mike Nichols who quickly emerged as Jackie's leading man. Mike and Jackie danced the night away in close embrace, the beginning of a long and intimate friendship.

The other personal loss Jackie suffered was Maude Shaw who had been with Caroline all her life and, at fifty-eight, felt a need to go home to England and take things easy. Fortuitously, just as Lee and Maude were bound for England, the old country invited Jackie to attend the ceremonial inauguration of a monument to John F. Kennedy at Runnymede where King John had signed the Magna Carta and where the British government had set aside a corner of an English field which would be forever America. Travelling with Jackie in an aircraft made available by President Johnson were Bobby and Ted Kennedy, six American Secret Service men, two officers of the British Special Branch and her usual entourage of servants and secretaries: the 'Queen of America' going to meet the Queen of England, someone remarked. At the ceremony, the Queen of England saw Jackie shed a discreet tear as speaker after speaker sang her husband's praise; but Caroline, sitting between the two elevated ladies, could not suppress a big yawn.

The children were in a happier frame of mind when embarking on an unusual adventure, a final weekend with their English nanny in her small house on Sheppey Island in the Thames Estuary. Watched by Maude and her sister Hetty, they built sandcastles and romped about until sightseers and photographers drove them back into the house. As a farewell present, Jackie gave Miss Shaw a scrapbook with pictures of the children and an inscription which said: 'You brought such happiness to our lives, and especially to President Kennedy, because you made the children what they are.' Jackie's two-week visit to London ended with the usual search for antique bargains, shops closing their doors to other customers while Jackie made her choice.

Her next public appearance in New York was nothing if not spectacular. Escorted by two cardinals, Cushing and Spellman, she met the Pope who was on a visit to the United Nations. She knelt and kissed his ring and the Holy Father helped her up, held her fondly and spoke so kindly about Jack that tears came to her eyes again. Another change of scene: it was getting increasingly difficult to keep up with her. One week she was on an Argentinian *hacienda* – John-John put a stone on a stone monument laid years earlier by his father – the next she was with Ken Galbraith in Gstaad, the Swiss wintersports resort. Then it was Rome where every palazzo opened its doors to her. She allowed Princess Galitzine, the aristocratic seamstress, twenty-four hours to make her a black dress suitable for her return visit to the Pope but it was Valentino, then a little-known couturier, who showed her such delightful designs that she appointed him on the spot her dressmaker-in-chief over and above Oleg Cassini and Hubert de Givenchy. Her spending spree was well under way: in the next two years Valentino designed one hundred dresses for her, and already the popular estimates that her clothes cost her $40,000 a year were wildly below the real amount.

Had she not been spotted holding hands with Mike Nichols at Arthur (Sybil Burton's noisy New York discotheque) it would not have occurred to people that she was back in New York. She did not stay long either but turned up in Spain, and in the headlines, with the Duke of Alba. The aging grandee was suspected of pursuing her but there was nothing between them, except the Duchess and their eight children. It was Jackie who was in hot pursuit – of foxes. In an eye-catching Spanish-style outfit she rode to hounds with the Marquess de Villaverde, Franco's son-in-law, and other nobles, and went to a bullfight where the successful matador presented her with his black hat. While taking off her magnificent Spanish clothes to put on a swimsuit, she was caught by a hidden camera and the photograph of her graceful bare backview was published by the illustrated *Gente*.

Americans, too, continued to be fascinated by her attractions and her love-life (if that was what it could be called). Countering the speculation whom she would marry, her half-sister Janet declared a little pompously that she, and mother, felt Jackie would never remarry. No man would dare marry her because no man could equal her in fame and status and she would not marry a man who would be content to be known as 'Mrs Kennedy's husband' or, worse, 'Mr Jackie Kennedy'. Still, every man with whom she was seen was examined for his qualifications as a prospective husband (although most of them were already married and this earned her the reputation of husband-borrower). The magazines' – and Jackie's – favourite choice was Lord Harlech, who returned to the U.S.A. for a lecture tour, stayed with Bobby Kennedy on his farm in Virginia and, naturally, called on Jackie. Romance, the gossip columnists decided. No question about it, Jackie and David were fond of each other.

The story, if not the romance, was revived when Jackie took the children to Ireland for a long holiday and was met by Lord Harlech at Shannon Airport. Since Jackie had lost her husband and Harlech his wife, the gossips reasoned, they were made for each other. Were they holidaying together? Two hundred Irish policemen, thirty armed detectives and two F.B.I. agents stopped people finding out. They kept sightseers and press away from Jackie's holiday home, the forty-room Woodstock House at Waterford on the south-west coast of Ireland. The Irish government implored people to refrain from keyhole peeping and shore-line prowling but Jackie and the children were seen riding and swimming. Lord Harlech was soon back in England but this did not stop the magazines speculating. Jackie could never marry a foreigner: it was unthinkable for President Kennedy's children to live abroad! Having investigated Lord Harlech, the mags came to the impudent conclusion that he was unsuitable as a husband for Jackie but added, paradoxically, that they were certainly going to marry. Another grotesque report claimed that she and the Spanish Ambassador to the Vatican . . . Whatever it was, Jackie denied it publicly.

She and the Kennedys had borne the torrent of gossip, disclosure and comment about them long enough. Now they showed signs of acute irritation and started to answer back. Writing about the Kennedys was becoming a hazardous occupation. The author of a debunking biography of JFK complained that he was being harassed by the Department of Immigration; another claimed the family had tried to tamper with his book on Ted Kennedy's campaign for the Senate; and Paul Fay, an old friend of the clan, was sternly rebuked for writing about 'Jackie' instead of 'Mrs Jacqueline Kennedy' and punished for his *lèse majesté* by having his contribution to the Kennedy Library rejected.

One publication which had Jackie's blessing and co-operation was her biography by Mary van Rensselaer Thayer, an old friend of her mother's who, like Jackie herself, looked on her past as *la vie en rose*. 'To read Mary van Rensselaer Thayer's official biography of Jacqueline Bouvier Kennedy,' remarked Jackie's cousin John Davis, 'one would conclude that the Bouviers had never known anything but wealth, health, extraordinary achievement, and uninterrupted terrestrial bliss. Not to mention a thoroughbred pedigree worthy of the *Almanach de Gotha*.' The public seems to have needed a sacrosanct figure like the Pope who was above criticism.

No more! It was William Manchester's book, *Death of a President*, commissioned by Jackie in the interest of historical truth which did much of the damage. Muttering started as soon as the book was completed. Though neither Jackie nor Bobby would read the finished manuscript ('Too painful') friends who studied it had reservations. Manchester was asked very forcefully to make substantial changes and pressure became so strong that the sensitive author's health failed. Jackie wrote to him: 'Please know how disturbed I am that you are sick and how much I hope that you will be better soon.' He soon was, but the badgering continued with Bobby and Jackie joining in and calling a small army of lawyers and advisers to assist them. Weeks and months of haggling produced no agreement.

Harper and Row, the distinguished publishers with old Kennedy associations, were anxious to publish; *Look* Magazine had acquired serialisation rights for $650,000, and big international deals for volume and serialisation rights had been set up when Jackie announced that she was taking legal action to stop publication. In a statement issued in her office at Park Avenue she described the book as 'a tasteless and distorted invasion of privacy'. Publication would violate her rights and cause irreparable harm. Commenting in private, she did not sound very sure of herself: 'I have to try,' she declared. 'We might lose this but I have to try . . . I can't lose what I have tried to protect for these years.'

Since there were scores of copies of the Manchester manuscript floating around newspapers' and publishers' offices, what Jackie was trying to protect was already common knowledge. Her most strenuous objection was to descriptions of her last night with the President, of the moments after the fatal shots and the scenes in Parkland Hospital where she was said to have kissed her dead husband's instep, to the story of her last letter to Jack and the children's first hint of the tragedy. She did not deny saying what she was quoted as saying but did not want Manchester to publish what she told him while under an intolerable emotional strain. Bobby Kennedy largely objected to passages denigrating President Johnson which were no longer politically opportune.

Manchester denied that the book implied what Jackie had found offensive. He thought she had behaved superbly but added that she was 'as inscrutable as Mao Tse Tung' and 'as isolated from the world as Marie Antoinette'. She was, he said, fully aware of her place on America's pedestal and had told him: 'Unless I run off with Eddie Fisher, the people will think anyone who is in a fight with me is a rat!' Manchester came to the conclusion that the men around Bobby were all thinking in terms of another Kennedy administration.

Legal action did not stop behind the scenes negotiations. As amendments went backwards and forwards between Kennedy advisers and Manchester lawyers with the press providing a running commentary, the public was getting increasingly irritated by the undignified squabble. Far from siding with her, people assumed, according to a Gallup Poll, that the Kennedys were fighting publication lest it damage their semi-deity image. Jackie's popularity dropped sharply. For the first time since 1963, she lost her lofty position as 'the woman Americans most admire'.

On a personal level, the fracas opened wounds which she had tried to heal, revived and compounded painful memories from which she had tried to escape into social whirl and non-stop jet-setting. The Manchester affair pulled her right back. And the Kennedys did not make things easier by dragging her back into the political arena. Once a Kennedy, always a Kennedy. Her nerves suffered but not her determination. She won some of the skirmishes in the battle with Manchester – *Look* and Harper and Row cut a few thousand words – but lost the war because her prized secrets were common property. The book's impact was strong and substantially reflected the author's points. From the proceeds, he donated about $1.5 million to the Kennedy Foundation which still left him with a handsome reward for a most impressive job. Exhausted by the long struggle, Jackie fled to Antigua to swim and play (behind the shield of her Secret Service guards) and forget.

CHAPTER THIRTEEN

Jackie – she is sexy. A hard woman who knows what she wants.

Henry Kissinger

Towards the end of 1967, Lord Harlech paid the penalty for associating with the world's most publicised woman. A peer of the realm? A brilliant British diplomat? Forsooth! As far as the Americans were concerned, he was 'the man Jackie travels with'. The steam the press had been working up blew off the lid when *Women's Wear Daily* told its readers that an engagement was imminent. Lord Harlech issued a denial which, unhappily, coincided with an announcement that Jackie was going on a private trip to the Far East and would be accompanied by – Lord Harlech.

It looked as if something was afoot after all. The trip to Cambodia and Thailand was presented as a pre-marital honeymoon or, at best, a prelude to marriage. Lord Harlech may have had intentions and Jackie thoughts of a much longer journey in David's company but this was no jaunt by two lovers. It was something quite different, a minutely prepared semi-political mission, discreetly sponsored by the U.S. government and camouflaged as private enterprise. Washington had some notion that Jackie might be able to stem the growing anti-American tide in Cambodia, a by-product of the war in Vietnam, and perhaps work her charm on the ruling playboy Prince Sihanouk who was getting increasingly hostile to the U.S.A. but was known to be susceptible to a pretty face. If Jackie's forays into foreign fields by the side of her late husband were anything to go by, her visit might well be rewarding.

To guide her on the delicate mission, Jackie was accompanied by a well-chosen entourage. Apart from Lord Harlech, her party included the Bartletts, her oldest Washington friends, and another potential beau, New York lawyer Michael Forrestal: journalistic, diplomatic legal expertise of high calibre.

Setting out from New York, they stopped over in Rome where they boarded an Alitalia aircraft whose first-class compartment had been turned into a bedroom for Jackie for the twelve-hour flight. The Pope was given no better treatment, was one comment.

Prince Sihanouk's welcome at Pnon Penh confronted Jackie's advisers with their first political problem. Scrutinising an advance copy of his speech, they spotted a remark which was bound to give offence. What the Prince proposed to say was that, had President Kennedy lived, there would be no war in Vietnam, a slap in the face of the Johnson administration. Lord Harlech advised Jackie to appeal to Sihanouk to cut out the passage. The Prince agreed and to reward him Jackie said in her reply that 'President Kennedy would have loved to visit Cambodia'.

Jackie then turned to a sight she had been anxious to see for a long time, the temples of Angkor Wat, the most intriguing remnants of Asia's great past. For three days she wandered among the historic ruins gathering up mementoes. She skilfully glossed over Sihanouk's anti-American remarks which threatened to spoil her public appearance to dedicate a John F. Kennedy Street. Not even lunch at Sihanouk's villa was free from embarrassment. After presenting a gift to her host and accepting his offering in return, Jackie performed another official task, feeding the royal elephants, and was glad to get away. An American Air Force C-45 took her to the less fraught atmosphere of Thailand where she was received by more congenial hosts, King Bhumibol and the glamorous Queen Sirikit, the 'Jackie of the East'.

At Bangkok, Jackie and her friends were installed in a royal palace. She was assigned a royal prince as an escort and guide, entertained at a royal reception and treated to a gala performance of the Royal Ballet. In her honour, the Temple of the Emerald Buddha was lit up in all its glory: 'The most beautiful thing I have ever seen,' she gushed; no private person had ever enjoyed similar privileges. For Jackie, these experiences and the visit to Angkor made the costly expedition immensely satisfying. For her American sponsors it was vexing that newspaper reports concentrated on her association with Lord Harlech to the exclusion of almost anything else. But while he was publicly presented as a 'Lord Consort to the American Queen', the trip was in effect the grand finale of their romance.

Still, Lord Harlech looked back on it with unqualified delight. With extreme discretion, he asked me not to repeat any of the flattering things he told me about Jackie's high intelligence and diplomatic skill on this as on many other occasions. They have remained friends and, though he has since married another lady, he is as loyal to her as all her old friends.

A few months after Jackie's Far Eastern tour, I flew to New York to show Onassis the manuscript of his life story on which we had been working together for the better part of a year. We met at his apartment at the Pierre Hotel: 'I want Mrs Kennedy to read a true account of my life,' he said out of the blue, 'and not all that rubbish that appears in the newspapers.' Only at this point did it occur to me that his purpose in co-operating with me so enthusiastically had chiefly been to present her with his version of his turbulent personal history in black and white. We drove off in his car to 1040 Fifth Avenue. Clutching my manuscript, he got out: 'You won't breathe a word about this,' he said waving a warning finger in my face. He was confident of my discretion and I denied myself the scoop of revealing the sensational romance. They were already discussing marriage, he eagerly, ambitiously, Jackie as yet hesitantly and beset by doubts.

A couple of days later, he told me he was taking 'Mrs Kennedy' on a cruise in the Caribbean: he did not think the newspapers would make too much of it. She had been cruising with others, Mr Wrightsman, Mr Nomikos, and conveniently the gossips were still preoccupied with Lord Harlech. He was a pastmaster of hiding behind smokescreens but it also occurred to me that his secret was safe because, his being such an unlikely suitor nobody would suspect the truth.

Their problems were daunting. If the news got out too soon, there was a risk of Maria Callas reacting like a woman scorned; the temperamental diva was not the kind of person to be silenced by even the most generous settlement. A more formidable obstacle when contemplating marriage to a prominent Catholic was Onassis's background and his previous marriage and divorce. It was a constellation liable to touch the American psyche on several raw spots. Where even such an impeccable suitor as Lord Harlech had roused the latent xenophobia in the American mind, here was a much more controversial foreigner ('That Greek!') and a divorced man to boot whose first wife was still alive, a wheeler-dealer who had clashed with the American authorities, perpetrating another rape of the Sabines and carrying away the widow of a President of the United States who was now wedded to the American people. They would not stand for it!

And what about the Catholic Church? Jackie was confident a solution could be found but clever and patient groundwork was needed. Had not Lee been able to marry her Polish prince while her first husband was still hale and hearty? Was not the Catholic Church adept in finding formulae which would not have shamed a Machiavelli? But premature disclosure before the obstacles were removed could make things more complicated. The idea would first have to be sold to the Kennedys, not so simple considering Bobby was campaigning for the highest office and a link between his name and that of Onassis was no help. Cardinal Cushing would have to be recruited as an ally. Jackie's approach was defiant: whatever any of them thought or said she had a right to live her own life and make her own decisions. What remained were technical problems.

When Onassis returned from his cruise, I tackled a technical problem of my own. He was tight-lipped and anxious when we met in London and tried to brush the delicate subject aside. 'Are you going to marry Maria Callas?' I asked a little deviously, though explaining truthfully that I needed to know because his life story would be incomplete if it did not register such a major event. 'Definitely not!' he answered firmly but could not resist a tell-tale wink when I suggested that he might perhaps have another bride in mind. We did not get further than that.

Thoughts of marriage were overshadowed in Jackie's mind by a new American tragedy, the cold-blooded murder of the civil rights leader Dr Martin Luther King. Had Jack not held Dr King in such high regard, the assassination would still have shocked her. She rushed to visit Dr King's wife Coretta, no empty formality; their embrace symbolised common suffering

206

and was a rare gesture on the part of Jackie who usually shrank from physical contact. Once more she was anxious to get away from tragedy. 'Borrowing' her old friend Ross Gilpatric, she flew to Yucatán, Mexico, to swim, dive for corals and talk, mainly talk. She felt a need to consult without disclosing her purpose, to review her condition and situation without revealing the sensational turn ahead. Much more was read into her association with Gilpatric but then too much was being read into almost everything she did.

Bobby Kennedy was hard on the presidential trail contesting the primaries. In the wake of Martin Luther King's death, he felt acutely morbid. He was certain that more blood would flow and mentioned it within Jackie's hearing if not as explicitly as in conversation with the French writer, Romain Gary, whom he told: 'I know there will be another assassination attempt sooner or later . . .' Not necessarily, he thought, for political reasons but 'due to contagion and emulation'.

The words were hardly spoken when it happened. The next time I met Onassis, in June 1968, he looked dejected. Before him was a newspaper with a shattering headline: 'Robert Kennedy Assassinated'. The report said that the assassin, a young Jordanian called Sirhan, had killed in revenge for the Arab defeat in the six-day war in the Middle East. It was only much later that Onassis admitted how much the news had shaken him, not only because he mourned Bobby but because of the ominous implications for him and Jackie. Developing a tortured analysis of Jackie's likely reaction, he feared, quite wrongly, it turned out, that the violent death of her brother-in-law, the terrifying carbon copy of Jack's tragic fate, would revive her depression and put her off marriage. Onassis was facing another crisis but Onassis's reaction to crisis was no more predictable than Jackie's reaction to tragedy.

At this stage, Onassis could only guess how Jackie felt as she flew to Los Angeles where Bobby was precariously hanging on to life some twenty hours after being shot. The day it happened he had gained a big lead in the Californian primary and greatly improved his chances of nomination as the Democratic presidential candidate. With Bobby's wife Ethel, and his sisters Jean and Pat, Jackie waited by his bedside at the Good Samaritan

Hospital while neuro-surgeons battled for his survival; saw him die, as she had seen Jack die, flew his body, as with Jack's, in the presidential Boeing 707; attended the service at St Patrick's, New York, and travelled with the coffin for the late-night funeral at Arlington in the shadow of Jack's memorial overlooking the city and the Potomac.

Onassis did not know her well enough to realise that Bobby's death filled her cup to the brim leaving no more room for suffering; that anger was replacing sorrow and turning her against the violent society which she held responsible for her own bereavement. If America ever had a claim on her after Jack's death, that claim was now forfeited. If she had felt any doubt or obligation to consider the impact of her action on the political prospects of the Kennedys, they were resolved by the shots that ended Bobby's life. For her, escape was the only way out. Jackie was shedding the Kennedy shackles. To put it bluntly, her decision to marry Onassis was made at the grave of Robert F. Kennedy.

She was looking after her own. Young John was difficult to manage, more so in school than at home where Mother's authority was rarely challenged. But teachers at St David's who knew her as a dutiful partner in teacher-parent consultations had to tell her that the boy was inattentive and restless and not making enough progress to merit advancement to the next grade. They suggested he ought to stay in second grade for another year 'until he matures a bit'. Certainly not, was Jackie's angry reply, as if such criticism was a reflection on the family honour. It so happened that the son of McGeorge Bundy, an old Kennedy loyalist, was getting on splendidly at another school, Collegiate. When she heard that Leonard Bernstein's boy was also at that school, she promptly enrolled John.

For the children's sake she decided to spend a long summer holiday at Hyannis Port and, at the same time, pay her last dues to the Kennedy connection which she was about to strain to the point of snapping. Having lost Bobby as a confidant, she talked to Ted about her plans and his plans – a third Kennedy aiming for the presidency? – and was not, could not be, surprised that the last bearer of the Kennedy standard did not cherish the prospect of Jackie, who had for long been the family's not-so-secret weapon, becoming Mrs Onassis. She behaved as if all was well, gathered up a gang of nephews and nieces and took them for a picnic to an island off Cape Cod, went to see Rose and Joe who were obviously perturbed about her prospective marriage but knew better than voice their opposition too strongly. To celebrate her birthday, her thirty-ninth, her in-laws, gave a family dinner party but it was a muted affair and everybody was glad to retreat into the enforced silence of the traditional post-prandial film show (*The Thomas Crown Affair*, a story of a millionaire who could never have enough money and became a bank robber).

In a final attempt to reconcile the Kennedys to her wedding plans, she asked her prospective groom to drop in at Hyannis Port, hoping that his charisma would swing opinion in his favour. Rose Kennedy, no pauper herself, was so overwhelmed by the wealth of Onassis that she forgot the Kennedy millions and sighed with relief when her guest did not notice the paint peeling off her garden chairs. More than the other Kennedys, she wrestled with doubts about the difference in Ari's and Jackie's ages, about Onassis being Greek Orthodox and a divorcee. She wondered whether John and Caroline would accept him as a stepfather, whether he would give them guidance – as if Jackie would allow her children to be guided by anyone but herself. But when Jackie informed *Belle Mère* officially, Rose told her to go ahead if that was what she wanted: 'Don't worry, my dear!' she said. Characteristically, Jackie interpreted her acceptance of the inevitable as support.

In the passage of time, Rose found Onassis pleasant and amusing. It was not long before he waved his magic wand and transported Jackie's mother-in-law into his kingdom which offered luxuries such as few contemporary royals could afford. She enjoyed his hospitality on many occasions and Ari – well: 'Ari adores her,' Jackie noted before long. He dropped in at Hyannis Port again a few weeks later bringing a load of toys for the children who were getting to know him, but the gulf between a man of sixty-two and such small children could not easily be bridged.

Having stayed in one place longer than in any other for some time, Jackie smoothly slipped away to join her future husband and a party of his friends on Skorpios and in his gleaming yacht *Christina*, anchored in the harbour. There were the inevitable oil tycoons, several Greeks and Ari's sister Artemis – rarely had the former First Lady found herself in less congenial company. It was a typical Greek atmosphere, noisy bands playing and Jackie anxious to enter into the spirit trying to dance the *surtaki* and *bouzouki* while Ari sang his favourite melancholy ballad, *Adios Compagnia* (Farewell to old Companions).

When Ari's children, Alexander and Christina, joined the party, Jackie's polished and superficial social chit-chat, designed to hide her underlying tensions, found little response in the two youngsters. Alexander at twenty-one and Christina at eighteen were deeply attached to their mother and, since their parents had parted in 1959, had been irreconcilably hostile to the women with whom their father associated, particularly Maria Callas whom they blamed for breaking up their mother's marriage. They did not deny Jackie the respect her background deserved but there was no love lost and, like most young people, they did not fall in readily with the sophisticated hypocrisy which disguises true sentiment in the artificial world of jet-set society. Jackie's refusal to recognise their antagonism avoided an open clash. She was confident that time and closer contact would improve the relations which had got off to such a poor start.

The guests dispersed but another visitor was on the way. Before August was out, Onassis took a transatlantic call on the *Christina*'s temperamental radio-telephone. Ted Kennedy, at the other end of the precarious link, just managed to get across that it might be perhaps useful if he and Ari could get together for a little talk: 'Of course, of course!' Onassis replied without a hint of apprehension. If the Senator would care to come to Skorpios, they could talk undisturbed and – Onassis's favourite expression – 'have a little fun', swimming, cruising . . .

Onassis gave me several versions of their encounter varying in detail (purposely, so as to prevent him being identified as my source) but not in essence. As was his habit, he discussed the serious subject in a jocular manner. He had no doubt that his unofficial engagement was what Ted wanted to discuss with him: 'As I did not expect a dowry,' he said with a chuckle, 'there was nothing to worry about.' He recalled his negotiations about a dowry with Stavros Livanos, his first wife's father, from whom he received a down-payment on a tanker, and a house in New York in his wife's name. 'I knew Mrs Kennedy did not have a lot of money,' he said – not by his standards and not measured by her expenditure.

Quite correctly, he suspected that Ted might try to talk him out of the marriage in the hope that he would yield more easily than Jackie. Whatever Ted's purpose, Onassis did not want Jackie directly involved: 'They were not on Skorpios at the same time,' he told me. Anticipating the obvious implication, he added forcefully: 'Mrs Kennedy and I never discuss money.'

It appears that the Senator, fulsomely greeted by his host in the idyllic atmosphere of a glorious Ionian summer, raised the matter of the political aspects of the marriage, not for himself and the Democrats, God forbid, but for Onassis: 'It will not be popular,' he said. Was he harping back on the old story of Onassis being arrested and fingerprinted in Washington in 1954? Ari still thought of it as a bit of a joke although it was, of course, as a result of his clash with the American maritime laws that the courts instructed him to put his American shipping corporations under a trust in the name of his American-born children. Ted hinted that it might not be easy either to be stepfather to the late President's children – they belonged to America – but this was not the kind of consideration Onassis really appreciated or wanted to. If Ted had harboured any real hope of preventing the inopportune marriage at this late stage, he quickly abandoned it.

'We love Jackie,' the Senator said – 'So do I!' Onassis interjected – 'and want her to have a happy and secure future.' We are getting to the crunch, Onassis thought. Ted continued: 'She will be losing her income from the Kennedy Trust when she remarries.'

'How much?'

Kennedy threw out a figure: '$150,000 a year.'

'She will get more from my trust,' Onassis countered.

Recounting the conversation, Onassis explained apologetically: 'It is quite common for wealthy Americans to make marriage contracts.' But this was not what he had in mind. One of his lawyers later amplified: 'Some form of contract was as much in Ari's interest as in hers. At this stage, Onassis would gladly have assigned half his fortune to Jackie.' In the event, more cautious counsel prevailed. The children had to be considered – his and hers – Onassis was hoping to hand over his empire to Alexander and Christina. He had to provide for his three sisters and the rest of the family – 'I am the head of a tribe of fifty,' Onassis was fond of saying. But with the huge funds under his control, $500 million at a conservative estimate, a solution was not difficult and the Senator from Massachusetts did not have to fight very hard.

Without much ado, Onassis agreed to allocate to Jackie and her children a share of the trust from which only American-born citizens were qualified to benefit. Since it was impossible to guarantee the value of the trust – $20 million when it was instituted in the late fifties, ten times as much at the height of the tanker boom, now on the decline again – he suggested that she should have a fixed income from her share, that is $480,000 a year whether he was alive or dead. His lawyers, if not Jackie, well versed in the realities of the tanker business where the creditor often has the upper hand and even cast-iron obligations are subject to renegotiation, were already thinking in terms of a possible tanker crisis when Jackie's income might have to be readjusted.

At this stage, though, Onassis did not want his wife to come to him for spending money and arranged to deposit $3 million in her account plus one million each for her children and held himself responsible for her expenses while the marriage lasted. It was obvious to Ted Kennedy that such items as clothes, jewellery, travel, a new house here, a Picasso or a Braque there or the *objets d'art* which Jackie avidly collected would not bother a man whose tax-free income was in the neighbourhood of $20 million a year and who would not skimp his wife even if she was often described as the most extravagant woman alive.

The Onassis Trust Agreement was due to run until 11 December 1971, the twenty-first birthday of his daughter when she and her brother would come into their share of the trust out-right. At this stage, again, Onassis did not anticipate that it would be changed as it was in fact, first when Christina married against her father's wishes; then when Alexander died and when Christina was reinstated after her divorce. When the trust was wound up in 1972, Jackie's entitlement was incorporated in a new agreement designed to remain in force irrespective of his will.

Over the radio-telephone, Onassis gave instructions to his New York lawyers to prepare the necessary documents. Within the limits of his native sophistry, he could say truthfully that he had not discussed money with Jackie before their marriage, and she also spoke the truth when she said years later that there was no marriage contract. With various amendments the Skorpios agreement has remained in force, although by the time of Onassis's death the value of his tanker fleet had shrunk considerably as a result of the oil crisis. But there were intricate renegotiations of shares all round which would obviously affect Jackie's position (though even a year after Onassis's death they were far from complete).

But that was in the future. In the summer of 1968 when Jackie joined her late husband's brother and her future husband on Skorpios the subject of money was exhausted. But the suspicion that she had married for money, and only money, has bothered her ever since. Truman Capote was quoted (in an interview in a magazine called *Playgirl* which trades in male nudes) as saying – in a tone which suggested that his information came from the lady's own mouth – that Jackie 'married this man Onassis for reasons of her own that were not greedy', and that she never got any more out of the marriage than a free ticket on Olympic Airways. 'I mean, she was alone,' Capote said. 'She had two children to think of, take care of. Why shouldn't a woman who is alone, a widow . . .' He did not say more but, if he was correctly quoted, he sounds like a humbug. If Jackie had reasons that were not greedy, what relevance had his remark that she had two children to take care of? Jackie's silence in the face of all conjecture was a better defence of her motives than that put up by her literary friend.

Although I came to know Onassis rather well – he could be

remarkably, naively frank about his hates and loves – and met Jackie, albeit briefly, I cannot offer a simple explanation for the chemistry which brought them together. For Onassis to fall in love with an exquisitely handsome woman, with her ambience of excellence, with admirers like de Gaulle, Kruschev and Nehru, with friends from the top ranks of literature, the arts, society, with her 'historic' background and personal qualities, who but a few dedicated anti-establishment intellectuals would not want to marry her? That she was not very profound and did not indulge in philosophical thoughts, that she could be irreverent as well as imperious, were assets rather than defects in Onassis's eyes.

For him who pursued excellence in every shape, cultivated Greta Garbo and Winston Churchill, delighted in the company of Taylor and Burton and was reverential to Paul Getty, Jackie was the supreme prize, and never mind the suggestion that he expected her to open doors for him his vast fortune could not unlock, there were few worlds left to conquer. And it was the other way round. Onassis offered her release from the prison in which American public opinion had tried to confine her; a chance to find safety in a golden cage of her own choosing and the protective devotion of a man who was able to provide it and was yet prepared to let her fly wherever and whenever she wanted. Onassis who, if the days and weeks were added up, had never spent more than three months in a year with his first wife, was not likely to insist on much more togetherness with his second. Like other men of great wealth and power he was attractive to women who were impressed by the massive sum total of his personality rather than his physical attributes.

Love comes in many variations and combinations. As far as Jackie was capable of this many-splendoured thing, with her resource of emotion depleted after so many harrowing experiences, she loved Ari although no two persons could have had less in common. It was like Mohammed Ali marrying Margot Fonteyn because both relied on nimble footwork, Billy Graham and Germaine Greer, both hot gospellers, Mick Jagger and Mary McCarthy or Garbo and Lenny Bruce who shared a common denominator not obvious at first glance.

214

Onassis, without much formal education, ignorant of literature and the arts (notwithstanding cheque-book forays which brought him his El Greco with whom he identified as much as with Ulysses), raucous raconteur with a touch of vulgarity; and Jackie, élitist, dilettante painter and writer who had read, if not digested, every vogue and coffee-table book over twenty years, collector of art and interesting people, mistress of refined conversation, what did they have in common? Jackie associated Onassis with the Greek argonauts rather than with modern tankers and boring shipping executives, with the Greek antique of Homer and Sophocles, a mental equation which raised him to her own standard. He saw in her the incarnation of an ancient goddess. More immediately, she was an eager recruit to the jet-set of which Onassis was the undisputed leader, craving the freedom of movement and range of opportunity he offered which were aphrodisiac and unlimited. That freedom as much as the hope that his wealth would ensure her privacy was the lure. To be attracted to it was a form of love although to many it was still spelt M-O-N-E-Y.

Onassis was fully aware that he was acquiring a precious and costly wife but never thought or had to think about the price. Jackie was demanding but not mercenary. She was marrying on her level. There was no one else like Jackie; there was no one else like Onassis. He would never be 'Mr Jackie Kennedy', she would never be smothered by the Onassis label. They were on their own up there as they prepared to join forces in the marriage of the decade.

The dissimilar equals went along the final lap to the altar by separate avenues. Jackie made for Boston to consult, or rather tell, Cardinal Cushing as if confession of her intent to sin was deserving of absolution in advance. The Cardinal had to make the best of a bad job for one of his eminent parishioners, the friend of the head of his church who was marrying a man of a different faith, whose first wife was still alive. A pragmatist, he thought that even if the marriage offended against canonical law, it was better to open the door to Jackie's nuptial chamber smoothly than to have her kick it in rudely. Since there was not the slightest chance of dissuading her, the Cardinal accepted the situation with good grace and offered comfort and support.

Ari was euphoric, but not a man to get his priorities mixed up. Simultaneous with the transaction of his marriage he was engaged in a big deal with the Greek colonels concerning an investment of $500 million in industrial projects in Greece. Commuting between Skorpios and Athens in his Piaggio aircraft, he spent hours in consultation with Premier Papadopoulos (to whom he let one of his villas at a peppercorn rent). Having reached a critical stage, the negotiations were so intensive that they left Onassis little time for wedding preparations save for a visit to his doctor who gave him a clean bill of health, and to take delivery of a ruby and diamond ring and matching earrings, cost one and a quarter million dollars, his wedding gift to the bride.

Artemis Garoufalides and a large staff were working day and night to make the wedding an occasion. Invitations and air tickets went out to friends and relatives; plane-loads of tulips were flown in from Holland. The Skorpios work force of forty clothed the island in festive garb and put the finishing touches to the restoration of the tiny Chapel of Panayitsa (Little Virgin) overlooking the sea. The yacht *Christina* was dressed overall, the pier was swept clean and garlanded, a fleet of mini-mokes waited to take the guests to the chalets on top of the island. Archimandrite Polykarpos Athanassion of Athens was standing by to perform the ceremony and, as important, hairdresser Angelo of Athens to attend to the bride's coiffure. There would be a wedding reception aboard *Christina* – a new hundred-forty room villa was still a-building and a smaller one ready, if, as yet, bare of decorations – and then, hopefully, a honeymoon cruise.

Two days before the appointed hour, Onassis sounded apprehensive when I asked him about the impending wedding: 'Not a word!' he said, not a word before the official announcement which would have to come from Boston. He was aware that the Kennedys were still groping for a wording that would convey their misgivings without being offensive to Jackie. When it came it was cryptic and coldly formal and Edward Kennedy's personal wishes sounded even chillier. Jackie was about to leave her New York apartment for the flight to Greece when Joe Kennedy was wheeled in to give her a silent blessing.

Kennedy sisters Jean Smith and Pat Lawford were in Jackie's entourage when she flew out on an unscheduled flight of the Onassis airline. Caroline and John went along as if it was just another outing with the usual fuss that attended most of their mother's activities. Caroline seemed uneasy as if aware of a new rival for her mother's affection, an unfounded fear, but John looked unconcerned and when asked what he thought of Onassis replied laconically: 'Nice guy!'

Only fighting between hordes of reporters trying to invade Skorpios and the guards pushing their hired boats back into the sea mirrored the excitement of the world outside; some boats were overturned before Jackie gave in to Ari's plea to admit half a dozen pressmen. By contrast, the wedding ceremony in the chapel was a quietly dignified anti-climax. Caroline and John, on either side of the couple, held ceremonial candles and kept their eyes on their mother who was wearing a long-sleeved ivory lace dress with a matching ribbon in her hair. She seemed locked in deep thought as the Archimandrite recited the wedding lines in Greek, and smilingly translated the key passages into English for her benefit: 'The servant of God, Aristotle,' he intoned, echoed by the cantors, 'is betrothed to the servant of God, Jacqueline, in the name of the Father, the Son and the Holy Ghost.' Acting as sponsor, Ari's sister Artemis placed two thin crowns of fine leather and lemon blossoms on the couple's heads and exchanged them three times. There followed the Dance of Isaiah, the priest leading the couple three times around the altar, chanting all the while. Husband and wife now, Ari and Jackie embraced and stepped from the chapel into the pouring rain which fed the parched earth of the island – a good omen.

Some of the wedding guests thought the bridegroom had fortified himself for the occasion and did not need the glass of champagne that was pressed into his hand; he looked happy but tired and emotional. Then Mr and Mrs Onassis led the way down to the *Christina*, followed by his children and her children, his sisters, his sisters-in-law, mother and stepfather, Lee and Stas Radziwill and the rest of the small congregation.

After a brief respite in the master's stateroom, Jackie made a grand appearance in the panelled lounge provoking the 'ohs' and 'ahs' which were the only adequate comment on the new jewellery she was wearing for the first time: 'Mummy, you look so pretty!' exclaimed Caroline and that was how everybody else felt. The band played throughout the wedding breakfast which went on for four hours and Ari sang until the exhausted couple retired and the privileged guests repaired to their staterooms and the others to chalets on the island.

Peace reigned in the remote Ionian sea until the following morning by which time the world's newspapers with their reports and comments were on sale. The most articulate bitches of the gossip columns had racked their brains for the most biting insults or approached those who could supply them. One of them obtained an offensive sour-grapes remark from Maria Callas: 'She did well, Jackie, to give a grandfather to her children. Ari is as beautiful as Croesus.' Gore Vidal was in his element saying: 'I can only give you two words – highly suitable!' 'I am sure,' was another notable comment, 'she married him to secure the finances of John-John's presidential campaign in 1983.' Less acidly, Bob Hope quipped (in a reference to Spiro Agnew, the Republican candidate for Vice-President): 'Nixon has a Greek running mate – now everybody wants one.' And *Le Monde*, referring to Onassis's friendship with the Greek colonels, editorialised that the bridegroom's career contrasted rather strongly with the liberal spirit that animated President Kennedy. 'America has lost a saint,' a German newspaper said, adding more compassionately: 'They wanted her to be a widow for ever,' and an American commentator was certain that Jackie had married Onassis to escape from the Kennedy clan which was not a bad guess. The view of Coco Chanel, the aged couturière who did not count Jackie among her clients, was harsh: 'Everyone knew she was not cut out for dignity. You mustn't ask a woman with a touch of vulgarity to spend the rest of her life over a corpse.' The most prevalent sentiment was voiced in the banner headline of the Stockholm *Expressen* which screamed: 'Jackie, How Could You?'

American Catholics pronounced the new Mrs Onassis 'a public sinner' and bombarded Cardinal Cushing with protests.

Some Kennedy voices were identified in this angry chorus which demanded that she be publicly rebuked. Gravely, the old cleric went on television to defend Jackie and, instead of rebuking her, denounced those who were 'knocking her head off': 'My advice to people,' he said, 'is to stop criticising the poor woman. She has had an enormous amount of sadness in her life and deserves what happiness she can find.' He recalled that after consecrating her marriage to John F. Kennedy he had promised him to be good to Jacqueline if anything should happen to him – and this was what he was doing.

The pack snapping at Jackie's heels was not appeased. The Cardinal was accused of being the architect of an unholy alliance, had he been bribed by Onassis? Attacks became so virulent that he offered to resign but the Pope who had been fully apprised of the situation pretended not to hear. When the commotion did not subside, the Holy Father made the Vatican's position clear: Mrs Kennedy, as she was referred to, must be considered to be in a state of mortal sin, his spokesman said, and was barred from receiving the sacraments. She was not a child, the denunciation continued, and must have known perfectly well what were the laws of her church; she must have known that in the eyes of the church she could not legally marry Mr Onassis.

Charitable views were few. Reporters seeking the reaction of men they took to be Jackie's former boy-friends approached Ross Gilpatric (ignoring the existence of his wife Madelin): 'I hope she has a happiness that certainly is entitled to her,' he told them. 'I wish her that.' And a solitary partisan of Onassis appeared in the person of Elizabeth Taylor who described him as charming, appealing, kind, considerate.

Kind and considerate but not conventionally so to Jackie at this time. The echo of the wedding bells had not died down when a plane was seen taking off from Skorpios but it was not, as was thought, carrying the couple to warmer climes; it was the bridegroom alone flying to Athens to attend to his business. With $500 million at stake and a lifetime with Jackie ahead what did one or two days count? Ari was in a hurry to conclude his mammoth transaction. While riding with Premier Papadopoulos in his car he cleared the last remaining points at

219

issue, noted the main clauses on the back of an old envelope and got Papadopoulos to initial them. A huge deal and a sensational marriage in one week! Ari had pulled it off – or had he? The deal, unlike the marriage, was never consummated. But Ari did not know that as yet and was in a triumphant mood.

Rain and storm upset arrangements for the wedding guests to be ferried by motor boats to the west coast of Greece where an aircraft of the Onassis airline stood by to take them to Athens. When the weather cleared, Jackie took a tearful farewell from Caroline and John and put them in charge of her mother. They flew to Athens where they spent the night at the Hotel Grande Bretagne ('Dumping the children in an hotel!' the critics grumbled). Next morning they caught a plane home to New York and school. The other guests departed for their various destinations.

The sun came out over Skorpios. Jackie and Ari relaxed, went swimming and fishing. Most afternoons while he was doing his sums she attended to her correspondence: things had been so hectic and secrecy so important, the first some of her friends knew about the wedding was when they read about it in the newspapers. She had a lot of explaining to do. One of the people who received a handwritten letter datelined 'Aboard *Christina*' was Ross Gilpatric: 'I would have told you before I left,' she wrote, 'but then everything happened so much more quickly than I'd planned. I saw somewhere what you had said and I was very touched – dear Ross – I hope you know all you were and are and will ever be to me – with my love, J.' (The letter with four earlier ones addressed to Gilpatric was later stolen and turned up at a public auction. Gilpatric, incidentally, was soon divorced and married again.)

Onassis, too, was closing old chapters. He was being informed about the state of an embarrassing lawsuit over a half share in a vessel worth some £1.2 million which he had made over to Maria Callas as a camouflage parting gift – her investment in the venture was £60,000, a tenth of her share's value. In a complicated legal move before the London courts, the late Greek shipowner Panaghis Vergottis, part-owner of the vessel, had tried to block the transaction out of jealousy or spite; his motive was manifestly not financial. The news from

London was that a verdict in favour of Callas was imminent. Account settled.

When *Christina* finally raised anchor, the world's most energetic travellers did not venture far afield and never left Greek waters. But Jackie flew to Athens with Ari several times and on one occasion told him: 'I have asked Billy Baldwin to come and see me and he is arriving in Athens today.' Ari guessed why Jackie had summoned her favourite interior decorator. He sent a car to collect Billy at the airport and bring him to his villa where Baldwin was treated to his first Greek lunch: 'I will kill you if you pretend to like it,' Jackie told him. They were joined by Ari's two sisters: Artemis, according to Baldwin, spoke passable English but Merope just smiled and said 'No English'. The next day Jackie took Baldwin with her to Skorpios and showed him the empty building on the island: 'It'll have to be furnished by Christmas when the children come back,' she said. They settled down to discuss the details and Baldwin sketched out designs for furniture and decorations: 'Ari made it clear that he did not want to be involved in the details,' Baldwin noted. For Ari, it was his first experience of Jackie's decorating mania and he was still indulgent.

By mid-November Ari and Jackie were back in Athens where Jackie met the press in the garden and with wifely humility told them that 'future plans depend on Ari'. The plans turned out to be a trip to London and Turville Grange, the Buckinghamshire home of the Radziwills. While they were there the house was burgled and the thief got away with $5,000 worth of Lee's jewellery; a reminder that by her marriage Jackie had not only lost her $30,000 presidential widow's pension but also her Secret Service guards. Lee asked a few 'interesting people' to come and amuse her sister, among them Rudolf Nureyev, a star in her collection of prominents. Ari saw business associates and lawyers. As if reluctant to end the honeymoon, or return to the hostile United States, they lingered in England longer than originally planned, then took separate planes to New York where they were reunited for their new life.

CHAPTER FOURTEEN

'Is it true what they say about – Jackie?'

It is difficult not to write a satire or a gossip column; difficult to separate the facts from the fictionalised accounts which accompanied the early stages of Jackie's married life. Some of the most lurid fables were dreamed up by Pulitzer Prize-winner Fred Sparks who worked out how much Ari and Jackie had spent in their first year of marriage and came up with fifteen to twenty million dollars, or around 400,000 dollars a week. Not that this would have strained Onassis's resources but even with the running costs of *Christina* at around $15,000 a week, a new $1,500 couture dress every week, travel (free for the owner of an airline), half a dozen homes and Skorpios Island to run, the amount was wildly exaggerated. (His calculations, for instance, included, quite unreasonably, the forty part-time labourers from neighbouring Lefkas who tended Skorpios twice a week at insignificant wages, in the list of highly-paid personal staff.)

The rumours were accepted at face value even when they were flatly contradictory and self-defeating because, incredibly, people believed everything that was printed about Jackie. The same people who accepted the Sparks account of her extravagance as gospel truth, devoured Mary Borelli Gallagher's reminiscences (*My Life with Jacqueline Kennedy*) which portrayed her as an almost pathologically penny-pinching miser. The book made her sad rather than angry, Jackie said.

It started the day she and Ari took up residence in New York. When Ari moved into 1040 Fifth Avenue, the professional gossips unearthed a dramatic upstairs-downstairs situation, a clash between his and her servants. 'Ridiculous!' said the ever-faithful Nancy Tuckerman who continued as Jackie's factotum. What was wrong with the rumour was that Ari was not in the habit of travelling with servants and had not brought any with him to the States. Reports about a clash of temperaments between Jackie and her new stepdaughter, Christina, were less fantastic than premature.

How was the marriage affecting his lifestyle, I asked Ari. 'Not at all!' he answered emphatically. As if to demonstrate the fact, he was airborne almost as soon as he had deposited his bride in New York and turned up in Paris where he was discovered (by Sam White, the London *Evening Standard*'s able correspondent) dining with Callas. 'Triangle', 'Divorce', 'Calamity', was the public reaction. As this was only the first of several dinners with Callas the theme cropped up at regular intervals. Their first encounter was to clear up financial business arising from the London court decision confirming La Callas's right to half the vessel Onassis had steered into her bank account. What worried Ari about these reports, long before they disconcerted Jackie, was the memory of the breakup of his first marriage which was precipitated by the revelation of his clandestine meetings with Callas. To dispel the impression that he still hankered after his old flame, he went on the town with gamine Elsa Martinelli and, unrecorded by the press, her husband. Two thousand miles away in New York, Jackie was lunching with André Meyer, the Lazar Frères banker, which was interpreted as her having an affair with Meyer which threatened her marriage, or that she had financial problems, or both. On one of their outings, Jackie and Meyer were pursued by photographer Ron Galella all the way from 1040 Fifth Avenue to the Twenty-One Club, an incident which Jackie later included in the list of her complaints against Galella who was doing a big trade in Jackie photographs. According to other reports she was either expecting a baby from Onassis or leaving him or, again, both.

Confounding the prophets of marital doom, Jackie and her children flew to Greece to join Ari for Christmas and New Year celebrations on Skorpios. Having restored Caroline and John to their respective schools in New York early in the New Year, Jackie returned to Athens where Ari was still wheeling and dealing. Doing her own thing, she went in search of books on Greek art in the company of Alexis Minotis who was a more congenial companion than Ari's business friends. She made a quick trip to Lausanne where Lee was in a clinic to put on some weight. 'Jackie is buying a Swiss chateu,' the press reported. She had no intention of buying anything in Switzerland and was back in New York in no time joining up with Caroline who, in her mother's jet-set fashion, had been on a quick holiday in the Caribbean.

Come April and cruising time, Ari and Jackie made for Lyford Cay and a Terence Rattigan situation. They were entertained by the William Paleys – he a communications czar, she a star of the best-dressed women's list – whose house guests included Rose Kennedy. Also in Lyford Cay were Ari's ex-wife Tina and her husband, the Marquess of Blandford, but her only link with the Onassis camp was daughter Christina who was staying with Maria Goulandris, the uncrowned queen of the Greek shipping clan, to whose son Peter Goulandris Christina was unofficially engaged. The social life of Lyford Cay was conducted across many separate tables.

A second cruise later that year took the *Christina* to other seas. Jackie enjoyed every minute of it and was content to be alone with Ari, except for the crew of fifty including two chefs, one French, one Greek, maids, valets, stewards, coiffeur. Coming ashore at Capri, they looked perfectly happy in each other's company. Jackie wore slacks and a clinging jersey which, while not see-through, showed off her figure. She was barefoot which added spice to their shopping expedition for Italian shoes (to add to the three hundred pairs in her closet). Ari also bought her a few trinkets at a local jeweller. He was still anxious to give her things but the story of him sending her a bouquet every day with a piece of jewellery hidden among the flowers was a charming invention and totally out of character. They went to Villefranche, Sardinia, Marbella, the old route of the cruising élite.

In New York in June, Jackie persuaded Ari to take her to the Royal Ballet season at the Met, a considerable feat. Having yawned through many an opera to please Callas (he told me how ridiculous he found opera, much like the Greek priests in his youth chanting their *kyrie eleison*), he kept up his spirits with the thought of the dinner party to follow. On the first anniversary of Robert Kennedy's death, Jackie flew to Washington to attend the memorial mass at Arlington National Cemetery. Business kept her husband in Europe while she was busy meeting relatives and friends who queued up to entertain her.

Presently a new cloud appeared on her horizon. It can be identified in one word – Chappaquidick, the little island off Cape Cod, and Senator Edward Kennedy's mysterious night out with old faithfuls, one of whom, the pretty secretary Mary Kopechne, lost her life when he drove her home and his car plunged over a parapet into the water. There were howls for Ted's indictment, negligence, manslaughter, and all manner of constructions were put on the fatal accident in the dark of the night which was reported to the police only the following morning. The Senator, third of the accident-prone Kennedy brothers to nurse presidential ambitions, was not indicted but has been in deep water over Chappaquidick ever since. Jackie dashed off one of her famous letters overflowing with commiseration.

Ted's ordeal coincided with Jackie's fortieth birthday which she planned to spend with Ari in Greece. Returning to Europe she was greeted with a different kind of speculation. 'Onassis, the Next Greek President' the headlines predicted. Jackie, it appeared, was destined to become a First Lady once more, if not in Washington then in Athens. Not true? Ah well, perhaps it was true, then, as the next rumour suggested, that she was forcing Ari to sell *Christina* because she regarded her as an unlucky ship and did not want to be reminded of Callas queening it in the yacht. Not true either, of course, but proof, if needed, that, if she had hoped to find privacy, marrying into the Onassis notoriety was the least likely means of getting it.

The Kennedy era was coming to an end. Old Joe Kennedy died on 18 November 1969, and as Jackie stood by his graveside the Kennedy mystique gripped her once more with all its contradictions. Joe was a man to inspire awe but few other emotions. Jackie had felt his presence in the background long after he had lost the power of speech and movement. For better or worse, with him went part of her life. Onassis was blotting out the Kennedy past.

For a while the drums of publicity which beat to the rhythm of Jackie's progress were muted until they exploded with a fearful noise when she and Ari were photographed leaving the cinema after watching *I am Curious, Yellow*, a pastime which told something about their relationship. They reached a new crescendo when Jackie turned on her tormentor, photographer Ron Galella, who had been dogging her and her children's footsteps since 1970. She had had enough, she said; went to court to seek an injunction against him molesting her, and gave a lurid account of the persecution to which he had subjected her. Jackie's right to privacy became a public issue. She claimed the photographer had lurked outside her house, had used disguises to get near her, made friends with one of her maids, unbalanced young John while he was riding his bicycle in Central Park. Galella counter-claimed that she was preventing him from earning a legitimate living and asked for $1.3 million damages. The case dragged on until the evidence submitted by both sides filled 4,700 pages.

The issue was whether the right to privacy overrode the First Amendment (rights of the press) of the constitution. In the event Galella's suit was dismissed. 'We see no constitutional violence done,' said the judge, 'by permitting the defendant to prevent intrusion on her life which serves no useful purpose.' Galella was ordered to stay at least fifty yards away from Jackie, seventy-five from the children and a hundred yards from her home. The wider issue of privacy versus press was left undecided. Jackie's legal costs came to nearly $250,000 which Ari was slow to pay. She was unhappy when she discovered that he had not settled her attorney's account, and exasperated when stories about her husband's tardy approach to her obligation became publicly known. There were some heated arguments foreshadowing later complications with her bills. For publication Onassis said that the delay was due to 'paper work'. Ron Galella promptly settled down to write a book about his experiences with Jackie: 'Jackie, Jackie. Did it have to end like this?' he asked – and went on a profitable lecture tour illustrating his theme with four hundred slides.

Such incidents dominated the conversation across the Onassis dinner table which otherwise would soon have dried up. There were problems as the first anniversary of their wedding drew near but it was manifestly absurd to regard every little local difficulty as a step towards divorce. Ari was so concerned about the recurrent insinuations and convinced that Jackie was being treated unfairly that he promised to help me, 'strictly unofficially', with an account of her life as he saw it (beyond our original plan to extend his biography): 'She is like a diamond,' he said lyrically as we talked in the Bar of the Hotel Grande Bretagne in Athens, 'cool and sharp at the edges, fiery and hot beneath the surface.' But the sparkle was often dimmed by the mist of their respective burdens which, rather than becoming more bearable when shared, became weightier when added together.

Although Onassis did not complain when the memory of John F. Kennedy obtruded at every step – was not Jackie's past as First Lady one of her attractions? – it was not easy for a proud Greek husband to live in the shadow of another man. It created an inner conflict which he had not foreseen but which flared up whenever Jackie observed one of her numerous anniversaries – the anniversary of Jack's birth, the anniversary of their wedding, the anniversary of his death, the anniversaries of highlights in his career which Jackie drew to the children's attention. At home or abroad, it was either her time with Jack at Hammersmith Farm of which the Kennedy shrine was a constant reminder, or their triumphant trip to Paris. At the same time, the domestic and scholastic misadventures of Caroline and John were magnified out of all proportion. What might have passed as a minor irritation in another family became a public issue when it concerned the infants of the late President of the United States.

Ari's children, if anything, complicated matters. There was Christina commuting between London (her mother's home), Lausanne (her maternal grandmother's residence), Paris (and the good life), Athens and New York where she did not fit easily into Jackie's scheme of things. A restless girl with a disturbed family background and at a difficult age, yet, like most Greek girls, mature for her seventeen years, she was no ideal companion or example, Jackie felt, for the younger and less sophisticated Caroline. The mantle of stepmother did not sit as easily on Jackie's shoulders as her couture clothes and, though she tried, relations with her husband's daughter were forced and hedged in with mental reservations. It was worse with Alexander whose hostility was a constant threat because it gnawed at Ari's conscience. The young man was wrestling with his own emotional problem, his fierce love for Fiona Thyssen, the Scottish-born model and ex-wife of one of Europe's wealthiest industrialists, fourteen years older than he and mother of two children. Jackie could not keep aloof from the quarrels between Alexander and his father who opposed his plan to marry Fiona across such a wide age difference. That Alexander, reluctantly, bitterly, deferred to his father's wish did not improve his view of the stepmother 'this preposterous marriage', as he called it, had imposed on him.

There were other aspects of Ari's past which Jackie found as intrusive as he regarded her Kennedy connection; the embarrassing family constellation (which had confronted her in Lyford Cay), not to speak to Ari's sisters who regarded Jackie as a rival and interloper who monopolised his affection and was likely to scoop up the bulk of his fortune at their expense. Then there were the Greeks, friends, associates, managers, who sailed in Ari's wake: Jackie could no more get acclimatised to them than he fitted into the world of opera, literature, architecture and art in which she liked to move.

On a more humdrum level there were minor irritations. Ari was due to fly to the States the day after another of our meetings. As we walked through the London night – he loved walking at night – I asked him where I could contact him in New York: 'It's difficult to say,' he replied, looking troubled and embarrassed. 'Call the office, they'll know where I am.'

It took some time to find out why he was so touchy about his New York address. More often than not when he announced his impending arrival, Jackie would say that there was no room for him at 1040 Fifth Avenue: 'The decorators are in,' she would say ('She likes decorating the apartment,' Ari remarked with an air of resignation). Or: 'Caroline has friends staying . . .' Or: 'John and his tutor are here.' So Ari would settle, unhappily, for the Pierre Hotel. Decorating became a bugbear. His apartment in Paris was one of the costliest in Avenue Foch (round the corner from Callas's place) but lacked the woman's touch since his divorce from Tina some fifteen years earlier. The precious carpet in the huge drawing room was threadbare, Tina's portrait looked down on the new mistress of the home. Jackie's broom swept such remnants of his past away, off with the painting, on with the new carpet, but Ari did not easily adjust to changes. As with the Paris apartment, so with the Athens villa and the two houses on Skorpios and, worst of all, with *Christina* which he regarded as his real home but which to Jackie was only a plaything. The allegorical panels (by Vertesz) depicting Ari, Tina, Alexander and Christina in various ethereal poses with lambs and flowers were not exactly tasteful; they soon disappeared.

Jackie's conduct of the household on terra firma could not be easily reconciled with Ari's. He did not bother unless when things went wrong while she was accustomed to keeping staff on a tight rein at all times, checking expenditure, issuing firm instructions, providing for every contingency. In a Greek marriage, the husband is master: no husband of Jackie's could hope to be her master. It was impossible to avoid flare-ups over the minor issues which arose from their different approaches. The magnificent stateroom Ari occupied in the yacht was not suitable for two. Tina and, after her, Callas were content to leave it to him and settle for one of the less spacious eight staterooms with marble bathrooms and precious furniture, regal boudoirs indeed. But it was inconceivable for Jackie to inhabit a cabin which was smaller or in any way inferior to any other, and Ari soon found himself relegated to the stateroom called Chios which, though it had perfectly adequately accommodated Garbo and Churchill, was still a rung below his own with the El Greco over the desk and the mosaic bath with the Minoan design and the gilded faucets. For the first time since he had transformed the old Canadian frigate into the world's most luxurious yacht, the owner felt like a guest aboard. Happily the new house on Skorpios was nearing completion and Jackie, if she wished, could put up at the smaller one – his and her villas. Small as the island was, husband and wife would not need to jostle in narrow space.

Though Skorpios with its olive groves, miles of riding paths and secluded beaches might have been designed with Jackie in mind, it did not tie her down for long. Much as they pretended to crave privacy, neither really enjoyed seclusion. They never stayed long and their restless wanderings back and forth across the Atlantic drew a pattern on the map which looked like a fever chart gone mad. While she was dining with André Meyer in New York (again), Ari was living it up in the nightspots of Athens. As she tried, and failed, to shake off Ron Galella in Fifth Avenue, Onassis hit out at photographers who pursued him in Constitution Square in Athens. She flew to Europe, gave Ari a peck on the cheek and was off to Corfu before flying on to Rome to take a hand in his family affairs, trying to dissuade Christina from breaking off her engagement to Peter Goulandris, Ari's favourite prospective son-in-law. Her efforts were of no avail.

She and Ari met up in New York for a few days (with the obligatory visits to Manhattan's nightclubs), then went their separate ways again, Ari roaming across Europe, Jackie riding and hunting in Maryland, but came together again at Skorpios with the children and Rose Kennedy among the guests to celebrate Jackie's birthday. His present: a pair of earrings with a space design. Ari invited a couple of American astronauts to Greece but, much to Jackie's chagrin, the visit was blocked by the State Department which Ari interpreted as a personal affront. He indulged in one of his spasmodic anti-American tirades which offended Jackie.

On the surface neither separation nor domestic squabbles affected their relationship. When they were together, they were affectionate, walked arm in arm, sat close together with his hand on hers, his cheek rubbing against her cheek. Jackie felt the shadow of the Kennedy jinx lifting and her friends thought she appeared secure in Onassis's comforting embrace until the misfortunes of his own tribe began to rival those of the Kennedys. Yet she did not easily understand Ari's consternation about the mysterious death of his erstwhile sister-in-law, Eugenie Niarchos, on her husband's private Aegean island of Spetsopoula. She did not realise what deep old wounds the island drama opened in Ari's mind. They took him back to the early forties when he first met Eugenie and Athina (Tina) Livanos, daughters of the wealthiest Greek shipowner of his day, and to his courtship with Tina without suspecting that she was secretly in love with his friend Stavros Niarchos, another young Greek shipowner, and he with her.

When Onassis carried away Tina, Niarchos, in the quaint manner in which Greek unions are arranged, married Eugenie. The brothers-in-law fell out, the beginning of their lifelong feud, each trying to score over the other with bigger tankers, better yachts, more sumptuous homes, more fabulous parties to which they lured royalty and headliners to spite each other. Niarchos, who had been married twice before, had left Eugenie briefly to marry Henry Ford II's daughter Charlotte, then left her and their baby to return to Eugenie. They were alone on Spetsopoula (quarrelling over Charlotte's child) when Eugenie died under suspicious circumstances. Had she taken her own life or died, accidentally, from an overdose of drugs? Were the wounds on her body caused by Niarchos's attempts to revive her? Niarchos was not allowed to leave Greece while the authorities investigated the affair, confused by political implications, pro-Junta magistrates versus anti-Junta judges, until Niarchos was cleared of culpability (though the issue flared up years later). Jackie could not remain untouched by the morbid obsession with which Onassis followed the misfortunes of the hated Niarchos. He was difficult to live with.

Excitement over Genie's death had hardly died down when Ari was informed that Tina was parting from the Marquess of Blandford. She was looking after her late sister's younger children and, incredibly, planning to marry – Niarchos! The thought of his former wife and that man was more than Onassis could bear. If Genie's death had opened old wounds, the prospect of this marriage poisoned his whole system. Never a moment of peace! As if this situation was not grim enough, Jackie and Ari had to cope with a new menace, a threat to kidnap young John in England which they regarded as the safest country in the world. The police traced the would-be kidnapper, an electronics engineer, who was later found to be insane and confined to an asylum. (A year later another kidnap plot was uncovered in Greece and frustrated.)

Less violent but still disturbing was the news from London. After fourteen years of marriage, Lee was being sued for divorce; it was another twelve months before the parting became official. Jackie flew to be with her sister who planned to move back to New York. The sisters pursued their hobbies as if nothing untoward had happened, went to the theatre and on shopping expeditions. As Jackie returned to New York, the newspapers reported that Ari had dropped in by helicopter on Callas who was holidaying on a Greek Island. If Ari read the gossip columns which he did, he could not overlook the snide little references to Jackie dining out with William van den Heuvel, a personable young lawyer whose name was added to the list of her romantic attachments. Could these respective extra-marital activities be the reason why their winter cruise was delayed, or was it abandoned? Much was read into it until it was announced that *Christina* was having her 'bottom scraped and her face lifted' at the Hamburg shipyard which had originally fitted her out.

The social round continued unabated. Jackie went to see Rudolf Nureyev dance in New York and, naturally, visited him in his dressing room. In February 1971 she was invited to the White House for the first time since 1963 for the hanging of her and Jack's portrait: Jackie's replacing Eleanor Roosevelt's which was moved to a new place. President Nixon sent a military jet to fly her and the children to Washington, and made it a jolly party. The children were shown over the Oval Office which they hardly remembered but for Jackie the memories were vivid and painful.

With yet another Kennedy occasion out of the way, she joined up with Ari at Martinique, briefly visited the Mellons at Antigua, then sailed via the Canary Islands to Skorpios. The holiday was spoiled by yet another crisis in the Onassis family. Footloose after the break-up of her engagement to Peter Goulandris, Christina had met a man called Joseph Bolker, and planned to marry him. Who was Bolker? All the agitated father could find out was that the man about to become his son-in-law was forty-seven years old, more than twice Christina's age, with four teenage daughters; that he lived in Los Angeles and was a real estate dealer (or something).

Ari was up in arms. He telephoned Christina and implored her to give up the plan: she would not yield. He sent Alexander to see her but the young man's mission was no more successful. Tina flew to the United States and tried to dissuade Christina, but since she herself was marrying 'Uncle' Stavros Niarchos, the family ogre, her chances of changing her daughter's mind were negligible. For Ari there was only one thing to do. If he could not stop the marriage, he could stop this man getting his hands on Christina's trust fortune. In a few exchanges with his New York lawyers, he excluded Christina from the trust in the nick of time, for her twenty-first birthday when she was due to get her share of some $61 million was only months away. She would not be getting a penny, and never mind California's community property law on which Bolker may have banked. Nothing would stop Christina. The marriage was concluded in Los Angeles and not much later Tina became Mrs Stavros Niarchos. The wife of a man with Onassis's temperament could not expect to remain unaffected by his emotional upsets. Jackie suffered with Ari.

This was not a time for her to return to America where she would be liable to meet her stepdaughter or cause speculation if she did not. Unhappily, the complication coincided with a Kennedy celebration to which Jackie had been looking forward, the ceremonial opening of the Kennedy Centre for which she had asked Leonard Bernstein to compose a Mass. It was to have been Jackie's night. Over two thousand guests nursed their invitations, most of them dying to meet her or see her at close quarters. Jackie did not attend. Instead she turned up in Paris in style, wearing an outsize Yves St Laurent monogram on her coat as she entered the salon of Pierre Cardin.

One restful interlude in the ding-dong journeying of the peripatetic couple was a family Christmas in England. Ari seemed to have recovered his spirits and stayed on with Jackie for a few days after Caroline and John had gone to New York. He was due to follow them, and Ari took her to Heathrow Airport where they waited in the VIP lounge for her plane's departure. Their conversation was lively, Ari's rasping voice rising as always when he spoke with feeling. He grew noisier and noisier and disregarded Jackie's attempts to quieten him down. Their row was overheard and reported in the newspapers. When Jackie boarded the plane alone, the implication seemed to be another bust-up. To avoid attention, she had booked under the name of Simpson – Colin Simpson was an associate in London – which made things look even more suspicious. Her pseudonym blew up in her face.

'It was nothing,' Ari said when I asked him about the row. He could flare up and forget all about it the next minute and there certainly was no danger to their marriage. It was not affected either by the publication of a sensationalist book, *The Fabulous Onassis – His Life and Loves*, by Christian Cafarakis, a former mess steward on *Christina*, who claimed to have seen the Onassis marriage contract with one hundred and seventy clauses some of which he quoted. One of them was said to stipulate that Onassis should not insist on Jackie having his child. Others were similarly absurd. The book was littered with obvious mistakes, among them the ridiculous suggestion that Callas had been on the 1963 cruise with Ari and Jackie. It also listed virtually every shop in Manhattan claiming that Jackie was a regular free-spending customer in all of them. Such was the hunger for material about Jackie and Ari that the book, however unreasonable, still provided dozens of newspapers with lengthy series, and was said to have earned the author a small fortune.

The view of Jackie from the galleys of *Christina* was as nothing compared to the eyeful Italian readers had of her at the end of 1972 when the girlie magazine *Playmen* published four pages of colour photographs of her in the nude. They had been snatched by a photographer from a boat while she was sunning herself on Skorpios, and left nothing to the imagination. ('Only pictures of Howard Hughes's face would fetch more,' it was said in the trade.) Though she had no reason to be ashamed of her body, she was upset by this ultimate intrusion into her privacy. 'It spoiled Skorpios for her,' Ari said later. Although he tried to treat the incident as a joke, neither he nor Jackie liked the whispers and sniggers following the publication.

As if competing with his wife for international attention Ari, spotting a *France Dimanche* photographer lurking on a beach while he was changing on the deck of *Christina*, exclaimed 'It's my turn now!' and gave the snooper a full view of himself which soon adorned the pages of the French paper. Not much later he burst into the news again – with a bang. Having summoned his favourite acolytes to Athens to celebrate the twenty-fourth birthday of Alexander, he competed with Elsa Martinelli and Odile Rodin (widow of that other international playboy, the late Portfirio Rubirosa) for a world record in the Greek sport of plate smashing. Ankle deep in broken crockery, Ari had the time of his life and a shock when he was threatened with prosecution for violating the Colonels' ban on the destructive Greek pastime. Onassis being prosecuted in Greece? Once the newspapers had had their fun, nothing further was heard of his smashing night out.

Ari and Jackie never reproached each other for their respective highly publicised extravaganzas. But Ari's sisters, overlooking his behaviour, became highly critical of Jackie. Flaunting herself with all these men as soon as her husband's back was turned was not their idea of a loyal wife's behaviour. Was she treating their beloved brother with contempt? Comparisons between her handsome friends and the diminutive Ari did not show him in a favourable light. They were offended by jokes about Jackie's five foot seven inches towering over Ari's five foot five: 'When he stands on his money, he is taller than she,' it was said. Neither did they enjoy the apocryphal story about Nixon asking Chairman Mao: 'What would have happened if Kruschev had been assassinated instead of Kennedy?' and Mao replying: 'I don't know but I can tell you one thing – I don't think Mr Onassis would have married Mrs Kruschev!' Ari and Jackie were in danger of becoming a huge joke.

The persistent reports about their quarrels were no joke. Although Ari put a bold face on them – 'We enjoy these rumours more than the people who invent them' – he went out of his way to kill them. Each 'divorce imminent' disclosure was promptly followed by Jackie and Ari making a public appearance together. One such occasion was the reopening of El Morocco, an old Onassis haunt in New York, where America's upper four hundred turned up flashing their diamonds while Ari, it was said, arrived flashing Jacqueline.

Estate agents, at least, did not assume they were splitting up and offered them every house that came on the market, often as a means of getting publicity for a property on sale. A villa on the island of Hydra – perhaps Mrs Onassis was interested? Tell the press and a dozen customers turned up to get it first. An estate in Virginia, would Mrs Onassís care to inspect it? Mrs Onassis would not. New Jersey, perhaps? Yes, this one appealed but Jackie wanted to rent not buy. She chose Bernardsville as a base for her outings with the Essex Hunt, and later persuaded Ari to buy her a house in the neighbourhood.

One day she was hunting in New Jersey, the next she was in Paris on a shopping spree. By the time her presence was reported in the morning paper, she was on her way to Sardinia, the Aga Khan's holiday camp for millionaires, flying off for dinner in Rome and back to Sardinia for the night. Ari was in a happier frame of mind now that six months' intensive persuading and cajoling had wrested Christina from the grip of her unsuitable husband. After a week of wild chases back and forth across the Atlantic, Christina shook off Joseph Bolker and filed for divorce. Ari reinstated her into her benefits from the trust which was liquidated shortly after her twenty-first birthday with Jackie's share being embodied in a new agreement which, unlike the Trust Agreement, was concluded out of public sight. All seemed well in the Onassis camp, nothing sensational to garner for Jackie watchers.

In Greece the echo of the crockery crashing against a taverna's fireplace on Alexander's birthday had only just died down when Onassis received news of a crash in which the young man was gravely injured. The effect on Ari was shattering and had repercussions which threatened Jackie's peace of mind and her marriage. Alexander, Ari's heir and successor, had gone up in a Piaggio with an American pilot and a Canadian co-pilot, it was not clear who was at the controls, when the engine stalled and the plane crashed down on Athens airport. Unconscious and with severe head wounds, Alexander was rushed to hospital where doctors diagnosed severe brain damage: hopes for his survival were minimal. When told over the transatlantic telephone, Ari would not accept such a gloomy assessment of his son's chances. He commandeered a jet while Jackie asked an eminent neurosurgeon to fly with them to Greece. Aides were making arrangements for a chartered Trident to take a London brain specialist to Athens to join the Greek surgeons who were operating on Alexander.

Those who saw Onassis off at Kennedy Airport were struck by his appearance. He seemed to be aging by the minute, his skin paling and his hair greying before their eyes. His own eyes looked glazed under a film of tears. By contrast, Jackie's in-built defence mechanism kept her emotions below the surface. She was ostensibly calm but it may not have been her fault that her comforting words sounded hollow. Did Ari already suspect, as he did later, that she did not share his grief, his despair? It never occurred to him that this journey in the shadow of tragedy might make her feel as if she was forever travelling with death.

When all the available information about the accident was pieced together, it appeared that not Alexander but the Ameri-can pilot, Donald McCusker, had been at the controls when the Piaggio crashed, and was also injured; if only Alexander had been in charge, Onassis moaned quite reasonably, the accident would never have happened. The other pilot, formerly with the British Overseas Aircraft Corporation, had escaped injury.

By the time Ari, Jackie and the American surgeon arrived in Athens, Alexander's condition looked hopeless. At the Red Cross Hospital, Onassis was told that his son was clinically dead, his brain having ceased to function although his heart was still beating faintly. Only the desperate situation stopped Ari flaring up when Tina arrived with Stavros Niarchos. Chris-tina was there, so was Fiona Thyssen who, but for Onassis, might have been Alexander's wife. The three Onassis sisters completed the chorus of woe that rang through the corridors. Only Jackie was composed as if she could not mourn the pre-dicament of the young man who had treated her as an enemy.

There was no truth in the story that the disconsolate father had said 'An Onassis cannot live as a vegetable' and had asked the doctors to let his son die if his brain was irreparably damaged; it was already beyond the power of the doctors to keep Alexander alive. Twenty-seven hours after the accident he was dead. Tina cried over his body, Christina was prostrate, Fiona Thyssen buried her head in her hands and Onassis seemed on the verge of collapse. Jackie had no tears but her sympathy with Ari was strong and genuine. Words, she felt, were meaningless.

If he expected more demonstrative compassion, he must have forgotten that wringing of hands was not Jackie's way of expressing her feelings. Not in the mood to analyse his wife's manner, he felt that she was remoter than ever. What he said later suggested that he resented her 'Kennedys don't cry' discipline, her instinctive retreat from tragedy as if it did not exist. Mingled with resentment, his self-pity carried him further away from her than he had ever been in marriage. She had seen little of Alexander while he was alive; in death he loomed like a giant between her and her husband.

Alexander's remains were taken to Skorpios and buried by the Chapel of the Little Virgin. Ari went through the funeral as if in deep shock. When he came out of it, he was curt and abrupt with Jackie. Quarrelling with fate, he hit out in all directions and, as always in adversity, saw enemies all around him. Was it nothing more than a tragic accident that had caused Alexander's death? Had his enemies plotted to hit him by getting at his son whom he loved more than he loved himself? Had evil conspirators tampered with the aircraft? More bluntly: was it murder?

It was impossible to disabuse him of the idea. Once it had taken root he would not be diverted from the conspiracy theory. When Jackie tried to talk him out of his manic obsession, it only soured him, and the more readily his relatives echoed his vague suspicions, the more he resented Jackie's adamant refusal to join him in a campaign; just as, after Jack's assassination, she had refused to associate herself with the view that the President had been the victim of a conspiracy. Onassis carried on with his search for the guilty and offered a £220,000 reward for evidence of foul play. That Jackie was not in there with him to see that justice was done, or Alexander's death avenged, he never forgave her. But he did not think of leaving her or ending their marriage even though with Alexander's death part of his love for Jackie died too.

He felt a need to talk about the tragedy, she wanted to put it behind her. Rather than argue over their different outlooks,.

they were silent but their silence was aggressive, if not hostile. Ari seemed to undergo a change of character although there was as yet no overt hint of physical illness or incipient disease which may well have aggravated the psychological effects of his deep sorrow.

Cause and effect were impossible to separate. In the wake of the Athens disaster, the first symptoms of Onassis's ill health appeared but were not recognised. They coincided with business problems caused by the tanker crisis, the rise in oil prices, reduction of consumption and over-production of tankers and falling rates – an accumulation of troubles which preoccupied and equally affected his marriage. He and Jackie saw less of each other and were ill at ease when they were together. Superficially in every sense, they resumed their old pursuits. Refusing to look back, Jackie instinctively began to clear the decks: she did not know for what. She cleared her New York apartment and storerooms of surplus stuff that had accumulated as she had been buying and buying, acquiring new furniture, new clothes, new playthings for the children. Among the surplus were young John's old trombone and a couple of Louis Quinze commodes in Caroline's bedroom. Away with them! Five hundred items in all to be got rid of. Jackie sent them to auction raising a new hue and cry about her meanness.

Having discarded the old stuff, it was time for 1040 Fifth Avenue to be refurbished again; an upper-class version of the working-class woman's obsession with house cleaning which psychiatrists recognise as an attempt to wash away guilt or atone for forbidden desires. To show her home, to show herself, clean and pure, Jackie, in an astonishing volte face, invited a *Vogue* photographer to violate her privacy and take pictures of her library, 'a family hide-in', where she and the children spent much of their time at home. Cluttered up as it was, the room reflected Jackie's idea of comfort with its big settee, deep chintzy easy chairs, low tables, high tables, bookshelves stacked with albums of family photographs, lamps, busts, knick-knacks including Greek worry beads of blue glass, a present from Ari, a couple of Egyptian bronze cats, a relic from Angkor Wat, a black coral from Yucatán, baskets of fruit and flowers, paintings of horses and some of the children's handiwork: 'Comfort and texture must feel good,' she explained. Not to be outdone by this exhibition of Jackie's sanctum, Ari gave permission for a German photographer to visit Skorpios but, like Jackie, showed his hideout without appearing in the picture. The new view of Skorpios included Alexander's gravestone crowned by his bust.

While Ari was mournfully reticent, Jackie in her most sociable mood attended a party at the offices of the *Ladies' Home Journal* to launch a series of articles by Lee about their childhood and youthful travels, their letters home with the little drawings, a careful selection of harmless anecdotes for which Lee collected a handsome fee. With the accolade of Jackie's approval the book version was bound to be a success. A less welcome literary product appeared in France in the shape of a novel by Pierre Rey. Entitled *Le Grec* it was an uninhibited *roman à clef* with Jackie and Ari thinly, or hardly at all, disguised as the central characters. Only a few outrageous incidents departed too far from the reality which was fantastic enough. Jackie read it, Ari did not, while they were together in Skorpios for her forty-fourth birthday. She looked better than ever but Ari was losing weight and seemed to have put on ten years in the last three months. His eye was bothering him and he was experiencing the physical discomforts of old age.

CHAPTER FIFTEEN

The tenth anniversary of John F. Kennedy's death was approaching. Jackie's thoughts were on her first husband rather than on her second, and on a phase in her life in which Onassis had no share. Two people with a crowded past were in the grip of memories without a common denominator except grief. Retracing her steps, Jackie made the mistake of dragging Ari along with her. She wanted to visit Acapulco where she and Jack had spent their honeymoon, and when they got there told Ari that she would like a house, a house within a stone's throw of her erstwhile honeymoon home. Wherever they went in the Mexican resort, they were in the company of President Kennedy's ghost. Ari groaned. They looked at the house of Jackie's choice, inspected other villas, Jackie pressing for a decision, Ari prevaricating; he clearly did not want a house in Acapulco. Nothing was decided and on the flight back they argued, and argued themselves further apart. Jackie flared up and said she did not want or expect anything from him, he answered that she was not going to get anything.

He was working up to a crisis. Looking back later he thought that at this moment he had wanted to get out, break the Kennedy spell and the marriage, liquidate his emotional commitment. It was time to draw a line and close the account. His thoughts turned to his fortune: with Onassis everything came down to that sooner or later. He started scribbling away on a pad, filling page after page with an inventory of his property, dividing his holdings under many headings, the bulk to be shared between Christina and a tax-saving foundation in the name of Alexander, an idea he conceived after his son's death. There were provisions for his sisters, his nephews, his closest collaborators. It was the nearest thing to a last will and testament except that the document was neither witnessed nor submitted to his lawyers. They were working on the reconstruction of his empire and on his real will which was an immensely complicated document.

Having written his anger out of his system, he stuffed the notes into his pocket and forgot all about them. His exasperation with Jackie subsided as quickly as it had flared up. Yet, after his death, the Acapulco document was discovered and leaked to a Greek newspaper probably in an attempt to put Jackie in her place by showing how little she figured in Ari's plans. The document had no bearing on Jackie's life annuity.

When Ari left New York for his more congenial European abodes, Jackie settled down to work on a brief tribute to Jack as part of an impressive Kennedy symposium to be published in *McCall's* magazine. She dwelt on the decade since Jack's death and on how much 'we missed him in it', on the time he came to the Presidency 'when it was right to hope' and quoted a passage from one of Jack's favourite books, John Buchan's *Pilgrim's Way*, an epitaph to a British Prime Minister's son killed in World War One, which, she thought, applied equally to Jack: his great beauty of person; gift of winning speech; a mind that masters readily whatever it cared to master; poetry and a love of all beautiful things; a heart as tender as it was brave; and, poignantly, the one gift that was withheld from him, length of years. But, she added, she would not let herself be numbed by sadness. She was thinking of Jack as 'the bright light of his days'. Now he would have been older and wiser, and it was impossible to say how he would have coped but he would still have maintained his deep belief that problems can be solved by men.

Preoccupation with Jack's death blinded her to the threat of Ari's life. Early in 1974, Onassis was at last persuaded to consult a doctor in New York about his drooping eyelid. A specialist was consulted and sent him to hospital for observation; he registered in the name of Philips, and left after a week without telling anyone that his complaint had been diagnosed as myasthenia gravis, a debilitating disease of the muscles. He made light of it. When he could not keep his eyes open for any length of time, he attached his eyelids to his forehead with sticking plaster and showed himself without apparent concern in public, at New York's Twenty-One Club which is on the regular beat of gossip columnists. 'Onassis has suffered a stroke,' they reported. Onassis had not suffered a stroke. He was gravely ill though he still joked about it: 'If I spend as long with my make-up as Jackie,' he told a friend, 'I could use invisible tape and nobody would be the wiser.' To those to whom he had confided the nature of his illness, he said: 'Doctors keep telling me I ought to have an operation but they can't guarantee that it will help. So what's the point?'

Jackie did not know how dangerous his condition was and was hopeful that he could be cured: Jackie was always hopeful. In the meantime there was disturbing news from both wings of the family. Bobby Kennedy's youngsters were tumbling from one mischief into another (reckless driving with a fatal accident, possession of marijuana), Teddy Kennedy's wife Joan was psychologically disturbed and, presently, his twelve-year-old son Teddy Jr had to have his leg amputated. Much against her inclination, Jackie was drawn into all these problems.

Ari, too, grappled with family troubles. Christina was relentlessly flitting from city to city, from playboy to playboy without forming any real attachment. Like her father, she suffered from insomnia, was taking sleeping pills to find rest, and stimulants to give her strength after sleepless nights. One day she was found unconscious in her London apartment and rushed to hospital under the assumed name of Miss A. Danoi. An overdose of sleeping tablets? A suicide attempt? Onassis would not turn to Jackie. He was only too familiar with her views on Christina. He was too ill to go to his daughter's aid but her mother flew from Paris to London to be with her. Christina recovered quickly and not a word about the unhappy interlude leaked out at the time. She resumed her friendship with Peter Goulandris which was good news, and Onassis asked her to come to New York and familiarise herself with the business. Not even with her most impenetrable blinkers could Jackie overlook the significance. Ari was not only trying to give Christina a purpose in life, he was easing her into the shoes of her late brother, grooming her as a partner, heiress and successor. In his own way he was giving Jackie notice that Christina, not she, would inherit the bulk of his fortune although, at this stage, he was preparing for retirement and not death.

As if it was no business of hers, he never told Jackie about the major reorganisation of his empire which he had set in motion, streamlining and amalgamating some hundred companies under his control. With a serious tanker crisis looming ahead, even an industrial giant like his empire was forced to pull in its horns. The tightening up at his New York headquarters produced some awkward personal complications. Jackie had been blithely directing her bills to the New York offices and up to this point payment had always been prompt. In the new economy wave, managers were slower if not reluctant to pay out large sums for paintings, furniture and clothes without the boss's OK. But Onassis was rarely there to authorise payments, there were delays, bills remained unpaid, and Jackie was shocked to find that, through no fault of her own, her credit was no longer automatic while old accounts remained unsettled. Onassis had not intended his economies to affect his wife – there was enough in the kitty to satisfy her most extravagant demands. But the hitches caused friction and he was in no mood to listen to reproaches. One evening, at the Twenty-One, he was overheard discussing Jackie in his high-decibel voice and exclaiming in a moment of irritation: 'That woman . . .!' His outburst caused a lot of ripples in the gossip belt; so that was how he talked about Jackie!

While quarrelling with each other, they went off to patch up another quarrel: Ari's long-standing feud with Prince Rainier of Monaco dating back to their partnership in the fifties when the Prince forced Onassis to sell him his shares in the Société des Bains de Mer which controls the Bank of Monte Carlo. Jackie had kept in touch with Princess Grace, two American women with Mediterranean husbands, and suggested they all got together. As a result, Rainier and Grace invited Ari and Jackie to their palace for lunch, and Ari, weary and less combative than in his heyday, readily seized on the opportunity for a reconciliation. It was a placid occasion.

Next stop was Madrid where Jackie, as if she did not have a care in the world, tried her skill with castanets and even coaxed a reluctant Ari on to the dance floor where he performed like a wounded bear. On and on they went, to Egypt where they visited the pyramids, and down the Nile. Increasingly troubled by the progressive weakness of his facial muscles, Ari was thinking of this trip as a farewell cruise, not a farewell to Jackie but to the life he had led for fifty years. He was tired, very tired but Jackie with her never-say-die mentality glossed over his growing disability. It was almost like Jack in the first year of their marriage when he came close to death – and did he not recover to a bright future? She never allowed herself to accept that there was no future for Ari.

Death was once more edging towards her, the world's most inveterate bystander at tragedy, but it did not as yet reach out for Onassis. Instead, as if to endorse the theory that victims attract the same fate over and over again, it struck at two removes but no less hurtfully for that. Death's appointment was with Tina Livanos Onassis Blandford Niarchos who was found dead in her Paris apartment. Tina dead! A mysterious and unexpected death like the death of her sister, Niarchos's previous wife. Though, by her marriage to Niarchos, she had extinguished the last spark of Ari's old attachment, her inexplicable demise affected him deeply coming as it did so soon after the loss of Alexander. He may have thought, and said, that Tina had paid the price for marrying his arch-enemy but she was also Christina's mother and a large part of his life.

Jackie was no more than an impotent spectator when Ari exploded on hearing rumours that Tina had committed suicide; she was said to have tried to take her life a few months earlier in London. It was a reporting mistake but it seemed to confirm Ari's suspicions. He instructed Christina to press the French authorities to investigate her mother's death and conduct a postmortem. Incensed by the implication, Niarchos denied publicly that Tina had ever attempted suicide. Hitting back at the Onassis side, he revealed that she had flown to London in March to be with Christina who had tried to end her life. Thus Christina's secret came out. It was a nasty conflict to watch at close quarters and Jackie was deeply disturbed to be part, however inactively, of this sordid affair. In the event, the postmortem showed that Tina had died from natural causes. The Onassis tragedy was moving to a climax.

He refused to go to Tina's funeral, 'He's too old, too sick,' an aide explained. Christina was there cutting Niarchos dead but was comforted by her previous stepfather, the Marquess of Blandford. Old love and new hate were tearing Ari apart but Jackie could do nothing to help the wounded tiger who snarled at friends and foes. Gritting her pretty teeth, she went about her own concerns. From her New York base, she kept in touch with Caroline who was working with a film unit on a documentary about Appalachian miners, and was delighted when the mining family with whom Caroline lodged said in an interview that 'She's just folks!'; high praise indeed. Caroline was invited to exhibit the many photographs she had taken on this and other occasions but the announcement caused such a burst of publicity that Jackie decided against the exhibition, only, as so often, to change her mind a few months later and let the exhibition go ahead.

She was busying herself with a photographic project of her own. At the invitation of an old friend, Karl Katz, a Brooklyn-born Hebrew scholar, one-time director of New York's Jewish Museum and artistic adviser to the Metropolitan Opera, she went to a preview of a new museum sponsored by the International Centre of Photograph, and talked to its executive director, Cornell Capa, a top photographer. She stayed for lunch and made copious notes of all Katz and Capa told her about the Centre's activities, went home and wrote it up in her best reporting style. The *New Yorker* was pleased to accept her article as an anonymous contribution and published it in its second January 1975 issue making sure that the identity of the author remained no secret.

Early in February, a telephone call came from Athens to say that Ari had collapsed with excruciating pains in the abdomen. The insidious disease was beginning to affect his heart, and through the heart his lungs and his liver. Jackie summoned an American heart specialist, Dr Isidor Rosenfeld, and flew with him to Athens where Ari was being tended by his sisters. From Gstaad, the Swiss winter sports resort where she had been holidaying with Peter Goulandris, Christina hurried to her father's bedside. Neither Ari himself nor his sisters nor Christina, and certainly not Jackie, would admit that it was more than a passing indisposition. Ari had contracted flu and had some little difficulty in breathing, they said. But they could not shut their eyes to the gravity of his condition when Dr Rosenfeld decided that he should be flown to Paris where the American Clinic was better equipped to deal with his ailment. Jackie, Christina and Artemis Garoufalides accompanied him on the flight.

At Orly Airport, Onassis refused a stretcher and, against doctor's advice, insisted on going to his apartment in the Avenue Foch. Looking grey and haggard, a shadow of his former self, he shied away from the photographers and reporters but pulled himself together and rushed past them into the house unaided. Jackie's expressionless face did not betray her own ordeal. Next morning, evading the photographers, Onassis was driven to the American Clinic which he entered by the back door before the press could catch up with him. The family was still reluctant to spell out the danger. His condition was not really serious, they insisted. This was not Jackie's doing. As Artemis and Christina took charge, she had little say in the proceedings. She visited Ari every day but insisted on pursuing her social life and dined out with friends most evenings which did not endear her to Ari's grief-stricken family.

While he fought for his life, another battle was going on around him. Some members of his family resented this strange woman, Jackie, the intruder who might get away with the loot. They did not want her to come between them and their beloved Aristo. Alive or dead, he belonged to them not to Jackie. The less she saw of him, the better! And was not this what Ari wanted? As they saw it, he preferred their company which created warmth to that of Jackie who could not generate real feeling. Unwittingly, he may have intensified the conflict and set them off against each other leaving Jackie unhappy and bewildered. Drawn into the struggle, not too reluctantly, Christina refused to share the Onassis apartment with her stepmother and moved into the Hotel Plaza Athenée where she was reunited with Peter Goulandris. Ari was only semi-conscious but when he spoke it became evident that he was worrying as much about Christina's future as about his shipping empire whose executives were forgathering in Paris.

Realising that his great hope, perhaps his last wish, was that she and Peter would solemnise their long friendship in marriage, Christina wanted to reassure her dying father. She knew him well enough to guess what went through his mind, that she alone could not manage the complicated co-ordination of his American and European shipping operations, the financial arrangements involved, super-tankers on order at $25 million apiece which would have to be cancelled at high cost or sent from launching pad into mothballs. It needed a shipping man, a Greek, to deal with these problems; the question of Jackie taking over did not arise. What Onassis visualised was that his ships wedded to the Goulandris fleet would sail on and brave the storms of the tanker crisis. Christina took Peter with her to her father's deathbed and told him that they had decided to get married. Ari brightened.

It was a well-meaning deception, Peter generously playing his part. But there was no pretence in the attitude of the Onassis family who made it clear that Jackie's reign was coming to an end. The war of nerves was supported by the lawyers who were examining Ari's papers in consultation with his executives. Insidious leaks suggested that, whatever his plans for Jackie's future, whatever the signed and sealed agreements, she would have to take what they, and Christina, would let her have. With the tanker business at rock bottom nothing was safe, everything was negotiable.

For the next two weeks Ari hung on to life. He underwent an operation to assist his internal functions which his weakened heart could no longer stimulate with an adequate supply of blood. He was put on a kidney machine and on a ventilator to pump air into his lungs. It brought some relief. When Jackie visited him on Friday, 7 March 1975, he seemed to have weathered the crisis.

That evening she telephoned New York and spoke to her daughter. Was everything all right? Caroline's reply was not reassuring. Was the girl keeping something from her? Jackie was not happy with the company Caroline was keeping and her infatuation with a young man who was a pleasant, innocuous fellow by ordinary standards. She told herself that Caroline needed her – or was she looking for an excuse to get away from Paris where she was not wanted? Was it that she could not bear to witness another death struggle and the thought of her second husband dying in her arms like the first?

The following day when she entered Ari's sickroom he greeted her with a ghost of a smile. Christina and Artemis who followed her to his bedside gathered that she had told him she was off to New York to look after Caroline. It seemed that Onassis, well aware of his wife's intense concern for her daughter, did not try to dissuade her. He was beyond caring. As Jackie flew off, Christina was under the impression that she would be back in Paris on Monday, 10 March. Instead, that day, Jackie telephoned to inquire about Ari's progress. Progress? She was told that there was no progress but no deterioration either. She telephoned again the following day and throughout the week. On Friday she was informed that Ari's condition was serious, very serious. In that case she would be back after the weekend on Monday, 17 March. Although no angry words were spoken, the Onassis family did not react kindly. They thought Jackie was indifferent, casual if not callous.

But was it made clear to her that Ari might not live through the weekend? Was there not on the part of his closest relatives a superstitious reluctance to say 'dic' which concealed the imminent danger? Was Jackie aware that the sands were running out for Ari or did she, as often in the past, as in the last few days of her father's life, close her mind to the unpalatable truth? Or, if she fully realised the true position, did she really want to rush back and watch Ari die? The next message from Paris roused her from her sleep at eight a.m. (New York time) on Saturday, 15 March. Onassis was dead. Ari had died in her absence.

When Jackie returned to Paris that evening, only Ari's chauffeur was at the airport to meet her. The weather was fair but the hostility of the family hit her like a burst of hail from a storm cloud. Christina was coldly aloof, Ari's sisters reserved and silent. His aides from Monte Carlo, Athens and New York tried to avoid her. Conversations were studiously conducted in Greek and mostly beyond her comprehension. She was made to feel as if she was intruding on the Onassis family's private grief. There was no question of her taking charge of the funeral arrangements – 'Greek Orthodox rites, you know, Ari's instructions before his death while you were away . . . We know what he wanted.' He wanted to be buried on Skorpios by the side of Alexander.

Not a frown, no expression in the smooth features, no gesture or word revealed Jackie's feelings. Resentment? Sorrow? She was either indifferent or amazingly controlled. As Onassis once said about her: 'Sometimes even for me it is hard to know what she is thinking.' The truth was that, as after Jack's death, she would not allow herself to be numbed by sadness. And so, after the unpleasant confrontation with Ari's people, she went to the apartment in the Avenue Foch to rest before going to the chapel in the American Clinic to say her last farewell to Ari and to pray. The following day, with Christina and other Onassis associates, she boarded the aircraft which took his body to Greece. Senator Edward Kennedy flew in from the States with Caroline and John.

Stiffly and dry-eyed, Jackie walked slowly away from Ari's grave atop his island. Christina wiped tears from her cheeks and bid the mourners follow her down the steep path to the harbour and aboard the gleaming Onassis yacht which bears her name. On the poop deck they were joined by the crew and the island staff and, as is the custom after Greek funerals, offered hot black coffee. Standing aside with the children and Ted Kennedy, Jackie watched Christina turn to the sailors and workers with a sweep of her arms as if to embrace them: 'This boat and this island are mine,' she said in Greek. 'You are all my people now!' Whether or not she understood the words, Jackie could yet not mistake their meaning. It was more than a daughter's sentimental gesture to her late father who, as he had often told me, regarded the yacht as his home and Skorpios as his kingdom; it was a bold acceptance of the succession, the first autonomous pronouncement of the heiress. It sounded like a challenge to the widow but Jackie accepted it, true to her philosophy, as part of the indescribable whole that is called life.

She was in a hurry to get away. After a night in Athens, she sent young John back to the States with his uncle and flew to Paris with Caroline (who, a few days later, kicked out at a photographer who followed her in the street). By the end of the month Jackie was back in New York where lawyers and executives dealing with the Onassis estate told her that her financial position was secure. She was, of course, entitled to the jewellery Ari had given her – total value over $2 million; to the Onassis apartment in Paris; to a quarter share in *Christina* and Skorpios (if sold), the other three-quarters going to Christina, or the use of the island and the yacht at times to be coordinated with Christina. Her annual allowance would come to her partly from the American Onassis holdings, partly from his European and South American interests, subject to final arrangements and consultations with tax experts. Caroline and John were already provided for. Behind the legal explanations lurked a veiled threat that any further claim on her part would be contested – with the backing of the whole Onassis fortune.

Jackie had no intention of contesting the arrangements. It was not in character and she had no wish to give ammunition to those who surreptitiously persisted in painting her as a cool, calculating, money-grabbing, wildly extravagant latter-day Marie Antoinette. She could afford to let matters rest where they were. Shrewd investments had more than doubled her $3 million and the million more she had been worth before her marriage to Onassis. In addition to Ari's jewellery, she owned several pieces worth half a million dollars she had received while First Lady. She had a house in New Jersey (where she planned to breed horses), the Paris apartment, her New York home, her art treasures and, last but not least, her collection of personal records – these, of course, capable of yielding millions the moment she agreed to edit and publish them, particularly if she kept her name in the public eye which presently she set out to do. Her name was an asset that could bear dividends in many ways. She lent it, for nothing, to a campaign to preserve New York's Grand Central Station, and sold it deliberately cheaply (for $250 a week) to a publisher for whom she promised to read manuscripts and recruit new authors; Sinatra was one of the candidates whose autobiography would be a great seller. She had access to everybody.

Within a few days, she was back on her international round-about. She turned up at a bullfight in Madrid, flew into London to sign documents at a solicitor's office on the same day as Christina but did not meet her. When Christina was reported to have made snide remarks about her, lawyers warned both not to create the impression that they were fighting over Ari's inheritance lest it damaged the delicate negotiations to secure the future of the Onassis empire without Onassis.

From London, Jackie went to Skorpios to collect her personal belongings taking along her friend Karl Katz to assist with the transport of paintings, antiques and furniture from the island and the yacht. Artemis Garoufalides kept a watching brief. For Jackie it was not goodbye to Skorpios – not yet. Young John went to Moscow with his uncle Sargent Shriver and his family (Shriver soon announced his candidature for the Democratic nomination for President) and, true to form, was photographed at an official reception at the very moment he bit the hand of his cousin Maria Shriver which was resting fondly on his shoulder.

Back in the States, Jackie attended Caroline's graduation from Concord Academy at the same time as President Ford's daughter Susan. The indestructible Rose Kennedy and Senator Ted were there to signify Jackie's return to the Kennedy fold; she went to the Robert F. Kennedy Charity Tennis Tournament and spent a week in Hyannis Port which was like coming home. A little reluctantly she arranged for Caroline to spend a year in Europe to separate her from certain American friends but, rather than choose Paris where she herself had earned her European spurs, enrolled Caroline at an arts course in London.

In July she took John with her to Skorpios for a holiday which turned out to be a camouflage to preserve a secret until the last moment – Christina Onassis's surprise wedding to Alexander Andreadis, son of a Greek banker and shipowner, Professor Stratis Andreadis, whom Christina had known only for a few weeks. In spirit, if not in the person of Peter Goulandris, Christina fulfilled her father's last wish. It looked as though the Andreadis power allied to the Onassis fortune could create a mighty industrial combine until it emerged that Christina's new in-laws had not remained immune to changing economic conditions.

But all seemed as yet well at Christina's wedding at which Jackie was the star attraction. 'How I love that child!' she exclaimed within the hearing the press – that should scotch rumours of dissension in the Onassis camp!

The Jackie story was soon back in the familiar groove. A Greek shipowner announced that he hoped to marry her; her Skorpios trip with Karl Katz yielded rumours that they were contemplating marriage. She went out with Frank Sinatra – another possible romance – and the name of the Shah's former son-in-law was bandied about as yet another candidate for her favours. It was announced that she had agreed to appear in an Italian film playing the part of a witch (but she denied that she was supporting a film about her life with Onassis if it ever came about). Truman Capote, another perennial potential spouse, quoted – if not correctly certainly most appositely – her own explanation for the intense interest in her comings and goings: 'Because of an accident of history,' she was supposed to have said, 'I'll always be an object of curiosity, like something you go to see in a freak show.'

Poor Jackie!

BIBLIOGRAPHY

Adler, Bill *The Commonsense Wisdom of Three First Ladies*, Citadel Press, New York 1966

Bair, Marjorie *Jacqueline Kennedy in the White House*, Paperback Library, New York 1963

Baldridge, Letitia *Of Diamonds and Diplomats*, Houghton Mifflin, Boston 1968

Baldwin, William W. *Billy Baldwin Remembers*, Harcourt Brace Jovanovich, New York 1974

Birmingham, Stephen *The Right People*, Little Brown, Boston 1968

Birmingham, Stephen *Real Lace*, Hamish Hamilton, London 1973

Burns, James Macgregor *John Kennedy, A Political Profile*, Harcourt Brace, New York 1961

Cafarakis, Christian *The Fabulous Onassis*, William Morrow, New York 1972

Carpozi, George *The Hidden Side of Jacqueline Kennedy*, Pyramid Books, New York 1967

Curtis, Charlotte *First Lady*, Pyramid Books, New York 1962

Dareff, Hal *Jacqueline Kennedy, A Portrait in Courage*, Parents Magazine Press, New York 1965

Davis, John H. *The Bouviers, Portrait of an American Family*, Farrer, Straus and Giroux, New York 1969

Fay, Paul B. Jr *The Pleasure of His Company*, Harper and Row, New York 1966

Gallagher, Mary Barelli *My Life with Jacqueline Kennedy*, Michael Joseph, London 1970

Galella, Ronald *Jacqueline*, Sheed and Ward, New York 1974

Hall, Gordon *Jacqueline Kennedy*, F. Fell, New York 1964

Harding, Robert *Jacqueline Kennedy, A Woman for the World*, Encyclopedia Enterprises, distributed by Vanguard Press, New York 1966

Hawley, Earle *A Salute to Jacqueline Kennedy (1960–63),*
J. P. Matthews, Los Angeles 1964

Heller, Deane and David *Jacqueline Kennedy,* Monarch
Books, Derby, Connecticut 1961

Kennedy, John F. *Profiles of Courage,* Harper, New York
1956

Kennedy, Rose *Times Remembered,* Collins, London 1974

Lincoln, Anne *The Kennedy White House Parties,* Viking
Press, New York 1967

Malkus, Alida *The Story of Jacqueline Kennedy,* Grosset and
Dunlap, New York 1967

Manchester, William *Death of a President,* Harper and Row,
New York 1967

O'Donnell K. and Powers David F. with McCarthy J. *Johnny
We Hardly Knew Ye,* Little Brown, New York 1972

Pollard, Eve *Jackie,* Macdonald, London 1969

Posell, Jack (ed) *Jacqueline Kennedy: A Woman of Valor,*
Macfadden and Bartell, New York 1964

Rathi, Balder S. *Mrs Kennedy: The Negative Forces of Human
Reverence,* Bikaner 1965

Rey, Pierre *Le Grec,* Laffont, Paris 1973

Rhea, Mimi *I was Jacqueline Kennedy's Dressmaker,* Fleet
Publishing Corporation, New York 1962

Ridha, Muhd *Jacqueline Kennedy,* Pustaka Negara, Djakarta
1965

Schlesinger, Arthur Jr *A Thousand Days,* Houghton Mifflin,
Boston 1965

Shaw, Maude *White House Nannie,* New American Library,
New York 1966

Shulman, Irving *Jackie! The Exploitation of a First Lady,*
Trident Press, New York 1970

Sidey, Hugh *John F. Kennedy, President,* Atheneum, New
York 1964

Sorenson, Theodore C. *Kennedy,* Harper and Row, New York
1965

Sparks, Fred *The $20,000,000 Honeymoon,* Dell Publishing,
New York 1971

Thayer, Mary Van Rensselaer *Jacqueline Kennedy,* Doubleday,
New York 1961

Thayer, Mary Van Rensselaer   *Jacqueline Kennedy, The White House Years*, Little Brown, New York 1971

Vidal, Gore   *Two Sisters*, Heinemann, London 1970

West, J. B.   *Upstairs at the White House*, Coward McCann, New York 1973

White, Theodore H.   *The Making of the President 1960*, Atheneum, New York 1961

White, Ray Lewis   *Gore Vidal*, Twayne Publishers, New York 1969